Approaches to Teaching Dickens's *Bleak House*

Approaches to Teaching World Literature

Joseph Gibaldi, series editor

For a complete listing of titles,
see the last pages of this book.

Approaches to Teaching Dickens's *Bleak House*

Edited by

John O. Jordan

and

Gordon Bigelow

The Modern Language Association of America
New York   2008

© 2008 by The Modern Language Association of America
All rights reserved
Printed in the United States of America

For information about obtaining permission to reprint material from
MLA book publications, send your request by mail (see address below),
e-mail (permissions@mla.org), or fax (646 458-0030).

Library of Congress Cataloging-in-Publication Data

Approaches to teaching Dickens's Bleak House / edited by John O. Jordan and Gordon Bigelow.
p. cm. — (Approaches to teaching world literature; 105)
Includes bibliographical references and index.
ISBN 978-1-60329-013-5 (alk. paper) — ISBN 978-1-60329-014-2 (pbk. : alk. paper)
1. Dickens, Charles, 1812–1870. Bleak House. 2. Dickens, Charles, 1812–1870—Study
and teaching. I. Jordan, John O. II. Bigelow, Gordon, 1963–
PR4556.A86 2008
823'.8—dc22   2008031307

Approaches to Teaching World Literature 105
ISSN 1059-1133

Cover illustration of the paperback edition: Hablot K. Browne (Phiz), title page to
first complete edition of Bleak House, 1853. Courtesy of the Dickens Project,
University of California, Santa Cruz

Published by The Modern Language Association of America
26 Broadway, New York, New York 10004-1789
www.mla.org

CONTENTS

Teaching Specific Scenes, Patterns, or Problems

Intertextual Approaches

Specific Teaching Contexts

PREFACE TO THE SERIES

In *The Art of Teaching* Gilbert Highet wrote, "Bad teaching wastes a great deal of effort, and spoils many lives which might have been full of energy and happiness." All too many teachers have failed in their work, Highet argued, simply "because they have not thought about it." We hope that the Approaches to Teaching World Literature series, sponsored by the Modern Language Association's Publications Committee, will not only improve the craft—as well as the art—of teaching but also encourage serious and continuing discussion of the aims and methods of teaching literature.

The principal objective of the series is to collect within each volume different points of view on teaching a specific literary work, a literary tradition, or a writer widely taught at the undergraduate level. The preparation of each volume begins with a wide-ranging survey of instructors, thus enabling us to include in the volume the philosophies and approaches, thoughts and methods of scores of experienced teachers. The result is a sourcebook of material, information, and ideas on teaching the subject of the volume to undergraduates.

The series is intended to serve nonspecialists as well as specialists, inexperienced as well as experienced teachers, graduate students who wish to learn effective ways of teaching as well as senior professors who wish to compare their own approaches with the approaches of colleagues in other schools. Of course, no volume in the series can ever substitute for erudition, intelligence, creativity, and sensitivity in teaching. We hope merely that each book will point readers in useful directions; at most each will offer only a first step in the long journey to successful teaching.

Joseph Gibaldi
Series Editor

INTRODUCTION

Bleak House is a central text both in Dickens's career and in the history of the novel itself. Published in 1852–53, *Bleak House* comes midway in Dickens's career, which extends from the first of the young Boz's "Sketches" (1833–34) through the unfinished *Mystery of Edwin Drood* (1870). It marks a turning point in Dickens's art and in the progress of Victorian realism. The novel appeared in serial form over the course of nineteen months; thus it provides occasion to discuss the industrial transformation of publishing and reading in the nineteenth century and the rise of what we understand now as a media-driven mass culture. But unlike the sometimes looser serialized conglomerations of the 1830s and 1840s (*Pickwick, Old Curiosity Shop*), it represents a total narrative vision. Its social concerns are familiar from Dickens's early career: law, crime, family, education, money; but the scope of its social vision is almost uniquely broad. New characters appear in each of the first twenty-two chapters of the novel, and this enormous cast represents every stratum of English society, from the aristocracy to the homeless. In this way, in terms of scale, vision, and artistic control, *Bleak House* looks ahead to novels that declare themselves as modern *epoi*, George Eliot's *Middlemarch* and James Joyce's *Ulysses*. At the same time, its engagement with many institutions and settings (urban and rural, financial and agricultural, professional and artisanal) makes it a nexus for discussing the social and economic transformations that gave the Victorian period its enduring character and its continuing relevance to our own postindustrial world.

In writing and assembling this book, we hope to offer tools that will ease some of the difficulties inevitably encountered in teaching Dickens's novel. Given the scope of the critical debate it has inspired and the sweep of the narrative itself, *Bleak House* presents many challenges to the prospective teacher. The essays collected here offer an array of practical teaching strategies developed by seasoned instructors and tested in the classroom. Some describe courses organized exclusively around *Bleak House*; others offer strategies for teaching a single scene or topic in the novel. The essays spring from classrooms in Los Angeles and Johannesburg and Buffalo. They discuss high school advanced placement courses and graduate seminars, and they propose a variety of contexts, contemporary as well as Victorian, for studying the novel and considering different interpretive possibilities.

The sheer size of *Bleak House* poses an obstacle for teachers and no doubt discourages many from assigning it to undergraduates. In choosing a text by a major novelist for classroom use, instructors are often initially drawn to the shortest ones: *Silas Marner, The Turn of the Screw*, or, for Dickens, *Hard Times, A Tale of Two Cities,* or *Great Expectations*. But while these books may appear to be the most approachable, and thus the most teachable, they often convey quite imperfectly the contribution that the author made to his or her time and to the literary tradition. The experience of the instructors who have contributed to this book shows how *Bleak House* can be put to work in classrooms at all levels and how the novel can reward the work it demands of students.

We open the book with a discussion of the wide range of materials available to instructors teaching *Bleak House*. This section draws on the results of a survey conducted in 2004 of over sixty instructors who regularly teach *Bleak House*. We asked these instructors to describe the decisions they made when teaching the novel, from their choice of editions to their own preparation. We report on the pedagogical practice of our respondents, and we also attempt to provide a guide to the wealth of materials that might be of use to instructors, including reference works, critical studies, and background materials. Transatlantic interest in *Bleak House* climbed to a gentle peak in 2006, when a new BBC film adaptation of the novel aired in the United States and a new edition of the text was issued with a cover featuring Gillian Anderson in the role of Lady Dedlock. We offer a brief appraisal of this adaptation, as well as of an earlier BBC film version. Finally, we make some recommendations about useful materials available electronically through the World Wide Web (Web sites, electronic editions, electronic discussion groups, etc.).

Essays in part 2 of the book detail particular approaches to teaching *Bleak House*, which we have grouped into four categories. In the first section, "Victorian Contexts," contributors locate *Bleak House* in relation to different aspects of nineteenth-century British culture and describe ways of teaching the novel alongside other Victorian social texts. Essays in this section thicken the historical context of the novel by focusing on a variety of trends and events: the Great Exhibition of 1851 (Janice Carlisle); the disastrous Niger expedition of 1841 and the gulf between rich and poor, anatomized in the condition-of-England debate (Timothy Carens); the growth of advertising and mass culture (Andrew Williams, Gordon Bigelow, Kevin McLaughlin); and mid-nineteenth-century developments in science and technology (Shu-Fang Lai). The emphasis throughout this section is on ways of integrating historical information with specific passages in the novel and on pedagogical strategies that improve students' ability to make these connections on their own.

Respondents to our survey stressed the importance, especially for a novel as large and complex as *Bleak House*, of relatively small, tightly focused exercises that can be used as discussion units or discussion threads for teaching the novel. The next section, "Teaching Specific Scenes, Patterns, or Problems," attempts to meet this need. Contributors provide practical pedagogical handles for grasping Dickens's sprawling, multiplot narrative. Timothy Peltason and Lisa Sternlieb focus (in different ways) on Esther Summerson as character and narrator, a perennial subject of interest and controversy for students as well as critics. Barbara Leckie reads the description of Mr. Tulkinghorn's room and uses this scene as a way of encouraging students to explore the relation between character and architecture in the novel. Robert L. Patten teaches monthly number 10, the midpoint of Dickens's nineteen-part serialization, as an instance of Aristotelian recognition and reversal. Robert Tracy looks at *Bleak House* as a detective novel and describes an approach that first identifies various detective figures in the novel and then casts the reader in the role of detective. Working with the novel's illustrations, Richard Stein treats *Bleak House* as a multimedia production and suggests ways of engaging students in the practice of visual literacy.

The essays in the third section, "Intertextual Approaches," describe ways of drawing illuminating connections between *Bleak House* and other Victorian or modern texts. Robert Newsom describes a course in which *Bleak House* serves as a reference point for teaching nonfiction prose writers such as Thomas Carlyle, John Stuart Mill, John Henry Newman, John Ruskin, and Matthew Arnold. Jennifer Phegley explores connections between Dickens and nineteenth-century America, taking as her point of departure the United States publication of *Bleak House* in *Harper's* magazine in 1852–53. Also interested in the United States context, Daniel Hack proposes strategies for teaching *Bleak House* in conjunction with the antebellum fictional slave narrative *The Bondwoman's Narrative*. Lauren M. E. Goodlad locates *Bleak House* in relation to Victorian liberalism and twenty-first-century neoliberalism. Michal Peled Ginsburg outlines a comparative course, reading the novel alongside Victor Hugo's *Les Misérables*. Carrol Clarkson describes teaching *Bleak House* in South Africa, focusing on the theme of disease and drawing connections between Dickens's treatment of fever in Victorian London and the portrayal of AIDS in a recent South African novel.

In the final section of part 2, "Specific Teaching Contexts," teachers describe courses or extended course units on *Bleak House* that they have taught in different settings and at different educational levels. Among these contributors are a high school advanced placement English teacher from Kentucky, Kathleen Breen; a California urban community college teacher, Nita Moots Kincaid; and a Connecticut law school professor, Robert Googins. Two other essays, by Joel J. Brattin and Denise Fulbrook, describe undergraduate courses organized around library exhibits or special collections that feature *Bleak House* and other Dickens-related materials (manuscripts, essays from *Household Words*, original serial parts and illustrations, etc.). In the last essay, Hilary Schor describes a graduate seminar in narrative theory that takes *Bleak House* as its specimen text. Several of the contributors in this section present teaching strategies that adapt Dickens's practice of monthly parts publication in ways that allow students to approximate the nineteenth-century experience of reading in serial installments. They argue that their methods of teaching the book in its original serial format transform this lengthy novel into a satisfying and exciting series of episodes, which students are eager to pursue and discuss.

Two appendixes bring the volume to a close. Robert Tracy offers a chronology of events in *Bleak House*, which teachers may reproduce for their students (or may reserve for their own use). It helps clarify the novel's complex plotting and narrative structure and provides a time line against which to locate historical events alluded to in the narrative. Finally, as a complement to his essay on *Bleak House* and *The Bondwoman's Narrative*, Daniel Hack supplies an anonymous poem titled "Borroboola Gha: A Poem for the Times," published initially in *Frederick Douglass' Paper* in 1855. The poem appropriates Dickens's critique of telescopic philanthropy and resituates it in a presumably African American context.

JOJ and GB

ILLUSTRATIONS

SPECIMENS FROM MR. PUNCH'S INDUSTRIAL EXHIBITION OF 1850.

(TO BE IMPROVED IN 1851).

Fig. 1. "Specimens from Mr. Punch's Industrial Exhibition of 1850." From *Punch* 18 (1850): 145. Courtesy of McHenry Library, University of California, Santa Cruz

THE POUND AND THE SHILLING.
"Whoever Thought of Meeting You Here?"

Fig. 2. "The Pound and the Shilling." From *Punch* 20 (1851): 247. Courtesy of McHenry Library, University of California, Santa Cruz

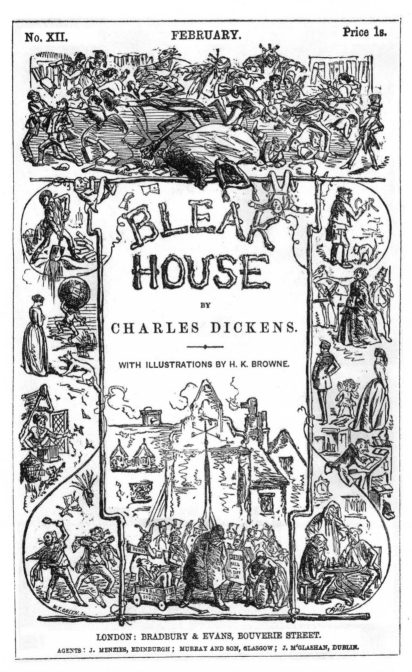

Fig. 3. Hablot K. Browne (Phiz). Wrapper cover, from *Bleak House* (1852–53). Courtesy of Special Collections, McHenry Library, University of California, Santa Cruz. Ada B. Nisbet Collection

Fig. 4. "Dakin & Co." From the *Bleak House Advertiser* (1852–52). Courtesy of Special Collections, McHenry Library, University of California, Santa Cruz. Ada B. Nisbet Collection

Fig. 5. Hablot K. Browne (Phiz), "The little old Lady." From *Bleak House* (1852–53). Courtesy of the Dickens Project, University of California, Santa Cruz

Fig. 6. Hablot K. Browne (Phiz), "The Young Man of the name of Guppy." From *Bleak House* (1852–53). Courtesy of the Dickens Project, University of California, Santa Cruz

Fig. 7. Hablot K. Browne (Phiz), title page to first complete edition of *Bleak House* (1853). Courtesy of the Dickens Project, University of California, Santa Cruz

MATERIALS

Editions

Our survey of instructors shows the Penguin Classics *Bleak House* (2003), edited by Nicola Bradbury, most often chosen for classroom use, and for this reason we have used it as our reference edition for this volume. The Penguin text is based on the 1853 first edition of the novel, though Bradbury silently modernizes spelling and punctuation throughout. Teachers concerned with textual variation will wish to consult the Norton Critical Edition, edited by George Ford and Sylvère Monod, which includes extensive textual history and notes. Our survey respondents also value the Norton for its collection of relevant material on pollution, government, and the legal system in mid-Victorian London, as well as its selection of critical perspectives extant at the time of the edition's publication. A drawback of the Norton as a teaching text is that it reproduces only a small number of the illustrations originally published with the novel. The Penguin reproduces all illustrations, though not the so-called wrapper cover of the serial parts, and it also provides reasonable explanatory notes. (For more on teaching the illustrations, see below 106–12.) Stephen Gill's Oxford World's Classics edition is preferred by a number of instructors. It contains complete illustrations, a map of legal London, and helpful explanatory notes. (See also Brattin on the Penguin and Oxford editions of the novel.)

Bibliographies

The primary and secondary sources available for teaching and studying Dickens are vast in number. The best bibliographical overview and guide to this enormous body of material will be Duane DeVries, *General Studies of Charles Dickens and His Writings and Collected Editions of His Works: An Annotated Bibliography*, a projected four-volume work of which only the first volume is in print at the time of this writing. Comprehensive, intelligently annotated, and usefully indexed and cross-referenced, DeVries's compilation will supersede all previous general bibliographies of Dickens. According to DeVries, an annotated bibliography on *Bleak House* is in preparation for the Dickens Bibliographies series published by AMS Press, a continuation of the Garland Dickens Bibliographies series. This volume is sorely needed.

In the meantime, teachers of *Bleak House* must rely on the available sources. Philip Collins's entry on Dickens in *The New Cambridge Bibliography of English Literature*, volume 3, is complete through 1967. The Dickens entry by Ada Nisbet in *Victorian Fiction: A Guide to Research* and its sequel by Philip Collins in *Victorian Fiction: A Second Guide to Research* remain valuable. The casebooks on *Bleak House* edited by A. E. Dyson, Harold Bloom, and Jeremy Tambling have selected bibliographies, as does the Norton Critical Edition. The selected bibliography in Susan Shatto's *The Companion to* Bleak House is especially useful for its list of relevant articles by Dickens (and others) in *Household Words* and *All the Year Round* and for other historical and background sources. For more recent critical studies of the novel, teachers may consult the annual *MLA International Bibliography*, available on CD-ROM and online at many universities. *Dickens Quarterly* contains in every issue a checklist of recent primary and secondary sources and is the best way to keep up-to-date on new work in the field. A review essay of the previous year's work in Dickens studies appears regularly in *Dickens Studies Annual*. A convenient starting point for research on *Bleak House* is the bibliography prepared by Robert Newsom for the 2001 Dickens Universe conference at the University of California, Santa Cruz, which lists sixty-eight books and articles and emphasizes recent materials up to 2000. Available online, Newsom's bibliography contains links to other resources, including a map of *Bleak House*'s London neighborhood and an image of the *Bleak House* wrapper design.

Reference Works and Other Resources

Shatto's *The Companion to* Bleak House is an invaluable source of background information and commentary on the novel. Monthly number by monthly number, chapter by chapter, page by page, it provides illuminating explanatory notes with an emphasis on historical, cultural, and topographical references. It also reproduces Dickens's number plans for the novel and contains useful maps and illustrations. Breezier in style but also rich in contextual information and commentary is John Sutherland's *Inside* Bleak House: *A Guide for the Modern Dickensian* (not yet available in the United States), published to coincide with the BBC television adaptation in 2005. Among the dozens of other general companions, introductions, and reference works on Dickens, the *Oxford Reader's Companion to Dickens*, edited by Paul Schlicke, stands out for the excellence of its articles and the encyclopedic breadth of information it provides about Dickens's friends, the Victorian cultural context, trends in Dickens criticism, as well as individual works and characters. *The Dickens Index*, edited by Nicolas Bentley, Michael Slater, and Nina Burgis, contains a full list of characters and places referred to in the novels. *The Cambridge Companion to Charles Dickens*, edited by John O. Jordan, and *Palgrave Advances in Charles Dickens Studies*, edited by John Bowen and Robert L. Patten, are also useful.

Bleak House was first published in nineteen monthly installments, beginning in March 1852 and ending in September 1853. The manuscript of the novel along with the corrected publisher's proofs in Dickens's own hand are housed in the John Forster collection at the Victoria and Albert Museum in London.

They, together with other materials in the Forster collection, are available on microfilm. For information on Dickens's relations with his publishers and for details about the sales of *Bleak House*, Robert L. Patten's *Charles Dickens and His Publishers* is indispensable. The definitive, twelve-volume Pilgrim Edition of Dickens's *Letters*, edited by Madeleine House, Graham Storey, Kathleen Tillotson, and others (also available on a searchable CD-ROM), provides a rich look at the daily texture of Dickens's busy life. Volumes 6 and 7 deal with the period of *Bleak House*. Although a transcription of Dickens's number plans and of the alternative titles he considered for the novel is included in most teaching editions of *Bleak House*, as well as in Shatto's *Companion*, Harry Stone's edition of *Dickens's Working Notes for His Novels* usefully provides a facsimile of these documents. For contemporary reviews and responses to the novel, see *Dickens: The Critical Heritage*, edited by Philip Collins. George Ford's *Dickens and His Readers* traces the course of Dickens's subsequent reputation. In the introduction to a 1996 Longman casebook on Dickens, Steven Connor gives an excellent survey of Dickens criticism in the twentieth century.

Of special interest to teachers and students of *Bleak House* are the articles on contemporary social issues and current events that appear in the two magazines, *Household Words* and *All the Year Round*, that Dickens edited beginning in 1850. As mentioned, Shatto's *Companion* provides a list of these and other contemporary sources. Topics discussed in these articles range from Chancery reform, public health, and electoral corruption to Dickens's excursions into the urban slums with Inspector Charles Field of the London Detective Police, his model for the character of Inspector Bucket (see esp. Dickens, "On Duty"). Dickens's attitude toward some of the important topics of his day can also be derived from his speeches, which have been collected and edited by K. J. Fielding. A third contemporary source used by some instructors when time permits is Henry Mayhew's *London Labour and the London* Poor, which began appearing as articles in the *Morning Chronicle* shortly before Dickens started work on *Bleak House*. Mayhew's survey of working lives among the London poor offers many productive points of comparison with *Bleak House*. His interviews with costermongers, mudlarks, and crossing sweepers (like the novel's Jo) allow access, mediated admittedly by Mayhew's middle-class persona, to seldom heard voices from the urban underclasses.

Visual, Audiovisual, and Electronic Materials

Bleak House is of course an illustrated novel, and many respondents in our survey chose the Penguin edition as a teaching text in part because it contains reproductions of all the original Hablot Browne (Phiz) illustrations for the novel (though not of the wrapper cover for its original serialization). Teachers interested in ways of integrating study of the illustrations into their classes should consult the essay by Richard L. Stein in this volume. Other valuable sources of information about the *Bleak House* illustrations can be found in Michael Steig, *Dickens and Phiz*, and Jane R. Cohen, *Charles Dickens and His Original Illustrators*, as well as in the entries by Patten in the *Oxford Reader's Companion to Dickens*. Stein's essay "Dickens and Illustration" also deals extensively with *Bleak House*.

In recent years, considerable attention has been devoted to another paratextual aspect of the novel's original serial publication, the advertisements that preceded and followed the two illustrations and thirty-two pages of text that made up each monthly number. (The final monthly installment was a double number, with four illustrations and forty-eight pages of text.) Copies of the *Bleak House Advertiser*, as it was called, are not always easy to come by, unless one has access to a set of the original parts. Bernard Darwin's *The Dickens Advertiser: A Collection of the Advertisements in the Original Parts of Novels by Charles Dickens* contains a fairly random selection of ads from different novels and is by no means complete. Michael Slater's facsimile edition of *The Life and Adventures of Nicholas Nickleby* includes all the advertisements for that novel and can serve as a model for students interested in seeing an earlier example of the interplay of advertisement, illustration, and text. Reproductions of and commentary on advertisements from *Bleak House* can be found in a few places. Stein's "Dickens and Illustration" reproduces one such ad. Andrew Williams's essay in this volume discusses teaching *Bleak House* in connection with the *Bleak House Advertiser* and gives examples. Chapter 2 of Daniel Hack's *The Material Interests of the Victorian Novel* has an interesting discussion of the advertiser and reproduces two sample advertisements. Valuable commentary on Dickens and advertising can be found in Jennifer Wicke, *Advertising Fictions: Literature, Advertisement, and Social Reading*, and in Gerard Curtis, *Visual Words: Art and the Material Book in Victorian England*.

Two further visual aids for teaching Dickens more generally and *Bleak House* in particular deserve mention. One is the set of plates in Gustave Doré and Blanchard Jerrold's *London: A Pilgrimage*. Although they date from two decades after the publication of *Bleak House*, Doré's dark images of crowded streets and urban slums tangibly capture the atmosphere of certain passages in the novel and give students a good visual reference point for the broader social world of the Dickensian city. A second resource is Peter Ackroyd's *Dickens' London: An Imaginative Vision*, which contains a wide sampling of Dickens-related photographs of Victorian London.

None of the respondents in our survey reports using films, videos, or DVDs as an integral part of teaching *Bleak House*, although several mention the availability of such materials as something they call to the attention of students who have the time or inclination to find them on their own. Audiovisual resources for teaching *Bleak House* are generally of two kinds. First are films that focus on the life and career of Dickens himself. These include the ten-part, eleven-hour TV miniseries *Dickens of London,* written by Wolf Mankowitz, with Roy Dotrice as the adult Dickens; the three-part, three-hour TV miniseries *Dickens*, written by Peter Ackroyd, with Anton Lesser as Dickens and Ackroyd himself as the on-camera presenter-narrator; and the A&E biography *Charles Dickens*. Also available is a filmed version of Simon Callow's one-man performance *The Mystery of Charles Dickens*, a play scripted by Ackroyd and combining historical narrative with reenactments of Dickens's own dramatic readings.

Two modern screen adaptations of *Bleak House* are available, both TV miniseries produced by the BBC. The 1985 version, adapted by Arthur Hopcroft, features Diana Rigg as Lady Dedlock and Denholm Elliott as John Jarndyce. The 2005 miniseries, adapted by Andrew Davies, with Gillian Anderson as Lady Dedlock and Charles Dance as Tulkinghorn, appeared too late for respondents in our survey to use or even refer to. Both versions have their strengths, including strong supporting casts in the comic roles (Krook, Smallweed, Guppy). The 1985 version adheres more closely to Dickens's plot; the 2005 version moves at a faster pace and has more comedy. Neither successfully finds a way to deal with the novel's double narration, though the 2005 version uses editing to good effect, cutting crisply between scenes to create striking juxtapositions in a way that recalls the alternation between Esther and the other narrator. Purists will inevitably find points to disapprove of in both versions: oversimplifications of the plot, omissions of favorite minor characters (no Bagnets!), the introduction (in 2005) of a character (Tulkinghorn's clerk, Clamb) who does not appear in the novel, and so on. An entire course could be designed around the two versions, focusing on problems of adaptation and perhaps drawing comparisons to similar issues raised by the film versions of *Great Expectations* or *Oliver Twist*.

In recent years, electronic resources for studying Dickens have expanded rapidly. Not all Web sites are reliable, however, and they should always be used with caution, since information on them is sometimes posted without proper oversight or review. In addition, addresses change, sites close, and regular maintenance deteriorates. We mention here only sites that have shown signs of endurance and dependability. Other resources may be found by using standard search engines.

Project Guttenberg, a reliable source for electronic texts by Dickens and many other writers, provides a downloadable text of *Bleak House. The Victorian Web* offers a wide range of background information on the Victorian period generally and on many Victorian texts and writers, including Dickens. Mitsuharu Matsuoka's Web site *The Dickens Page* contains searchable texts of all of Dickens's novels as well as links to many other Dickens Web sites. *The Dickens Project* at the University of California, Santa Cruz, maintains a Web site with information about its annual Dickens conferences. The site also contains a searchable e-text of *Bleak House* as well as Newsom's useful *Bleak House* bibliography from 2001. *The Victorian Dictionary* site has good maps of the city and a wealth of information about Victorian social history. It also contains a Dickens search engine with access to most of Dickens's major texts. For more information on human spontaneous combustion, a valuable source is the Wikipedia Web site, which has references to *Bleak House* and to other uses of spontaneous combustion in fiction.

Finally, mention should be made of the valuable electronic discussion list housed at the University of California, Santa Barbara, and devoted to Dickens. Dickns-l provides a forum for Dickens scholars, students, and enthusiasts from around the world. It also has a keyword-searchable archive of previous postings. To subscribe, send a message to listserv@listserv.ucsb.edu with the command subscribe dickns-l.

Readings for Students

When we asked teachers which critical or contextual readings they assigned to students studying *Bleak House*, the most common response was none at all. Teachers seemed all too aware of the demands of the novel alone, and most devote at least two and up to four full weeks of a standard semester course to reading it. We found nonetheless a fair number of faculty members assigning required reading to accompany *Bleak House*, and their strategies fall into three categories.

Contextual Reading

The most common assignments are designed to introduce students to the cultural landscape of Victorian Britain and to illuminate aspects of the novel's social critique. Many instructors assign articles from Dickens's magazine *Household Words* or sections of Mayhew's *London Labour and the London Poor*. Some courses locate *Bleak House* in relation to other Victorian responses to the conditions of the Victorian city, assigning Thomas Carlyle's early essay on industrialism "Signs of the Times" or Friedrich Engels's detailed assessment of Manchester in *The Condition of the Working Class in England*. Others assigned selections from Isabella Beeton's *Book of Household Management* to help students analyze the novel's representation of domesticity and, by extension, of Esther Summerson.

Critical Essays

Although many instructors mentioned one or more critical essays on *Bleak House*, they agreed on few. Two, however, were mentioned again and again; they are discussed below. Faculty members who teach critical essays often use a casebook or ready-made collection of critical perspectives. Those who use the Norton Critical Edition often assign one or more of the critical pieces excerpted in that volume; those by G. K. Chesterton, W. J. Harvey, and H. M. Daleski were singled out. Many assign part or all of the *Bleak House* casebook edited by Jeremy Tambling, which collects ten essays on the novel.

Theoretical Essays

Virtually the only essays on *Bleak House* used by more than one or two instructors are the two now classic statements by J. Hillis Miller and D. A. Miller, each representing an important aspect of poststructuralist theory as it developed in American letters. Hillis Miller's essay was published first as the introduction to a 1971 Penguin edition of the novel. Though no longer part of the Penguin Classics paperback now in print, the essay is available in Miller's *Victorian Subjects* and is reprinted in the Tambling casebook. D. A. Miller's article first appeared in the journal *Representations* in 1983, then as a chapter in his 1988 book *The Novel and the Police*. It is also included in the Tambling casebook.

Hillis Miller's introduction illustrates one trend in the American adaptation of Jacques Derrida's philosophy of deconstruction. Considering the central role of Chancery in the novel, Miller focuses on the court's failure to manage the documents it produces. In Hillis Miller's hands the papers of Chancery illustrate the impossibility of ultimate and final interpretations and thus the openness of interpretation itself. If this approach represents the early adaptation of Derrida for criticism on the novel, D. A. Miller's "Discipline in Different Voices: Bureaucracy, Police, Family, and *Bleak House*" offers an early application of Michel Foucault's work, or, more precisely, Foucault's theory of power in the modern state developed in the book *Discipline and Punish*. The nineteenth century, for Foucault, was characterized by new government systems of surveillance to monitor populations (most famously Jeremy Bentham's panopticon), as well as the increasing internalization of state power by individuals. For D. A. Miller, *Bleak House* evokes a seamless world of discipline, internal and external, typified by the omnipresence of Chancery and the all but invisible work of Inspector Bucket. But he suggestively links the logic of the modern institution to the genre of the novel itself: a paper system in its own right, producing an experience of domestic freedom (i.e., the experience of private reading), while paradoxically constraining and shaping that experience.

Teachers who use these essays are often interested in addressing questions in critical theory and methodology with their students. But many have simply found it helpful to test students' interpretive skills by asking them to reconcile these two influential views or to take sides in an imagined debate between them.

Readings for Teachers

Biographies

There are two major contemporary biographies of Dickens, each very different in character and each attracting its own loyal following. Fred Kaplan's *Dickens* is a scholarly biography, providing scrupulous documentation for each assertion. Peter Ackroyd's *Dickens* aims to provide a readable and imaginative reconstruction of the writer and his world. Until Kaplan's book, Edgar Johnson's 1952 two-volume *Charles Dickens* was the standard life; it is exhaustively researched and still preferred by many. Also of great value is John Forster's *Life of Charles Dickens*, the official biography commissioned by Dickens before his death.

Shorter summary biographical introductions to Dickens's life and work have been standards of twentieth-century publishing: every major house seems to provide one. A contemporary standout is the Penguin volume by the novelist Jane Smiley, whose familiarity both with the practice of fiction and with the politics of academic life (see her *Moo*) give her a particularly useful angle. Robert Newsom's *Charles Dickens Revisited* was also recommended by survey respondents. G. K. Chesterton's short overview of Dickens's life and works is now a classic.

Critical Perspectives on Bleak House

Esther and Feminism

The critical fortunes of *Bleak House* in some ways parallel those of its conarrator, Esther Summerson. With the resurgence of interest in Dickens among American critics in the 1950s and 1960s came renewed attention to the rhetoric of Esther's narrative. William Axton's "The Trouble with Esther" and Alex Zwerdling's "Esther Summerson Rehabilitated" helped inaugurate this critical trend.

More recent feminist readings have found in Esther's writing not an emblem of domestic docility but the symptom of a damaged and damaging world. Virginia Blain's "Double Vision and the Double Standard" argues that, despite the satire directed at Mrs. Jellyby and Mrs. Snagsby, *Bleak House* provides, through its split narrative structure, a revealing examination of a world torn into separate male and female perspectives. Helena Michie's "'Who Is This in Pain': Scarring, Disfigurement, and Female Identity in *Bleak House* and *Our Mutual Friend*" shows how female selfhood in these novels is figured in the description of illness and suffering. Carolyn Dever, in her book *Death and the Mother from Dickens to Freud*, poses this stunning question: "Is it possible for an orphan to write an autobiography?" (85). She shows that, from the psychological perspective Dickens develops in *Bleak House*, the articulation of selfhood is founded on the symbolic loss of the mother. Hilary Schor's essay "*Bleak House* and the Dead

Mother's Property" focuses on the vexed question of female property in Victorian inheritance law. In Esther's narrative, Schor argues, "the orphan daughter writes to reclaim her property" (101).

Not exactly feminist in orientation but rehabilitative in emphasis is Timothy Peltason's "Esther's Will." Peltason traces the novel's "barely suppressed pun" on the word "will": the legal instrument in the Jarndyce case and the suppressed personal agency of Esther herself (671). While the former becomes moot, the latter, in Peltason's reading, emerges in a pattern of Esther's "growing self-assertion" (672).

Poststructuralism

The potential energy that poststructuralist theory leant to literary criticism in the 1970s produced innovative and striking readings of *Bleak House*, readings that recent critics of all stripes have felt compelled to address. The two central statements are the above-mentioned essays by J. Hillis Miller and D. A. Miller. Respondents also noted Katherine Cummings's "Re-reading *Bleak House*: The Chronicle of a 'Little Body' and Its Perverse Defense," which draws on French poststructuralist feminism in an analysis of Esther and her absent father, Nemo.

Bleak House and History

Critics have long been interested in *Bleak House*'s engagement with its time and place; an excellent introduction to the subject is John Butt and Kathleen Tillotson's chapter on the novel in *Dickens at Work*, which deals with poverty, law, politics, sanitation, and religion. In recent years critics have tried to understand more clearly *Bleak House*'s relation to the evolving liberal tradition in British politics. Lauren M. E. Goodlad's *Victorian Literature and the Victorian State* and Pam Morris's *Imagining Inclusive Society in Nineteenth-Century Novels* both include major chapters on *Bleak House*, which are notable for their reevaluation of the way critics, following D. A. Miller, have employed Foucault's reading of the panopticon, Bentham's circular prison, to understand the politics of the novel. Goodlad advances the concept of pastorship, developed by Foucault in later work, as a more useful point of reference, and she finds a model of pastoral politics developed through the story of Woodcourt. Chris R. Vanden Bossche's "Class Discourse and Popular Agency in *Bleak House*" also reads the novel as an attempt to envision a liberal society, in part through a critique of then current class discourse. Kathleen Blake's "*Bleak House*, Political Economy, Victorian Studies" examines the received view of Dickens as the enemy of utilitarian political economy.

If these recent historical readings, in varying ways, depart from the Foucauldian perspective of D. A. Miller, others have followed from critical reappraisals of J. Hillis Miller's Derridean approach. Among these are Gordon Bigelow, who examines the novel in relation to nineteenth-century economic thought, and

Kevin McLaughlin, whose *Paperwork* contains a superb analysis of the motif of paper in *Bleak House*.

Goodlad's essay focuses in part on Dickens's response to debates about public sanitation and public health. Laura Fasick's essay "Dickens and the Diseased Body in *Bleak House*" also considers the novel's representation of disease and contagion. The medical and scientific aspects of *Bleak House* have provoked perennial controversy, as Dickens's own preface indicates, with its reply to G. H. Lewes's skeptical view of spontaneous human combustion (for more on Lewes's view, see Haight). Ann Y. Wilkinson's "*Bleak House*: From Faraday to Judgment Day" suggests, as others have since, that Dickens drew on the concept of entropy, derived in nineteenth-century physics. In "Dickens's Science" K. J. Fielding and Shu-Fang Lai dispute the point, while at the same time illustrating Dickens's enormous interest in science.

Those interested in Mr. Bucket and the detective police will wish to consult Philip Collins's *Dickens and Crime*, as well as Ronald Thomas's "Making Darkness Visible" and Elizabeth Dale Samet's "'When Constabulary Duty's to Be Done.'"

More than half of Alexander Welsh's book *Dickens Redressed* is devoted to *Bleak House*. The essay is highly readable, blending biographical and historical interpretation with reflections on thirty years of criticism. His final take on the famous poststructuralist readings—he calls it "the cause of Miller and Miller" (140)—is worth the wait.

Narrative and Genre

Twinned narratives, the use of the present tense, an opening paragraph with no verbs, a sentence fragment for a closing—these and other striking formal features of *Bleak House* have generated strong interest among critics since Dickens's art began to be seriously considered. The most detailed attention to narrative technique is Audrey Jaffe's chapter in her book *Vanishing Points*, which examines the counterpoint between omniscience and self-effacement. Essays by Blain, Dever, and Schor, focused on Esther and described above, also discuss narrative structure or strategy. Robert Newsom's book-length essay *Dickens on the Romantic Side of Familiar Things:* Bleak House *and the Novel Tradition* has become a classic. Its approach is difficult to classify in any narrow way. Like Jaffe's book, it draws from psychoanalysis to help decipher the curiously halting and recursive narrative structure of the book. But, as its title suggests, it is also concerned with the question of genre, with the novel's crossing of gothic romance and novelistic realism.

Colonialism and Nationalism

In British literary studies as a whole, a once accepted indifference to the issues of colonialism and slavery has begun to dissolve, as the methods of postcolonial studies are increasingly incorporated into the critical repertoire of the discipline. Postcolonial studies of *Bleak House*, however, and of Dickens's work more generally, are an underdeveloped area, one that one hopes will not remain so for much longer. Bruce Robbins's essay "Telescopic Philanthropy" deals with the question of national identity, as raised by Mrs. Jellyby's enterprise. Timothy Carens looks at the novel's image of Africa in "The Civilizing Mission at Home." In "'Anywhere's Nowhere'" James Buzard sees in *Bleak House* a reimagination of Englishness, in part through a discussion of the Great Exhibition of 1851. Similarly, Robert Tracy provides a comprehensive discussion of the novel as Dickens's "alternate Exhibition to the one in the Crystal Palace" ("Lighthousekeeping" 46).

Part Two

APPROACHES

The Crystal Palace and
Dickens's "Dark Exhibition"

Janice Carlisle

"What connexion can there be" between a novel dealing with a Chancery case and an international exposition held in a building nicknamed the Crystal Palace? That variant of the famous question asked by the narrator of *Bleak House* about the relation between Jo and, among other places, Chesney Wold (256) highlights both the improbability and the relevance of my subject here. Dickens began thinking about the novel that would follow *David Copperfield* before the opening of the Great Exhibition of the Works of Industry of All Nations on 1 May 1851 and after he had participated, if only briefly, in the preparations for it; and he began writing *Bleak House* in November of that year, a little over a month after the Crystal Palace closed its doors (*Letters* 6: 298, 545). By setting the action of the novel more than seven years before Esther pens her final words, Dickens gave himself no occasion to mention the exposition or its astounding success in the pages of his novel. Yet before the exhibition opened and well before he began the first number of *Bleak House*, Dickens had called in *Household Words* for an alternate "great display of England's sins and negligences," a "dark Exhibition of the bad results of our doings!" ("*Amusements*" 313–14). As Robert Tracy has claimed, *Bleak House* became that "other exhibition, Dickens's Great Exhibition of 1852" ("Lighthousekeeping" 45). Fittingly, the novel, one of his darkest, both in its pessimism and in the visual qualities of Phiz's famous "dark plates," is a full, though indirect, commentary on the Crystal Palace, Dickens's "dark Exhibition" in response to the industrial show that had been staged in a giant, light-filled glass house.

Athough the Great Exhibition has been frequently analyzed as the event that inaugurated either Britain's entry into modernity or its embrace of commodity culture,[1] its unprecedented gathering of great numbers of people of different classes under one roof was among its most distinctive features and the one on which I focus here. Asking students to think about *Bleak House* in the context of the event that preoccupied national attention for more than two years helps them consider how Dickens treats some of the topics associated with it, particularly the relation between work and class. Sharing with students two *Punch* cartoons that commemorate the exhibition provides an effective basis for such a discussion. What follows here is a set of suggestions for preparing and teaching a class devoted to the "connexion" between Dickens's novel and the Great Exhibition, a "connexion" that encourages students to think about the people and places put on display not only by the Royal Commission responsible for the Crystal Palace but also, in their different media, by Dickens and the *Punch* staff.

Preparations

Although I hope to offer here all the information needed to set up this discussion—both the ingredients and the recipe, so to speak—there are some secondary sources on the Great Exhibition that it might be useful to consult. Especially helpful is the richly illustrated volume by C. H. Gibbs-Smith, *The Great Exhibition of 1851: A Commemorative Album*. Some of the images from this compendium are worth reproducing for students. "Oddities"—a stove "in the form of a knight" and a "Comic electric telegraph and key board" in the shape of a face or a knife with eighty blades and papier-mâché chairs (figs. 195, 203, 102, 166)—make some of the more wildly imaginative flights of Dickens's novel, eccentric characters like Krook and the Smallweeds, seem apiece with Victorian culture. Of the two books on the exposition published in 1999, Jeffrey A. Auerbach's *The Great Exhibition of 1851* is the more useful, though John R. Davis's *The Great Exhibition* includes a discussion of Dickens's ambivalent response to the event (187–90). Auerbach's chapter on workers' attendance at the Crystal Palace, "Integration and Segregation," is particularly pertinent here, even if he at times adopts a characteristically Victorian tone of self-congratulation, as he does when he inaccurately claims that "all classes" came together there (151). Most directly relevant to my purposes is Tracy's article "Lighthousekeeping: *Bleak House* and the Crystal Palace," a comprehensive exposition of the argument that Dickens's novel is "an alternate Exhibition to the one in the Crystal Palace" (46). As Tracy points out, the reader of *Bleak House* is treated to one exhibit after another: Tom-all-Alone's, a brickmaker's cottage, an attic housing destitute orphans. He offers useful information on the extent to which, *pace* John Butt and Kathleen Tillotson (180–82), Dickens commented on the Great Exhibition in his essays in *Household Words* (43–45), and he also describes the advertisements that enveloped the part issues of the novel, thus "placing the text . . . amid an exhibition of manufactured items, some of which had also been seen at the Crystal Palace Exhibition" (33–35). Stressing Esther's role in offering the readers of *Bleak House* one catalog after another (26–29), Tracy identifies what is, I think, the most obvious link between the novel and the Great Exhibition. Almost everyone writing about the Crystal Palace gives in at one point or another to the temptation to construct lists, and their prominence in *Bleak House* suggests that Dickens was no exception. One way of preparing for the class that I outline would be to ask students, as they begin their reading, to keep a list of the lists in the novel: the items in Krook's shop (67–68), the rooms and furniture in Bleak House itself (85–87), and, much later, my favorite catalog, that of the items in the Jellybys' closets (480). Students can also be encouraged to notice the ways in which characters in this novel become exhibits—Turveydrop, the "model of Deportment," is a good early example (225).

The class that I describe here, however, would take place after students have read at least twenty-two chapters of *Bleak House*, after they have accompanied Snagsby on his tour of Tom-all-Alone's. To prepare for this discussion, they should be asked, as they continue their reading of the novel, to reread specific sections of chapters 8, 15, and 22 (123–36, 243–49, 352–62). They should also study the two *Punch* cartoons available on the Web site https://classesv2.yale.edu/access/content/user/jc692/Punch/: "Specimens from Mr. Punch's Industrial Exhibition of 1850" (see fig. 1, p. 7) and an engraving after a design by John Tenniel, "The Pound and the Shilling" (see fig. 2, p. 8). Also well worth exploring is the site developed by the Kenneth Spencer Research Library at the University of Kansas: http://spencer.lib.ku.edu/exhibits/greatexhibition/index.htm. Enlarging and reading the street ballad "I'm Going to See the Exhibition for a Shilling" on the page "Humorous Asides" will prove the point that the lowest admission fee still excluded many members of the working classes: the speaker announces his determination to see the inside of the Crystal Palace even if he has to "sell the pig and donkey, / The frying pan and bed."

Adding some preparatory information is helpful when making this assignment: students should know that when the Great Exhibition opened on 1 May 1851, the cost of admission was high enough to exclude all but the well-to-do. On 26 May, the first day on which the fee was lowered to a shilling, the fears of "King Mob" that had complicated the planning of the Great Exhibition were again powerfully evoked—so much so that attendance dropped off initially, though by mid-summer, when specially priced excursion trains were bringing workers and their families to London from the industrial north of England, daily attendance figures at times reached over 100,000. Even so, shilling days (Monday through Thursday) were not the equivalent of free admission. The workers who built the Crystal Palace earned "a relatively comfortable daily wage of 3s–5s" (Auerbach 131), not enough to make the expenditure of even one shilling seem negligible. The entrance fee was, therefore, a way in which the largely middle-class organizers of the Great Exhibition rewarded what they took to be the respectability of the so-called skilled laborers who could save enough to cover the costs involved in seeing the Crystal Palace, including those for food, transportation, and lodging. Students should also be aware that the two *Punch* cartoons are examples of the most prominent visual feature of the weekly magazine: such full-page wood engravings, called "big cuts" in their time, represented the consensus that emerged from the weekly meetings of the entire staff, not the views of one artist. Although *Punch* had been skeptical about the Great Exhibition as it was being planned and although its attitude remained at times ambivalent (Pearson), by the summer of 1851, the paper, like most Victorians, was celebrating the success of the Crystal Palace and, in particular, the unexpectedly good behavior of the workers who went there on shilling days.[2]

Teaching the Class

At the beginning of this session, students will not know about Dickens's involvement in the planning for the Great Exhibition, which turned almost entirely on issues of class, and offering them the following information would be a good prelude to discussion. In 1850 Dickens readily agreed to serve on the Central Working Classes Committee, chaired by Samuel Wilberforce, the bishop of Oxford. The committee, which included such well-known members as Lord Ashley and John Stuart Mill as well as the Chartists William Lovett and Henry Vincent, was set up to counter fears that the working classes would use the occasion of the Great Exhibition to perpetrate violence or hold demonstrations like the relatively recent Chartist meeting on Kennington Common in 1848, and the committee's goal was to encourage workers to support and to visit the exposition. The committee's life, however, was short. At their first meeting in May 1850, the members voted to ask the Royal Commission for official recognition as a body working under its auspices. That request was turned down because such an action might have seemed to place Prince Albert, the president of the commission, "at the head of a 'democratic movement.'" Just a month later, therefore, Dickens moved that the committee be disbanded (*Letters* 6: 57n), and it was dissolved, an outcome proving to many that the planners of the exposition were not responding adequately to the needs and interests of the working classes.

Dickens was alternately unimpressed and overwhelmed by the Great Exhibition. He stayed away as much as he could, remarking on his "Expositional absence" from both it and London (*Letters* 6: 349). When he did attend, he mocked *Punch* for having "fall[en]" for the popularity of the Crystal Palace, explaining, "I have always had an instinctive feeling against the Exhibition, of a faint, inexplicable sort. I have a great confidence in its being a correct one somehow or other—perhaps it was a foreshadowing of its bewilderment of the public," which would finally issue in "boredom and lassitude" (*Letters* 6: 448–49). Earlier, Dickens had recorded his own sense of "bewilderment" when confronted with the plethora of objects in the Crystal Palace: "I find I am 'used up' by the Exhibition. I don't say 'there's nothing in it'—there's too much. I have only been twice. So many things bewildered me. I have a natural horror of sights, and the fusion of so many sights in one has not decreased it." Identifying two of the exhibition's most celebrated objects, he added, "I am not sure that I have seen anything but the Fountain—and perhaps the Amazon," references to the Crystal Fountain and an imposing statue of a female warrior about to kill the tiger that is attacking the horse on which she is riding (*Letters* 6: 428–29; Gibbs-Smith, figs. 33, 193). Stunned amazement was often the response to the Great Exhibition, one commentator describing the "state of mental helplessness" that it created in him (Auerbach 95; cf. Allwood 22). Despite all the light that the giant glass house afforded, then, the experience of going to the Crystal Palace might have been like Snagsby's in visiting Tom-all-Alone's, one of deepening confusion if not despair. In that sense the slums in London as Dickens evokes them in *Bleak House* are the dark double of the Crystal Palace—the places where England heaps up displays of its epitomizing phenomena, its impoverished workers or its glorious products.

This point suggests another that might be shared with students before turning to the discussion of the *Punch* cartoons. If it was difficult for the visitor to the Great Exhibition to grasp the magnitude of its 100,000 exhibits, it requires an equally challenging feat of historical imagination to conceive of the reasons for and extent of the hosannas of self-praise that greeted its opening. Whatever one's perspective, the building of the Crystal Palace must seem an extraordinary achievement—an act of imagination, organization, will, and even courage, an achievement not unlike the writing of *Bleak House*, a novel for which Dickens was planning the advertisements before having set down its first word (*Letters* 6: 518). The size of the building was unprecedented: covering nineteen acres in Hyde Park, it was made of nearly 300,000 giant panes of glass, 200 miles of iron framing, not to mention wood measuring 600,000 cubic feet. It took a crew that came to number over 2,000 men only six months to erect a structure so gigantic that it could enclose three impressive elms as well as groupings of smaller trees (Gibbs-Smith 32–33). As contemporary engravings reveal, it dwarfed the four-story residences across from it. No wonder that on opening day, with Queen Victoria in attendance, the Hallelujah Chorus was performed, and the archbishop of Canterbury invoked God's blessing on an event that many took to be evidence of the providential care that had rightly singled out for material success Britain and her industries. Charles Kingsley wept when he first saw the exhibition, and in a sermon that he preached four days later, he called it one of the "proofs of the Kingdom of God" (2: 21). Open for only 141 days, the Crystal Palace saw over six million visitors. Of those visitors, seventy-four percent bought shilling tickets (Gibbs-Smith 32–33). Writing on the day before attending the closing of the exhibition, Thomas Babington Macaulay described 1851 as "a singularly happy year of peace, plenty, good feeling, innocent pleasure, national glory of the best and purest sort" (qtd. in ffrench 274).

Dickens was no doubt repulsed by such self-congratulation, as Butt and Til-lotson speculate (182), but so also initially was *Punch*. Yet both paper and nov-elist adapted the methods of the Great Exhibition in their objections to it, as my references to the many lists in *Bleak House* suggest and as the first *Punch* cartoon, "Specimens from Mr. Punch's Industrial Exhibition of 1850," also dem-onstrates. When read from left to right, this engraving provides a pictorial list of destitute workers, and students can be encouraged to think about its visual logic, in particular the effect of the bell jars that separate the workers from their observers, Prince Albert and the wholly respectable Mr. Punch. Discus-sion could then take up the similarities and differences between this image from 1850 and the exhibits of the working poor that Dickens provided his public in 1852 and 1853, in particular the scenes from chapters 8, 15, and 22. In *Past and Present* (1843), Thomas Carlyle had famously described the "inarticulate" work-ing classes as too "almost stupid" to speak for themselves (22–23), but in these scenes from *Bleak House*, quite unlike that in *Punch*'s "Specimens," workers are allowed to speak—to have their say about their circumstances and to talk back when chided by their middle-class interlocutors, particularly when those exam-iners are as uncomprehending of the effects of poverty as are Mrs. Pardiggle and Inspector Bucket.

I do not want, however, to prescribe where the rest of this discussion might lead: for a teacher, the greatest satisfaction, I think, of talking with students about a novel as rich as *Bleak House* is the likelihood that they will come up with ideas and perspectives that one could not have imagined when planning such a discussion. In the case of the second *Punch* cartoon, the more famous "The Pound and the Shilling," that is particularly true. Although this engraving purports to offer a straightforward depiction of an imagined meeting between a navvy and the duke of Wellington within the confines of the Crystal Palace, a meeting that Mr. Punch himself seems to bless as he looks down on it from the gallery above, it quickly reveals complexities and problems that invite in-terpretation,[3] and students will soon discover them if invited to talk about its depiction of the material differences between members of different classes and the alignment of their bodies. Why *Punch* chooses a navvy as its archetypal worker is also worth considering, especially in relation to Dickens's decision to make servants—domestic workers like Charley and Snagsby's maid-of-all-work Guster and even the French maid Hortense—the most numerous workers in his novel, as their real-life counterparts were in England at the Victorian mid-century. Although the goal of this class is to increase students' appreciation of both Dickens's sympathy for the working poor and its limitations, the direction that this discussion takes will reflect the interests of the students engaged in it.[4] Dickens's "dark Exhibition" contains so many human "specimens," as *Punch* would call them, that their meanings, like the exhibits on display at the Crystal Palace, may seem at times almost inexhaustible.

NOTES

[1] Purbrick offers a comprehensive account of the use of the date of the Great Exhibition as a historical marker (Introduction 1–6). See also Briggs, chapter 2; Hopkins. On the Great Exhibition and commodity culture, see Richards, chapter 1; A. H. Miller, *Novels*, chapter 2. The linking of the Great Exhibition and *Bleak House* has become a feature of the criticism of the novel; see, for example, Buzard 109, 154–56.

[2] *Punch* also deserves credit for one of the Great Exhibition's most signal characteristics: in November 1850, it christened as "the Crystal Palace" the glass structure designed by Dickens's friend Joseph Paxton.

[3] See Edwards for a discussion of the sexual tensions evident in this image (28–34).

[4] After this class, students may want to continue to use the Great Exhibition as a touchstone. Lists and catalogs, as well as characters presented as models or exhibits, proliferate as the narrative of *Bleak House* moves toward its conclusion, as do questions that could frame a discussion of the last turn of its plot: "What connexion can there be" between the Crystal Palace and the house that Jarndyce prepares for Esther Summerson and Allan Woodcourt?

Bleak House, Africa, and
the Condition of England

Timothy Carens

Before students begin reading *Bleak House*, I call attention to a statement that falls near the end. "We are a prosperous community," Mr. Kenge insists, "a very prosperous community. We are a great country . . . we are a very great country" (950). With this comment in mind, first-time readers better appreciate the extent to which the novel shows just the reverse. Dickens depicts a nation in which myriads live in destitute poverty, a "community" riven by the great gulf of class. As an extended satire on the sort of patriotic blindness expressed by Kenge, *Bleak House* offers one of the most interesting contributions to what has become known as the condition-of-England debate. This debate includes a broad group of mid-century writings: essays, poems, sermons, government reports, journalistic accounts, and many novels. In *Chartism*, Thomas Carlyle begins with the observation that a "feeling very generally exists that the condition and disposition of the Working Classes is a rather ominous matter at present; that something ought to be said, something ought to be done, in regard to it" (151). In addition to Carlyle and Dickens, writers such as Charlotte Brontë, Elizabeth Barrett Browning, Benjamin Disraeli, Elizabeth Gaskell, Charles Kingsley, Alfred Tennyson, and John Ruskin published works that are in various ways preoccupied with this "ominous matter." Their writings confront a diverse array of interrelated problems: poverty, urbanization, sanitation, dehumanizing labor, alienation of the classes, and degradation of the domestic sphere. At stake throughout discussion of such problems is the very identity of the nation. Victorian social critics anxiously considered whether England had irremediably marred its ideal self-image as a "prosperous community" and "great country."

Condition-of-England texts might easily fill an entire special-topics syllabus, but I have always taught *Bleak House* in a broad survey course, where an introduction that attends to the novel's historical and discursive context is particularly helpful. I begin with a brief overview of the socioeconomic turmoil that attended the Industrial Revolution, particularly focusing on urbanization and poverty. Some of the illustrations by Gustave Doré from Doré and Jerrold Blanchard's *London: A Pilgrimage* provide vivid contemporary views of the Victorian slumscape. Through discussion and analysis of excerpts from condition-of-England texts, the class begins to acquire a sense of how middle-class social critics sought to express and generate dismay about the state of the nation. I ask students first to consider a passage from *Chartism* in which, after manifesting frustration with "our Upper Classes and Lawgivers" for neglecting the problems that have given rise to working-class political activism, the narrator exclaims:

> We lead them here to the shore of a boundless continent; ask them,
> Whether they do not with their own eyes see it, the strange symptoms of

it, lying huge, dark, unexplored, inevitable; full of hope, but also full of difficulty, savagery, almost of despair? (197)

Many students (especially those who have read *Heart of Darkness*) recognize the implicit reference to Africa. After reconstructing the Victorian image of the "dark" continent, the class is prepared to consider why Carlyle projects it onto poor and working-class England. Students readily see that he seeks to alarm readers with the notion of a "huge" and savage region at home. If asked to probe the reference to "hope," they also see that he aims to cultivate responsibility as well as fear. The passage encourages the "Upper Classes and Lawgivers" to explore and conquer, to take on the role of wise colonial governors who alleviate despair with light and order. This colonial model of class relations implies a paternalistic attitude that tends to rouse students; a few words about the Chartist movement allows them to raise informed objections about a metaphor that characterizes working-class subjects as either violent opponents to be tamed or passive victims to be uplifted.

The passage from Carlyle begins to suggest the crucial role that conceptions of African otherness play in condition-of-England discourse. Simon Gikandi rightly argues that "it is through the black figure that Englishness acquires the metaphorical structure that enables it to gaze at itself in crisis" (69). A passage from Disraeli's *Sybil; or, The Two Nations* further confirms that Victorian social critics generate concern and fear by evoking the "black figure" and its connotations of primitive despair and savage hostility. The narrator describes coal miners emerging from the earth: as "the mine delivers its gang and the pit its bondsmen," the

> plain is covered with the swarming multitude: bands of stalwart men, broad-chested and muscular, wet with toil, and black as the children of the tropics; troops of youth—alas! of both sexes,—though neither their raiment nor their language indicates the difference; all are clad in male attire; and oaths that men might shudder at, issue from lips born to breathe words of sweetness. Yet these are to be—some are—the mothers of England! But can we wonder at the hideous coarseness of their language when we remember the savage rudeness of their lives? . . . circumstances that seem to have escaped the notice of the Society for the Abolition of Negro Slavery. Those worthy gentlemen too appear to have been singularly unconscious of the sufferings of the little Trappers, which was remarkable, as many of them were in their own employ. . . . With hunches of white bread in their black hands, and grinning with their sable countenances and ivory teeth, they really looked like a gang of negroes at a revel. (178–79)

Students enjoy picking out the details of this topsy-turvy world created by industrial labor. English workers, presumably self-governing agents within a free-market economy, appear as "bondsmen." The coal dust that blackens their skin

proclaims the socioeconomic limitations on their freedom. The "worthy" abolitionists the passage mentions are in fact the owners of this mine, and so, in this
world of Disraeli's, abolitionists become slave merchants. Their exploitation of
English children highlights, for Disraeli, the hypocrisy of their philanthropic
commitment to ending slavery. The blackened workers are not only figures of
pity. The depiction of a "swarming multitude" of "broad-chested and muscular"
men suggests a fearful consciousness of their power. This excerpt also illustrates
how anxieties about gender roles, especially those perceived as appropriate for
the "mothers of England," become intertwined in condition-of-England texts
with anxieties about poverty, the class system, and national identity.

Although passages from many other texts could work equally well, the Carlyle and Disraeli excerpts efficiently convey ideological positions and rhetorical
devices that arise in more elaborate form in *Bleak House*. As attention turns to
the novel itself, students are quick to note a similarity between Disraeli's swipe
at the "Society for the Abolition of Negro Slavery" and Dickens's satire on "telescopic philanthropy" (49). Throughout his career, as Norris Pope shows, Dickens
censures foreign missions for taking up "useless and vexatious projects" abroad
while "ignoring urgent social problems at home" (127). In condition-of-England
texts, recognition of this imbalance tends to generate hostility directed toward
overseas philanthropists and also toward the distant objects of their concern—as
when Caddy Jellyby bitterly responds to her mother's career by exclaiming, "I
wish Africa was dead!" (60). The sense that England has fallen into terms of
comparison with the "dark continent" produces a desire to obliterate Africa itself and, by extension, all exotic locales that distract attention from the effort to
recivilize the nation.

This desire emerges most frequently and poignantly in relation to Jo, the
pathetic crossing sweeper who, like Disraeli's blackened workers, functions as
an icon of the precarious state of English civilization. The narrator angrily observes that Jo is not "a genuine foreign-grown savage" but rather "the ordinary
home-made article. . . . Homely filth begrimes him, homely parasites devour
him, homely sores are in him, homely rags are on him" (724). Such passages
forcefully show how condition-of-England discourse discredits conceptions of
imperial supremacy by attacking supposed distinctions between the home nation and the sort of savagery that Victorian culture associated with Africa. As
Homi K. Bhabha observes, the "'locality' of national culture is neither unified
nor unitary," and the "'other' is never outside or beyond us" (4). Although Jo is
the primary example of "home-made" savagery, students can find other varieties
in the Jellyby and Pardiggle families. Most writers who evoke "the black figure"
apply it exclusively to working-class characters and their environment. Dickens
takes a further step, suggesting that problems associated with Africa can erupt in
the middle-class homes of England as well as in its workplaces and slums. Noting
the silence and passivity of Mr. Jellyby, for example, Esther Summerson reflects
that he "might have been a native, but for his complexion" (57). Caddy, who
must forego an education in domestic femininity in order to work as her mother's

secretary, eventually rebels, insisting, "I won't be a slave all my life" (219). Bullied by their mother, the Pardiggle children become "absolutely ferocious with discontent"; their faces, "darkened" with rage, suggest a racial transformation (125). Prompted by discussion of the Disraeli passage, students will perceive a similar irony at work. Female philanthropists, like the "worthy gentlemen" who own the mines, produce at home the conditions they claim to redress abroad. With students, I try to emphasize that this irony serves different ideological interests in the two texts. In *Bleak House*, the responsibility for contaminating the nation with versions of "the black figure" shifts from captains of industry who exploit their workers to middle-class "mothers of England" who neglect their proper duties.

Because Africa plays such an important role in the novel's figurative structure, students benefit from learning more about Dickens's attitude toward the continent. After establishing the novel's preoccupation with "home-made" savagery, I turn attention to a short essay that Dickens wrote in response to the publication of *A Narrative of the Expedition Sent by Her Majesty's Government to the River Niger in 1841* (Allen and Thomson). In his review of this book, he mocks the grandiose objectives of a mission intended to eradicate slavery and establish a model farm in the African jungle. (See Temperley for a thorough historical account of the 1841 expedition.) As in *Bleak House*, Dickens blames female philanthropists for hatching a ludicrous colonization scheme. He also laments the death by malaria of the many English sailors, "more precious," as he describes them, "than a wilderness of Africans" (533). In the novel, the dismal end of Borrioboola-Gha reenacts the colonial tragedy in comic exaggeration. The review is a crucial supplement to the novel for a more significant reason, however, for it reveals the origin of a specific pattern of imagery that sustains the novel's diagnosis of the condition of England. In his review, Dickens depicts Africa as a site characterized by malignant nature. He imagines with disgust the "slimy and decaying earth," the "rotting vegetation," and the "pestilential air" of the Niger delta (533). Describing the Niger as a "fatal river," he endorses a grim metaphor coined by men on the 1841 expedition, who dubbed the entrance to the river "the Gate of the Cemetery" (533). For Dickens, tropical Africa represents decomposition, disease, and death.

Bleak House leads readers to "the shore of a boundless continent" at home, a London disfigured by the very marks of savage darkness that Dickens associates with the abhorred Niger delta. The memorable opening chapter depicts an urban metropolis in which malignant nature has begun to encroach on London. The "decaying earth" of the Niger delta becomes the "decaying houses" of England; the pavements and roads disappear beneath "crust upon crust of mud" (15, 13). Jo's life and death enact an uneven conflict between the English outcast and this decomposing matter. Jo tries to "keep the mud off the crossing" (256), but his effort to defend the intersection of civilized transport from "slimy and decaying earth" goes unnoticed and unpaid. By the end of his life, his clothes have come to look "like a bundle of rank leaves of swampy growth, that rotted long ago" (713), an image that recalls the "rotting vegetation" of Africa. While the plight of exotic inhabitants of the Niger delta captures the interest and compassion of Mrs. Jellyby and her ilk, the "home-made" savage carries the burden of England's degeneration.

Both symbolically and literally, the dense fog of London carries a pestilence as deadly as African malaria. John Jarndyce discerns a "subtle poison" in Chancery that "breed[s] . . . diseases" and "communicates some portion of its rottenness to everything" (560). A literal pestilence emanates from the "pestiferous and obscene" graveyard where Captain Hawdon is buried (180). The narrator emphasizes that the graveyard illustrates the fragility of the distinction between London, the supposed "heart of a civilized world," and sites such as the Niger delta (719). He predicts that it will provide "a shameful testimony to future ages, how civilisation and barbarism walked this boastful island together." Like the corpses of English sailors buried on the banks of the Niger, planted only to rot and breed more disease, Hawdon is "sow[n] . . . in corruption, to be raised in corruption." The "poisoned air" that exhales from his grave "deposits its witch-ointment" on the "iron gate," London's own "Gate of the Cemetery," at which both Jo and Lady Dedlock in turn catch the fever that kills them and infects others (180). If asked to recall the threat of revolution that Disraeli's *Sybil* embodies in the muscular frames of blackened English workers, students will perceive that *Bleak House* projects this fear onto a contagious disease that Dickens associates with the "pestilential air" of Africa. This comparison can lead to a fruitful discussion about why English writers persistently associate "home-made" social problems with versions of "the black figure." What conflicting feelings about the identity of the nation do such paradoxes expose?

If the Africanization of England works to justify the repudiation of overseas philanthropy, students should also be encouraged to see that it leads Dickens to a more problematic issue. Surveying Tom-all-Alone's, the narrator suggests at one point that "in truth it might be better for the national glory even that the sun should sometimes set upon the British dominions, than that it should ever rise upon so vile a wonder as Tom" (710). This statement marks a fascinating redirection in the novel's effort to sort out national priorities. Here, it is the geographic extent of the formal British empire rather than a private philanthropic scheme that rises in opposition to the reform of English barbarism. But Dickens is ultimately reluctant to call for a retrenchment of British dominions (710); he seeks instead to craft a policy that contains compassionate reform impulses within the nation without diminishing its imperial power. He suggests, in fact, that certain expressions of imperial power actually enhance the nation's ability to alleviate suffering and care for the destitute at home. Crucially, this resolution requires a careful realignment of those gendered spheres of influence confused by Mrs. Jellyby. This aspect of the novel provides compelling instances of how, as Deirdre David observes, "writing about empire . . . elaborates Victorian gender politics" (5).

Esther Summerson illustrates Dickens's approved model of female reform, in which order, cleanliness, and enlightenment expand incrementally through the agency of a middle-class woman. Enacting her principle of being "as useful as [she] could . . . to those immediately about [her]," Esther conducts a small-scale civilizing mission in the Jellyby household, where the distinction between England and the Niger delta is as precarious as on the streets of the slum (128). Her ability to light a stubborn fire symbolically conveys her capacity for bringing the comforts and necessities of civilization to a household where the rooms "had such a marshy smell" and "almost raw" meat is served for dinner (55). Her influence on the Jellyby children further demonstrates a talent for bringing "home-made" savages of the middle-class domestic sphere into the fold of civilization. Esther washes the youngest child, removing the filth that obscures the difference between the complexion of the English boy and that of the child of Borrioboola-Gha. She achieves a more lasting accomplishment by helping to transform Caddy from a sullen and disempowered "slave" into a competent middle-class wife.

The geographical restriction that the novel places on the philanthropic duties of middle-class women notably does not apply to men. Although John Jarndyce does not range far from home, other men do. A productive coalition between imperial military service and the work at home emerges in the depiction of heroic male characters who return from imperial adventure and military service equipped to reform savagery at home. Immediately after the narrative ponders that conflict between empire and social reform, it turns to a picture of Allan Woodcourt walking through the heart of urban darkness. Dickens at first identifies him only as "a brown sunburnt gentleman" (710). The physical trace of the doctor's recent imperial tour emerges as he makes this philanthropic excursion through the London slum. Just as the Jellyby household offers a domestic wilderness for Esther to civilize, the public streets of London supply men with a duty that corresponds to their gender. While Mrs. Jellyby misdirects scarce resources to the "banks of the African rivers" (49), Woodcourt ministers to those he encounters "on the banks of the stagnant channel of mud which is the main street of Tom-all-Alone's" (711). The alliance that he and George Rouncewell form to care for Jo further reveals the impress of their imperial careers. The "trooper" detects the "air" of a sailor in the doctor; he mistakes him for a "regular blue-jacket" (722) and defers to him with a respectful "military salute" (721). George suggests, "in a martial sort of confidence, as if he were giving his opinion in a council of war," a plan for washing and clothing Jo (725). Traces of George's military experience, like Woodcourt's adventure, emerge as the narrative depicts a compassionate corrective to the indifference that has produced "savages" like Jo. Richard Carstone, who fails as a soldier of empire and as a husband and citizen, provides an interesting counterexample.

By conveying the severity and extent of social problems at home through language used to describe the Niger delta, Dickens ironically thwarts the success of imagined reforms. The rhetoric he appropriates to redirect attention from Africa to London succeeds, as it were, too well. The English space figured as tropical Africa becomes as indomitable and deadly as its outlandish counterpart. Impenetrable to reform, it can only be escaped. Those characters who correspond to the surviving members of the Niger expedition eventually abandon their missions in the public and private wildernesses of the imperial metropolis. Like their predecessors, they muster their forces only to make a tactical retreat from the region of disease, death, and despair. The conclusion of the novel, featuring their escape to an idyllic rural locale far from London, furnishes interesting points of discussion in relation to problems foregrounded earlier in the narrative.

After students have spent four or five classes investigating the unique historical context of the novel's themes and imagery, they might also find it worthwhile to leave the text by considering the extent to which it speaks to our own moment. Are there, for example, contemporary Kenges who blindly proclaim the greatness of the nation? Does such rhetoric still function, as Dickens suspected, to hide inequalities? Are we disturbed by the imbalance of commitments abroad and at home? Do we abhor a distant, supposedly savage place? And are we tormented by the return of that which we abhor? Do we respond to crises by prescribing separate roles and responsibilities for men and women? Students who reflect on such questions might well discover that *Bleak House* can tell us something about the modern world we inhabit as well as about the Victorian past we study.

NOTE

Portions of this essay are adapted, and used with permission, from two previous publications of mine: "The Civilizing Mission at Home: Empire, Gender, and National Reform in *Bleak House*," *Dickens Studies Annual: Essays on Victorian Fiction* 26 (1998): 121-45, and *Outlandish English Subjects in the Victorian Domestic Novel* (Basingstoke: Palgrave Macmillan, 2005).

Bleak House and the Culture of Advertising

Andrew Williams

I teach *Bleak House* not as the object of literary criticism that has been handed down to us but as a cultural event at the time of its publication. This approach involves inviting students to read Dickens's words (and Phiz's illustrations) in the immediate context of the other elements that made up the monthly serial numbers of *Bleak House* as it was first published. The most important of these paratextual elements, for me, are the many advertisements that form the *Bleak House Advertiser*, the sizable advertising supplement that accompanied every one of the nineteen monthly parts as it was published between March 1852 and September 1853.

A good way of allowing students to think of such a canonical novel as the multimedia popular-cultural text it once was is to first ask them to critically read an early-twenty-first-century serial (Fox TV's *24*). We discuss the narrative effects of the modern television serial's convention of summarizing the story so far ("Previously on *24* . . ."). We also look at how narrative time in the show is affected by the presence of advertising (*24* is supposedly a real-time serial. Each of its twenty-four episodes lasts for one hour, but in reality there are only forty-five minutes of drama, the other fifteen minutes being taken up by advertising breaks).

Students are then introduced to Phiz's cover illustration and selected advertisements from the *Bleak House Advertiser* in the form of a twenty-page handout copied from an original version of the serial *Bleak House*. To help them visualize the novel as it would have looked, I provide facsimile copies of other Dickens novels in parts (Scolar Press's *Nicholas Nickleby* and the more recent Durrant Editions' version of *David Copperfield*, both of which include the advertising supplements).

Looking at the material composition of the monthly numbers, we discuss how they share some traits with the modern serial. For example, the engraved pictures on Phiz's cover page often act in a similar way to the title sequences and summarizing preambles of television serials, giving clues about future plot developments and providing reminders about what has already passed in the narrative. The placement of the illustrations before the text in each serial number fulfils a similar purpose, sometimes offering a pictorial prompt to where the last number ended and often giving the reader repeated visualizations of the main characters throughout the nineteen-month reading period required by this form of serialization. The advertisements in the supplements, of course, allow the students to locate the serials in cycles of commodity production, distribution, and consumption that are analogous to those of the television serial (as the vehicle for advertisements in a way not unlike those made for commercial television and as a marketable commodity itself).

After introducing students to the original form of the novel, I return to *Bleak House*'s cover page for closer inspection (fig. 3, p. 9). Having already invited them to analyze its narrative effects (they are usually very good at interpreting the small vignettes that constitute the piece), I ask them to think about the thematic significance of the way the images are organized on the page. They are quick to point out the importance of the illustrations relating to Chancery (at the top of the page), Exeter Hall (at the bottom), and the representation of Jarndyce's Bleak House with smoke billowing out of its chimney stack, alluding to the cozy hearth within (in the center of the composition). After considering the centrality of the domestic enclave on the cover page, they are invited to examine the way the novel itself posits the middle-class home and its cultural values as a positive force for good that counterbalances destructive state institutions and misguided philanthropic ones. With this in mind, we discuss how the text inscribes an ideal, middle-class, domestic feminine identity in the figure of Esther Summerson. From close readings of key passages, students analyze how the reader is led to sympathize with the values of devotion to feminine domestic duty, thrift, and deferred gratification espoused by Esther in her role as keeper of Jarndyce's Bleak House and as selfless friend to the needy. In particular, we look at two passages in which Esther reminds herself of her duty as keeper of Bleak House by repeatedly jangling her housekeeping keys (103, 609).

From here we move on to the ideological implications of the proximity of the advertisements to the text. The monthly numbers (taken as a whole) addressed the nineteenth-century reader as the subject of diverse and often contradictory cultural values. Readers of the serial text of *Bleak House*, then, were offered conflicting subject positions derived from two sets of very different cultural ideals. We turn to a number of the advertisements in the *Bleak House Advertiser* and propose that these texts addressed their readers with consumerist cultural values that differ from, and are sometimes opposed to, those offered by the novel. For reasons of brevity, I here describe only one advertisement in detail.

The first advertisement in the supplement to the novel's sixth serial part is a complex pastiche of Phiz's cover illustration (fig. 4, p. 10). The reader, encountering this illustration on the front of the pamphlet-like number, might have been slightly disorientated by what seems like an uncanny replica of the image on the cover. The similarities between this advertisement for Dakin and Co. (a tea merchant) and Phiz's cover illustration are many, and students are as adept at pointing these out as they are at isolating the differences between the two compositions. An intricately illustrated border, composed of miniature tableaux of London life, frames a textual center. The wooden frame of Phiz's drawing is replicated by two poles displaying messages advertising the shop, and cords from the top of each pole spiral off to create the words "Number One," which form the top horizontal bar of the frame. At the bottom of the pole, the cord turns out to be an extension of the pigtails of two caricatured Chinese men. Whereas in the Phiz engraving the pigtailed Chinese man illustrates the folly of Exeter Hall philanthropists like Mrs. Jellyby, in the advertisement these figures are emptied of such moral significance, symbolizing only an exoticization of the imported foreign commodities sold by the company. The image that forms the top third of the document is by far the most dominant and eye-catching part of the whole.

The undoubted center of the scene is the enclosed consumerist sphere of the shop on the right. All life either emanates from, or is drawn to, this point. Carts and delivery boys go about their business taking orders to the outlying suburbs or delivering goods from the dock areas of the Thames. People of different social backgrounds—roughly dressed workers, portly housekeepers, and top-hatted and bonneted members of the leisured classes—flock toward the doors of this all-important building. Even the imposing presence of Saint Paul's Cathedral cannot wholly draw attention away from the shop in the narcissistic world of the nineteenth-century mercantile publicist.

Having directed students to pay particular attention to chapters 17 to 19 in their preparatory reading (the chapters included in this original serial part), I ask them how the advertisement's use of Saint Paul's is echoed in Dickens's words. This compelling pictorial narrative scene is linked with another that is situated at the end of this installment of the novel proper. On the last page of written text, in chapter 19, Jo the crossing sweeper has been "moved on" from Snagsby's home after being interrogated by Mr. Guppy. He sits down to eat a piece of meat given to him by the housekeeper Guster:

> And there he sits, munching and gnawing, and looking up at the great Cross on the summit of St Paul's Cathedral, glittering above a red and violet-tinted cloud of smoke. From the boy's face one might suppose that sacred emblem to be, in his eyes, the crowning confusion of the great, confused city; so golden, so high up, so far out of his reach. There he sits, the sun going down, the river running fast, the crowd flowing by him in two streams—everything moving on to some purpose and to one end—until he is stirred up, and told to "move on" too.   (315)

The first page of the advertising supplement and the last page of the installment are linked, mutually punctured, by representations of the cathedral. The advertisement bonds with the seemingly discrete novel by means of this shared image; the two scenes are placed in dialogue with each other. Having pinpointed this shared image, we then try to isolate the differences between its uses. Discussion reveals that in the novel the dome of the great cathedral is a symbol of the chaos and inequality of the city. The anonymous crowd streaming past Jo as he sits alone emphasizes his sense of confusion and isolation. The only certainty in this passage is provided by the leveling inevitability of everyone's death. This depiction of Jo is also one of the most radical in Dickens's text because of its protomodernist representation of the alienation and inequality of life in the city. In the advertisement, however, the dome of Saint Paul's is ignored by all present. It is emptied of the sociopolitical meaning the novel imbues it with. Any value it might have in the novel is coopted in the advertisement, which endlessly reproduces its image as a trademark, or brand image, for the shop itself. Cathedral after cathedral disappears into the misty background on the sides of Dakin's delivery wagons. Elsewhere, at the bottom of the advertisement's main text, the cathedral is relegated to the status of a secondary landmark that consumers can use to navigate their way to the bold capitalized world of Dakin and Co.'s establishment. The bourgeois shop, shrine to conspicuous consumption, vies with the church as the center of the advertisement's mid-nineteenth-century universe. In parallel fashion, the advertising supplement as a whole can also be seen to unseat Dickens's text as the sovereign source of meaning in the original serial editions of *Bleak House*.

The occurrence of this shared image in the advertisement pinpoints for the students the first intimations of an alternative mid-nineteenth-century ideological project in the serial text of *Bleak House*. A division can be identified between the divergent ideological projects of the text and its advertising supplement. The class can further examine these varying sets of cultural values by reading the rest of this complex advertising image. The illustrations that border the central text are also important, and students are asked to interpret them and compare them with those that form the margin of the novel's cover illustration.

It seems that all social life is here. The lowest classes are presented in the idealized picture of the sandwich-board men sitting in a circle with a makeshift table, conversing and pouring tea for one another. There is a lower-middle-class tea-drinking and gossiping session going on in the lower left-hand side. Above this we have a tableau of working-class life, again more than slightly idealized: a working man coming home to his family, the children sitting around a table and his wife carrying a steaming pot of Dakin's. The last picture on this side deals with a picture of female domestic labor: a woman is hunched over a piece of sewing, aided in her work by candlelight and a pot of tea. The opposite margin mainly shows a more privileged section of Victorian society. At the top there is a writer, perhaps a student. Below him members of the upper class are pictured holding a piano recital, and below that rich ladies are being served tea by a butler. Students are usually quick to point out that the commodity, tea, is present in all the small images.

The central text hammers the message home: "Even in the midst of the excitement of a general election, and of anxiety felt with regard to future fiscal arrangements, the domestic tea-table cannot be altogether forgotten." Class and sociopolitical tensions are erased by the universal assertion of the domestic ritual of taking tea. Social inequality is glossed over to posit a universal middle-class consumer. Both the working- and upper-class tableaux mimic the behavior presented in the bourgeois ones. In the bottom third of the document, a triangle presents itself in which the middle-class ritual of tea taking is repeatedly replicated, the only differences being in the material wealth of those partaking in it. The homely bourgeois tea party is presented as a central and universal social structure that elides class difference, or differences in income. The core of these drawings remains the same; the only difference can be found in the trappings of wealth or the lack of it.

The illustration of the sewing woman marks the height of the advertisement's borrowing from the imagery and ideology of the novel. It exemplifies the Esther-like middle-class values of duty, self-help, hard work, and domesticity that the novel fosters, but it also has a more specific counterpart in the same serial number as the advertisement, this time in chapter 17. After a visit from the Bayham Badgers, during which Allan Woodcourt's name is mentioned, Esther finds she cannot sleep. Her desire for the doctor is made as clear as its repression, by the gently ironic split between the narrator's voice and the reader's consciousness of its limitations: "I was wakeful and rather low-spirited. I don't know why. At least I don't think I know why. At least, perhaps I do, but I don't think it matters" (274). Immediately after this the narrator finds the perfect cure for her malaise:

> At any rate, I made up my mind to be so dreadfully industrious that I would leave myself not a moment's leisure to be low-spirited. . . . I took out of my basket some ornamental work for our house . . . and sat down to it with great determination. It was necessary to count all the stitches in that work, and I resolved to go on with it until I couldn't keep my eyes open, and then, to go to bed. (274)

The two needlewomen operate in a similar way to the images of Saint Paul's. It is only a short imaginative leap from the image of the woman working by candlelight to that conjured up by Esther, counting the stitches in her needlework in an act of domestic ascetic self-denial.

It would, of course, be a mistake to read only the similarities between the advertising image and the novelistic one. What at first might seem like a reinforcement of the homely feminine cultural values and domestic ideology displayed by Esther turns out on closer inspection to be something quite different. The idealized middle-class perspective the advertisement depicts is not one that sees these domestic values as a positive force for social change, as the novel does. The egalitarian vision of the advertisement cannot be accessed by any means other than continued consumption of the commodities tea and coffee; values integral to the ideological project of the novel become hollowed out and commodified. The paradox is that some of these values—for example, thrift and self-denial—exist in opposition to the advertisement's project of increasing the consumption of its product.

Just as the shop heretically unseats the church at the center of the advertisement's sociopolitical vision, so the act of consumption associated with the shop usurps the power of the bourgeois domestic values it also displays. The advertising supplement can be seen to intervene against Dickens's text, suggesting an alternative set of Victorian cultural values. The Dakin and Co. publicity draws attention to a real ideological friction in *Bleak House*. The novel's ideal bourgeoise, Esther, has inscribed at her core the conventional middle-class values of duty, thrift, deferred gratification, and self-sacrifice. The advertisement works in opposition to these values. They become commodified, transformed into selling points. Emptied of the significance they have in the novel, they become advertising images used to spur the reader on to repeated acts of consumption. The advertisement's overriding ideological project is to address the reader as a consumer, a middle-class subject very different from that favored by the novel. Who needs thrift, and why defer gratification when it can be got at Dakin and Co.'s, the "Number One"? The difference between the modes of subjectivity inscribed by the novel and its supplement reveals a doubleness in bourgeois ideology at the time of the novel's publication and points to a conflict between two competing sets of Victorian cultural values: the residual values of selfless duty, thrift, and hard work and the need of an emergent commodity culture to address individuals as consuming, spending subjects. Reading the novel alongside its advertising supplement in this way allows students to gain a fuller understanding of the complexity of Victorian subjectivity and encourages them to see the mid-nineteenth-century subject as a site of competing ideologies.

Bleak House and the Culture of Commodities

Gordon Bigelow

The first time I taught *Bleak House*, I felt as if I was always waiting for something. My students and I talked about Chancery, about the Dedlocks, about Jo and the Brickmakers and Esther. But the stunning thing about *Bleak House* is the way each of its multiple plots grows to inform and enlarge all the others. I was able to illustrate this to students only in the most pedestrian of ways, showing how a single lawsuit touches so many lives and how the buried secret of Esther's parentage returns with widely felt consequences. But there was a level I could never seem to get to: the way all of life begins to feel like a case in Chancery, the way Esther's search for her mother, and herself, is another case that can never be settled. At this level of abstraction, where stories converge, *Bleak House* is as much concerned with economics and politics as it is with the law. The image that for me has always crystallized this dazzling refractive quality of the novel is the snow that falls on the night Honoria Dedlock flees from the house in town: the snow flakes circulate like papers in Chancery, covering the face of Esther's mother, reducing a world of uniqueness and subtlety to a flat landscape of indistinguishable objects. But you can't wait until the snow flies to teach this book.

I found a hook on which to hang these multiple plots, a way of characterizing their common critique, in Marx's concept of commodity fetishism. Teaching Marx brings its own challenges; my first try was no more successful than my first classes on *Bleak House*. The initial failures I encountered with both Dickens and Marx inspired the teaching strategy I describe here. Judging both from students' writing and from their expanding range of interests, the strategy has worked fairly well. Before starting *Bleak House*, students in my nineteenth-century novel course read Marx's chapter on commodity fetishism, and we spend a class period discussing it. This reading seems to help students see the novel's critique of its society as much more systematic and complex than they otherwise might, on the first reading of a big multiplot novel. Commodity culture is their culture, and their expertise in its pleasures and pains can become an asset to their study of nineteenth-century literature.

Marx's chapter, "The Fetishism of the Commodity and Its Secret," is characteristically dense, allusive, and playful and thus easy for students to mistake. But strictly from a teaching point of view, it has one redeeming characteristic: its core idea is summed up in one dense introductory paragraph. If students can understand the argument Marx is offering there, they can read the rest of the chapter with insight, and they can talk about the phenomenon of market society that Marx is describing. I ask students to focus on this paragraph, and I spend virtually our whole class discussion dealing with it. It begins as follows:

> The mysterious character of the commodity-form consists therefore simply in the fact that the commodity reflects the social characteristics of

men's own labour as objective characteristics of the products of labour
themselves.   (164)

With some simple questions, the sentence yields pretty quickly to basic exposition: What are "the products of labour" here? (Any made or manufactured
things, objects created or transformed through human labor.) What are the
"social characteristics" of labor? (The social meanings attributed to different
forms of work, i.e., various types of physical labor, professional work, paid
or unpaid domestic work, the very freedom from labor that characterizes the
leisure classes.) So the sentence asserts that commodities are odd things because, although they are physical objects, it seems as if they carry extra significance, meanings that are widely recognized by the society that produced them.
"Hence," Marx goes on, "[the commodity] also reflects the social relation of
the producers to the sum total of labour as a social relation between objects"
(164–65).

But then what is a "social relation between objects"? This question is more difficult, and so at this point I draw examples of two objects—two commodities—
on the board. Or, rather, I draw two very shaky rectangles, and then I explain
to the class what objects I have in mind: they are notebooks, the kind of shiny,
complicated three-ring binders that preteens might buy for the start of fifth
grade. I ask students to imagine that the notebooks are identical, same design
and manufacture, except that they have different pictures on their front covers.
Here one has to choose images that students will know and understand. I use
some version of the following: one notebook features a stylized and airbrushed
scene of characters from a recent *Star Wars* film. (Other options: A pop star,
a sports star, Hello Kitty). The second notebook features the quaint and old-
fashioned animated characters Raggedy Ann and Andy, skipping hand in hand
through a cartoon meadow. (Other options: Smurfs, Elmo, the former cast of
the *Lawrence Welk Show*.) The point will already begin to clarify: the relationships between kids on the playground or on the bus will seem to be embedded
in relations between the objects the kids carry.

But Marx offers an especially clear way to approach this issue, and it emerges
in reference to the senses. In the next sentence, he says that commodities are
"sensuous things which are at the same time supra-sensible or social" (165).
What this means is that commodities always function, and can be analyzed,
in two ways. First, they are physical objects, things that come to be through
human labor, with physical characteristics we can perceive and judge with our
senses. But, second, the significance of commodities in a capitalist society always goes beyond strict physical characteristics, as they take on extra social
meanings, meanings totally unrelated to their physical makeup.[1] Marx takes the
point further:

> The commodity-form, and the value-relation of the products of labour
> within which it appears, have absolutely no connection with the physical

nature of the commodity. . . . It is nothing but the definite social relation between men themselves which assumes here, for them, the fantastic
form of a relation between things.   (165)

Again, we get two ways of understanding how objects can be related or compared
with each other: first, as physical things, with purely physical characteristics;
second, as commodities, things that appear to express human characteristics and
human social relations.

Now we return to the board, and I ask students to compare the notebooks in
the two ways Marx has laid out. First, describe the relation between these notebooks if we view them purely as physical things. How would you compare and
contrast them? describe their makeup? Students point out that they are made of
the same things, metal and plastic, configured in the same way, but have different patterns of colorant applied to the finish on the front cover. Otherwise they
are identical. Then, how do they compare as commodities? I ask students to
cast their minds back to their fifth-grade playground and to imagine the world
of social relations operative there. How are these different notebooks significant
in that world? The answer is that one is cool and one is not. It's a trivial example,
but students can readily see how pieces of functionally identical colored plastic
end up telling you who gets beaten up on the playground and thus how physical
objects, otherwise inert, can become the bearers of social meaning. The notebooks are a good example because, since they are physically the same, they re-
duce the problem to its simplest form. Students can then think of more complex
examples of brands and services targeted at unique demographic groups.

An entry into these ideas in the novel comes in monthly number 5, which
opens with chapter 14, "Deportment." To this point our discussions of the
book's emerging themes—law, poverty, family—have progressed in isolation.
The concept of commodity fetishism can help students bring these issues together. And so I ask, Why does a book about the wards of Chancery include this
portrait of a dingy and puffed-up dance studio? My students balk at the question, and their pause cues me to flip just a few pages farther into number 5, to
the crucial passage: "What connexion can there be . . . between many people in
the innumerable histories of this world, who, from opposite sides of great gulfs,
have, nevertheless, been very curiously brought together"? (256). Thus when
we ask what one set of characters has to do with another in the book, we're not
speculating idly; we're pursuing a question the book itself has pressed on us.

I ask students to describe what happens at Turveydrop's Academy. They understand that the school offers dancing lessons, but it takes some discussion to
reveal that dancing is a part of the regimen of aristocratic manner and dress
that the academy teaches. Turveydrop's, after all, enters the narrative because
Caddy Jellyby feels "so awkward" at her introduction to Esther and Ada that
she determines to improve herself (220). Students are then able to point out
that "deportment" is a set of behaviors associated with a dominant class, a set
of skills that are desirable because they have become fashionable (dancing, but

also how to bow or curtsey, choose the right fork/clothes/furniture). These skills and tastes—these personal attributes—are offered for sale at Turveydrop's, packaged as commodities. This detachment of personal attribute from person is depicted to us in Mr. Turveydrop himself, wearing "false complexion, false teeth, false whiskers, and a wig" (225). With some guidance, students can analyze the "Deportment" chapter with the tools Marx provides: in this passage, the social relations between Mr. Turveydrop and the rest of the world are imprinted onto a set of objects (wig, teeth, etc.), which signify (however absurdly) personal characteristics. These consumer goods, as well as the services that the academy sells, take on the appearance of social meaning.

Turveydrop's reveals two important aspects of commodity culture that are at the heart of *Bleak House*. First, a commodity-based economy functions through imitation. If goods for sale carry with them social meanings, those meanings—like the meaning of all signs—are understandable only if their significance is already known and fixed. Meanings do change: we can imagine Raggedy Ann to have once been a figure of devastating attractiveness, inspiring a generation of children with dreams to their own satisfaction and autonomy. But Raggedy Ann means nothing—to its owner or anyone else—if the social content of her trademarked image isn't current. In commercial society, choosing things to buy is not an expressive act but rather a kind of citation: a reference to an already existing concept attached to an object. Every purchase imitates a previous purchase; every object imitates another. And the system of social meanings represented by commodities always predates the consciousness of individual actors.[2]

Second, where things take on the characteristics of people, people start to become more and more like things. This is an idea implicit in Marx's argument but more fully developed by Georg Lukács, who called the process "reification." The process is apparent again in the example of Turveydrop,

> pinched in, and swelled out, and got up, and strapped down, as much as he could possibly bear. He had such a neck-cloth on (puffing his very eyes out of their natural shape), and his chin and even his ears so sunk into it, that it seemed as though he must inevitably double up, if it were cast loose. (225)

Mr. Turveydrop's things are killing him, distorting his person out of its natural shape. The work of the academy imparts a similar lesson. Turveydrop has worked his wife to death, and he is using his son in the same fashion (226–27). His family become instruments of his business, as he himself becomes an object to exemplify and advertise its dubious aims.

Turveydrop offers a self-contained illustration of issues cultivated in more subtle and complex ways elsewhere in the book. And so I ask students once again, "What connexion can there be" between this stupid man and the wards of Chancery at Bleak House, Jo, Nemo, Tulkinghorn, and the Dedlocks? The discussion of reification, as the effect on consciousness of a commoditized economic system, usually helps students think more broadly. For it is immediately clear to them that the court system in the book treats its claimants like objects, cycling them through systematic procedures like "a slow mill" (102), like things on an assembly line. The questions the court takes up become as clipped and distorted as poor Mr. Turveydrop's bulging eyes. A good example for discussion is the mutilated language of Mr. Kenge's letter to Esther (40). Moreover, this "connexion" between the court and "deportment" is enlarged in the very next chapter, "The Bell Yard," which introduces Gridley and the resonant description of the court as "the system" (251).

With students now thinking at this level of abstraction, the obvious absurdity of the deportment academy looks like an iteration of the same problem the novel documents much more deliberately and completely in its portrait of Chancery. Social "systems" turn people into objects, while human characteristics and relationships are transposed onto a marketable array of things.

If the lesson has succeeded, I can then ask students to point out other situations in the novel where we see the imitative and reified structure of the commodity illustrated. Mrs. Pardiggle comes quickly to mind, with her "mechanical" approach to charitable enterprise (133). So does Mrs. Jellyby, who, like Turveydrop, transforms her child into an instrument of production: Caddy says, "I am only pen and ink to *her*" (221). The other example that a bit of prompting usually turns up is Nemo, and his case is an especially revealing one. Nemo's task is to reproduce legal language. He moves papers through "the system," and so in that way is part of the bureaucracy reviled by Gridley. He creates language without producing meaning, reduced, like Caddy Jellyby, to the pen that he holds, a "hand" in the system of labor that runs the Chancery Court.

On this day or some other, I have also found it useful to ask students what it means to be bored. For some reason, unknown to me, it is a question students in my Victorian novel class seem to relish. But when reminded of the constant state of boredom Honoria Dedlock lives in, they may offer more specific reflections. The boredom that typifies the world of fashion in the novel is described as a state where no one thing or experience can be sufficiently differentiated from the rest. House in town or Chesney Wold, abroad or at home, with guests or family, objects and entertainments make no distinct impression on "My Lady," and this fact points to a further aspect of commodity culture the novel dissects for its readers. Lady Dedlock is so far from being moved by any of the objects around her that none makes any distinct impression. The arid luxuries that surround her provide no pleasure, provoke no reaction at all. Their meaning is the purely social one Marx describes, expressing merely the relations between their aristocratic owners and their dependents, tenants, and neighbors.

Commodities are things that can all be compared on a single scale of value: money. However distinctive they are, all their characteristics must be translatable into a price. This function of money as a universal equivalent has the effect of flattening the field of objects in modern society. Commodities are objects whose uniqueness is obviated from the start, partly because they exist as imitations of other objects, but also because they must always be reducible to price. As Lady Dedlock's boredom reminds us, the social meanings of commodities overwhelm their significance as useful things. This is the central paradox of commodity culture: while fetishized objects seem to offer a range of expressive choices that define the uniqueness of each consumer, they show, with their price tags, how similar they are, as points on a universal scale of value. This is the economic and social landscape of Lady Dedlock's boredom: objects lose their uniqueness. It is also the landscape opened to us in the first paragraph of *Bleak House*, where the mud renders all dogs "undistinguishable in mire" and where particles of soot fall like "full-grown snow-flakes." Thus the snow that cover's Lady Dedlock's face and the blizzard of papers that blinds the Chancery lawyers are like the November mud, "accumulating at compound interest" (13). They refer to that distinctly modern sensation of sameness, repetition, imitation, and boredom that arises in a world where manufactured goods become a social vocabulary. It is a sensation contemporary students encounter with a deep sense of recognition.

NOTES

[1] Marx offers a more detailed illustration of the point in this same paragraph, in a reference to the way the eye gathers information about external objects. It is a helpful illustration to discuss if class time permits.

[2] On literary implications of the imitative nature of commodities, see Kevin McLaughlin, *Writing in Parts*, especially 17–20, and Andrew Miller, "*Vanity Fair* through Plate Glass," especially 1051–52. McLaughlin's introduction to *Writing*, "Citing Fetishism," also provides an excellent close discussion of Marx's fetishism chapter. I am grateful to McLaughlin for his comments on an earlier version of this essay.

Bleak House, Paper, and Victorian Print

Kevin McLaughlin

Bleak House is one of the finest products of the Victorian mass media. Dickens's novel also draws on the mass culture of print to depict broader forces at work in Victorian society. This is especially evident in the handling of paper in *Bleak House*. Thomas Carlyle associates mass-produced paper with the revolutionary masses in his popular history of the French Revolution, which appeared at the outset of the Victorian period. Like mass-produced paper, the masses are portrayed as lacking all substance in Carlyle's work: they are the medium of nothing more than an "inarticulate cry" (*French Revolution* 36).[1] Dickens, of course, knew Carlyle's work well. But while *Bleak House* makes a similar connection between paper and the masses, these media carry a different kind of message in Dickens's novel. *Bleak House* provides students with an illuminating attempt by the most popular serial novelist of the Victorian period to assign meaning to the sprawling urban masses of mid-nineteenth-century London by comparing them to the mass-produced material support that made his own work possible.

A good place to begin a discussion that focuses on the peculiar link between the masses and the mass media in *Bleak House* is with the mounds of paper in the novel. Paper abounds in *Bleak House*: from the courtroom and law offices to the shops and homes of the novel's protagonists.[2] This is the students' overwhelming impression of the opening chapters. Indeed, a good question to pose to a class would be, How much paper can you find in the first seventy pages of the novel? There is, in order of appearance, the "tens of thousands of Chancery-folio-pages" copied by the copyists (17), the "eighteen hundred sheets" of the lawyers (18), the "heavy charges of papers" hauled off by the clerks (19), the papers copied by a certain Nemo and placed before Lady Dedlock by Mr. Tulkinghorn "on a golden talisman of a table" (26), the "bundles of papers" (45) in Kenge and Carboy's law office, "the nest of waste paper" from which Mrs. Jellyby dictates endless philanthropic letters to her daughter, Caddy (58), the piles of "waste paper" in Krook's rag and bottle shop (67), and the paper advertising the copying services of Nemo put up in the window of the shop along with a picture of a paper mill (68). Students will be reasonably inclined to interpret all this paper as a sign of the mechanical reproduction of the courts or the Victorian bureaucracy. And they would be right, up to a point. A good example of this association of paper with machinelike copying is the illiterate Krook. Amassing paper and taking on its capacity to bear reproducible marks, Krook ultimately merges with the very substance of the material he collects—the mingling of his ashes with "burnt paper" "is all that represents him" (519).[3] With Krook mass-produced paper becomes a metaphor for the faceless existence that was anxiously associated with industrial society. The death of such a subject, accordingly, has the character of a mere blank: it can bear "all names soever" and is in fact the very stuff of the "tissue-paper" used by the newspapermen of Dickens's day to produce duplicate copy (519, 533).

But how, then, do we explain Dickens's decision to make copied papers the medium of something singular in the early interview between Lady Dedlock and Mr. Tulkinghorn in the novel? This question opens up an issue that is fundamental to *Bleak House*: in what sense can copying bear a signature capable of distinguishing itself from the threat of blankness posed by mass society? How, in other words, can mechanical duplication be the medium of an experience of this kind of singularity? Or, to put it more concretely in the terms of the novel, what kind of signature is Nemo? It is worth examining again the details of the scene in which Lady Dedlock seems to notice something singular in the copies Tulkinghorn puts before her. There is, as the lawyer observes, a certain heterogeneous element—something "original" and thus "not quite" entirely legal (27)—in this "law-hand." This signature is what strikes Lady Dedlock and produces "her unusual tone" (26). J. Hillis Miller's suggestion that the signature Nemo expresses the copyist's intention "to escape the involvement in society inevitable if one has any name at all" is illuminating ("Interpretation" 190). But the signature of Nemo's copying is not a matter of will or intention. Nemo did not intend to sign with his copying.

The question for discussion becomes at this point one of an unreproducible element in copying that emerges in Nemo's writing and extends across the entire novel. The extent of this copying can be suggested to students with a series of questions: What gets into the "hand" of this scrivener as he mindlessly copies Chancery's proceedings? What gets into my Lady's bearing as the "hand" is placed at her "elbow" (26)? And what gets into the manner of the subjects collectively in the novel, or into the manner of the readers collectively of the novel, as they follow the court's repetitions (the mounds of paper in *Bleak House* are also, after all, to be compared to the piles of paper that served as the material support for the novel's monthly installments)? The answers to these questions raised by the remarkable hand of Nemo are ultimately beyond the grasp of all concerned, precisely because in each case the singularity of the copying in question derives from the scattering force of a mass movement, a force that works against the establishment of a stable perspective from which one could become aware of one's position in the movement. The force conveyed by the papers placed before Lady Dedlock early in the novel does not remain within the space circumscribed by the iconic golden table. The hand of Nemo spreads like a plague.[4] The copied papers are not only scattered throughout the homes, shops, and offices of the novel's opening passages. The copying that reproduces the duplications of Chancery Court is also doubled in the novel by the spread of contagious disease.[5] The physical and scriptural connotations of Nemo's hand point to a double mass movement—one involving masses of paper, the other masses of people. To the extent that the multiplication of the contagion is comparable to the spreading of copies (the hand of Nemo), the human subject resembles paper. In both cases a proliferating movement is made possible by a massive support—that of mass-produced paper, on the one hand, and of the urban masses, on the other.[6]

At this point, it is instructive to bring into a classroom discussion of *Bleak House*, as a possible source for the link between mass-produced paper and the urban masses, some passages from Carlyle's *French Revolution,* especially from the chapter entitled "The Paper Age," in which the revolutionary masses are associated with the mass production of paper that is seen to lead up to the revolution (29–38). But then, to bring out the peculiarity of the way Dickens adapts this connection, it is helpful to place *Bleak House* in the broader context of Victorian writing on the London populace. Highly illuminating in this respect is Henry Mayhew's classic typological survey *London Labour and the London Poor*, a work that not only was contemporaneous with *Bleak House* but also was published initially in the serial press.[7] While Mayhew's goals are philanthropic, his comprehensive taxonomy aims for a scientific mastery over a portion of the population that is threatening because it is unknown. In *Bleak House*, by contrast, there is Jo. Another nobody, the crossing sweeper marks the disintegration of the body politic, an unacknowledged and shifting point of social breakdown at which society fails collectively to recognize its truly scattered state. Jo moves in the zone of estranging familiarity about which Dickens began to write in his earliest journalistic sketches. From the beginning "Boz" was concerned with a society singularly distracted in a manner that itself repeatedly escapes attention— what is called "habit" in *Sketches by Boz*.[8] Habitually, Boz observes of Newgate Prison, for example, men

> pass and repass this gloomy depository of the guilt and misery of London, in one perpetual stream of life and bustle, utterly unmindful of the throng of wretched creatures pent up within it—nay not even knowing, or if they do, not heeding the fact, that as they pass one particular angle of the massive wall with a light laugh or a merry whistle, they stand within one yard of a fellow-creature, bound and helpless, whose hours are numbered, from whom the last feeble ray of hope has fled for ever, and whose miserable career will shortly terminate in a violent and shameful death.   (234)

Depicted in this passage is a massive repression: the collective's repression of the masses and of its own massiveness. The "throng" presses against the self-consistent and immortal image of the public as "one perpetual stream of life." Yet the wall constructed to contain the pressure is "massive"—the prison wall but also the wall of habit—and it displays, rather than shutting out, the vast exposure of the public to the heterogeneity and transience of the dying "throng."[9] In *Bleak House* Jo inhabits, or passes away, in such a public passage: "Jo lives— that is to say, Jo has not yet died—in a ruinous place" (256). From the start the crossing sweeper recedes, not just in the novel, but also from the novel's shifting perspectives. Even as he is introduced in the third-person narrative, Jo seems to remain nearly out of sight—in the midst of London and at the limit of the representational space from which Lady Dedlock, touched by Nemo's hand, is said to have "flitted away." Nemo's hand draws Lady Dedlock away from "the place in Lincolnshire," where she is "at present represented . . . by her portrait," toward the "whereabout of Jo the outlaw" (256). It is place itself, in the various senses probed throughout the novel, that here gives way.[10] If Jo is out of place—kept about by being moved repeatedly elsewhere—that is because fundamentally he is not presentable.

And yet, Jo's singular and unpresentable condition is precisely what binds the society in its scattered state. "What connection can there be," the narrator wonders, between Jo's "whereabout" and Lady Dedlock's "place" (256), between Jo's "state" and the state of the society that gathers in the unsettling experience of reading *Bleak House*? A partial response comes in one of the most familiar, yet still moving, passages in the novel, in which Jo's strange state suddenly turns into that of a reading public:

> It must be a strange state to be like Jo! To shuffle through the streets, unfamiliar with the shapes, and in utter darkness as to the meaning, of those mysterious symbols, so abundant over the shops, and at the corners of streets, and on the doors, and in the windows! To see people read, and to see people write, and to see the postmen deliver letters, and not, to have the least idea of all that language. . . . [Jo's] whole material and immaterial life is wonderfully strange; his death, the strangest thing of all. (257–58)

The rhetorical gesture may appear routine, but something remarkable happens in this passage: the strangeness of Jo's condition to the readers is illustrated by a description of the strangeness of the readers' condition to Jo. Strangeness is, in other words, the "connexion." The state of being like Jo must be strange. For it obliges readers to see themselves, indeed to read about themselves, as a strange state—to make themselves out at the threshold of reading. At this point reading becomes both condition and limit: a state marked by strange occurrences, like the life and especially the death of Jo. And undoubtedly the strangest thing about Jo's death in *Bleak House* is the sense in which it is collective. Instead of pulling together an integrated community of individuals, this death displays a collective coming apart and dispersing as a mass. From this strange perspective Jo's death is not individual. It is the death en masse of community in the traditional sense. The crossing sweeper passes away by becoming immediately one of the many, by disappearing into the crowd.[11] His death is abruptly carried off by a mass movement: "Dead, your Majesty. Dead, my lords and gentlemen. Dead, Right Reverends and Wrong Reverends of every order. Dead, men and women, born with Heavenly compassion in your hearts. And dying thus around us, every day" (734). The death here, like the life, is a matter of "moving on" for all concerned—including the narrator.[12] Jo passes away in the space of such a withdrawal in *Bleak House*. Yet the repetitive movement of Jo's life, and especially his death, leaves an impression on the collective that fails to recognize itself in the strange vision of the crossing sweeper. As with the hand of Nemo, the impression is not a matter of conscious transmission and so not a matter of transmission at all in the conventional sense. What Jo bears is the breakdown of the community's capacity to hand itself down and hold itself together through the reciprocal exchange of experience. Thus paradoxically Jo becomes an "unconscious link" in the novel because he has no experience. He sees everything but knows nothing: "He sums up his mental condition, when asked a question, by replying that he 'don't know nothink'" (256). Jo's blank vision transmits like an imperfect recording device.

The manner in which this optic marks, and comes to bind, the social collective is suggested by a series of incidents already under way when Jo gives his testimony at the inquest into Nemo's death. Lady Dedlock, who reads in the "papers" the report of what Jo has seen (260), asks him to "shew [her] all those places that were spoken of in the account [she] read" (261). The tour that follows unfolds mechanically like a series of illustrations and in fact ends with the appearance in the text of Hablot K. Browne's drawing of Jo and Lady Dedlock at the iron gate of the open mass grave where Nemo is also buried ("Cook's Court. Jo stops. A pause. . . . Krook's house. Jo stops again. A longer pause . . ." [261–62]). In return for the visit, Lady Dedlock "drops a piece of money in [Jo's] hand, without touching it, and shuddering as their hands approached" (264). This may well be, as Lady Dedlock promises, "more money than [he] ever had in [his] life," but Jo gets even more than he bargains for in the scene that ensues (261). For, while retracing the steps of his testimony, the witness keeps picking things up—in this case, taking in not just the impression of Lady Dedlock's veiled face, but also, it is suggested, the contaminating illness contracted from the mass of decomposing bodies with which the remains of Nemo are merging. This is the deadly combination that Jo will involuntarily bear to the "neighborhood" of Bleak House and to Esther, who is both the mistress of the house and the child of the flawed union (487). From this point on Jo becomes an unconscious and physically disintegrating material support for the unsettling force that finds its way into the hand of Nemo and, as we have seen, into the face of Lady Dedlock when she glances at the copied papers.

But this is not the end of the story Dickens has to tell in *Bleak House*. At this point, students should be encouraged to consider Esther's narrative in relation to the epidemic of social and physical breakdown figured by paper in the novel. In what sense does Esther's encounter with Jo and with everything that it entails represent a positive response to the forces of disintegration at work in the Victorian society represented in *Bleak House*? Why, for example, does Esther retrospectively introduce her meeting with Jo and the contagion he bears in the Wordsworthian language of a "spot of time" ("spot and time," 489)? In what sense is the encounter with Jo an opportunity? And by extension, how is Esther's autobiographical writing marked by the scattering force traced in the third-person narration? Does her writing simply resist this force or is it at certain points receptive to it? Finally, how does the interaction between the third-person narration and Esther's narrative indicate Dickens's negotiation as a writer with the serialized, mass medium—and the mass-produced paper of monthly parts publication—of his own work? Starting from an analysis of paper in *Bleak House*, students can be led to a better understanding of Dickens's complex response to the Victorian mass media and to the mass society for which the mass media becomes a metaphor in *Bleak House*.

NOTES

[1] I have dealt with this connection between paper and the masses in Carlyle in more detail in *Paperwork* 1–5.

[2] The abundance of paper in *Bleak House* is reminiscent of Carlyle's "Paper Age" in *The French Revolution* and also remarks on paper in *Sartor Resartus*. Passages from the latter on Monmouth Street in London (243) are recalled by Krook's rag and bottle shop. But Dickens's early sketch on Monmouth Street, one roughly contemporary with Carlyle's book, is decidedly different, as I point out later in this essay. For an interpretation of paper in *Our Mutual Friend* on the basis of a distinction between public and private spaces, see Altick (see esp. 252–53). Maxwell describes the great quantities of paper in *Bleak House* as a representation of the outbreak of bureaucracy in mid-Victorian London (see esp. 171).

[3] For an illuminating interpretation of Krook's shop as a site of recycling in Dickens, see Ginsburg 143–45.

[4] The association of "hand" with contagion is suggested at the beginning of the novel in the description of the "groping and floundering condition which this High Court of Chancery, most pestilent of hoary sinners, holds, this day, in the sight of heaven and earth" (14).

[5] It is noteworthy that the contagion in question is not clearly identified. Is it smallpox, typhus, or erysipelas? (See West.)

[6] The sense in which the masses become a support with the industrialization of culture is also made explicit in Walter Benjamin's essay on technical reproducibility, in which the masses' capacity to bear impressions is compared to the typographical device of "matrix" ("Work of Art" 239).

[7] There are in fact more than twenty entries in Mayhew's work devoted to the varieties of crossing sweepers (2: 465–507). For some astute observations and distinctions on the figure of the crowd in nineteenth-century British "mass journals" of the 1830s, see Klancher 76–97.

[8] See, for example, the beginning of "A Visit to Newgate": "'The force of habit' is a trite phrase in every body's mouth; and it is not a little remarkable that those who use it most as applied to others, unconsciously afford in their own persons singular examples of the power which habit and custom exercise over the minds of men, and of the little reflection they are apt to bestow on subjects with which every day's experience has rendered them familiar" (234). On this passage, see my *Writing in Parts* 89–91.

[9] The word "throng" in this passage implies pressure, in the sense that a crowd is said to press. "Throng" is etymologically related to the German word *Drang*, the root of Freudian "repression"—*Verdrängung*. The French translation of *Verdängung*—*refoulement*—evokes the crowd (*la foule*) more explicitly.

[10] The senses of place are especially crucial to the initial portrayal of Lady Dedlock, one of the "representatives of her little world" (24). See especially chapter 2, which closes with Mr. Tulkinghorn asking "permission to place" the papers copied by Nemo on the golden table (26).

[11] Aesthetic receptivity is likened by Benjamin to death in the sense of the Latin phrase "to go over to the many" (*ad plures ire*). See *Illuminations* 198n13 and *Arcades Project* 471: "The receptivity of great, much-admired works of art is an *ad plures ire*." Also see the note to the English translation of the *Arcades Project* 990n22.

[12] The blindness to Jo's death is emphasized by the first sentence of the chapter that immediately follows the passage just cited (and is part of the same serial installment): "The place in Lincolnshire has shut its many eyes again . . ." (734).

Bleak House and Victorian Science

Shu-Fang Lai

Having taught Dickens's *Bleak House* in postgraduate courses such as Nineteenth-Century British Novel and Victorian Fiction in the department of foreign languages and literature at Sun Yat-Sen University, Taiwan, I have found a cross-boundary approach—studying Victorian science in the novel—especially useful, not only for helping students with the language, but also for helping them understand a past culture and a foreign (European) history. The novel first appeared as nineteen monthly installments from March 1852 to September 1853. By this time several scientific societies were well established (such as the Geological Society, founded in 1807; the Astronomical Society, in 1820; the Zoological Society, in 1826; British Association for the Advancement of Science, in 1831; the Meteorological Society, in 1836; and the Chemical Society, in 1841). The public had just experienced the wonders of science in the Great Exhibition of 1851, and scientific discoveries were widening people's view of the world, stimulating their interest, and causing an intellectual upheaval. Changes and transformations streaming from the sphere of science were increasingly influential on general literary and intellectual culture. These changes had all the more effect because they coincided with wider world exploration, the extension of education, and the enormous acceleration of cheap printing. A deeper knowledge of the relation of science to society in the Victorian period is helpful in situating the novel within its cultural contexts. The classroom strategy proposed here offers a way to teach the relation between science and literature.

I begin by introducing Dickens's experience of science as a cultural element: his contacts with contemporary scientists (such as the naturalist and anatomist Richard Owen, the mathematician and inventor of the earliest calculating machine Charles Babbage, and the chemist and physicist Michael Faraday), his possible reading of scientific books, and his early satire of science in the *Mudfog Papers* (1838).

"What could Dickens think of science?" I then ask the students. To answer the question, we read passages from Dickens's review of Robert Hunt's *The Poetry of Science* in the *Examiner*. In this piece Dickens praises Robert Chambers, "the author of the *Vestiges of the Natural History of Creation*, who, by rendering the general subject popular, and awakening an interest and spirit of inquiry in many minds . . . has created a reading public" (131). The review not only reveals Dickens's delight in scientific speculation but also decisively links him to the most controversial scientific issue of the time: evolution. Before Darwin's *Origin of Species*, Chambers's "remarkable and well-abused" book, as Dickens calls it (131), was widely read, though considered offensive and fiercely attacked by clergy and many writers. Hunt, like many of his contemporaries, complains in his book that Chambers's hypothesis of "the gradual development of animals from the lowest up to the highest orders" (366–67) has no foundation, and he declares that readers should see "the forms of animal life as distinct creations . . . springing from the command of the first great cause" (367). In his review, Dickens strongly opposes Hunt's attack on Chambers's book. Although overall Dickens agrees with Hunt's idea that science may destroy "sirens, mermaids, shining cities glittering at the bottom of the quiet seas and in deep lakes" (131), in return, he asserts, it brings out new ideas and renews our imagination. The review, full of sentiments about science, shows Dickens's imaginative insight. From this piece students learn that Dickens's attitude toward science was as optimistic and liberal as his general attitude to life; he was in favor of common sense, a speculative spirit, and freedom of thought. Such a preliminary introduction leads the students to consider how Dickens might have used his understanding of science as a novelist.

After our warm-up reading, the students are asked to look for scientific metaphors and vocabulary in *Bleak House*. The task has practical advantages: it gets the students involved immediately and helps them keep reading the novel with a specific goal in mind. Instead of wandering through the text struggling to know the dozens of characters and intricate plots, they now have an incentive to carry on reading actively for discoveries. They find casual allusions or Dickensian quips: for example, "a Magalosaurus, forty feet long or so, waddling like an elephantine lizard up Holborn Hill"; "the death of the sun" (13); Ada "the child of the universe" (92); and remarks from Mrs. Badger, who owes her adaptability to "science," after her marriage with Professor Dingo: "custom, combined with science—particularly science—inured me to [change]. Being the Professor's sole companion in his botanical excursions, I . . . became quite learned" (208). They can also find references with structural importance, such as Krook's "Spontaneous Combustion" (519) and the theory of planetary motion. Lady Dedlock is described as the central sun in a solar system, while others are planets and "dim little star[s] revolving about her" (24), who "cannot hear the rushing of the larger worlds, and cannot see them as they circle round the sun" (20); claimants in Chancery "revolv[e] about the Lord Chancellor and all his satellites" (118); and the "brilliant and distinguished meteors" (331) of fashion move within "[t]he fashionable world—tremendous orb, nearly five miles round . . . [while] the solar system works respectfully at its appointed distances" (734). Some students may search for words such as "science," "energy," "force," "system," and "electricity" in the e-text. The results show that Dickens uses the word "system" at least thirty times and the word "science" eight times, including five times in the modern sense in connection with the comic character Mrs. Badger (208, 267–68) and once in a general way in connection with gossip about Lady Dedlock (888). The most direct discussions of science in the novel are in the 1853 preface (6–7) and in the passage that responds to G. H. Lewes's attack in the *Leader* on the absurdities of Krook's death by spontaneous combustion (532). The episode actually illustrates Dickens's concluding statement in the preface, "In Bleak House, I have purposely dwelt upon the romantic side of familiar things" (7). This statement also echoes his view on the poetic side of science in his *Examiner* review.

After the primary introduction and simple word search, the students can do the following activities, designed to help them encounter relevant scientific issues and events that enrich *Bleak House*.

Classroom Activity 1:
Outside Reading and Oral Presentation

The students are divided into different groups by subjects such as astronomy, geology, natural history, chemistry, and physics. Although these disciplinary divisions were just developing, even by the 1850s the terms indicated distinct and well-recognized fields of study. As noted above, between 1807 and 1841 specific organizations were launched for the advancement of geology, astronomy, zoology, and chemistry. Dickens clearly has these learned bodies in view in the *Mudfog Papers*, which chronicles two meetings of the Mudfog Association for the Advancement of Everything.

Once divided into groups, students are asked to find out about topical figures, discoveries, and developments in Dickens's time. In the class each group presents its findings and explains how they might help us understand Dickens's novel. After these presentations are made, the students are invited to discuss the opinions expressed. In what follows I suggest sources students can work with and outline some of the ways they shed light on specific aspects of *Bleak House*.

Astronomy

The metaphor of the solar system, which Dickens uses to characterize both the world of fashion and the world of Chancery, illustrates the importance of astronomy and cosmology in the text. Dickens owned a copy of the third edition of John Herschel's *Outline of Astronomy* (1849). From his journalism we know he was aware of astronomical events such as eclipses and the visits of comets. Students can be directed to half-serious articles such as "Mr. Bub on Planetary Disturbances" (1851) and "Mr. Bubb's [sic] Visit to the Moon" (1851); a cluster of articles on comets, such as "Meteors" (1856) and "A Sweep through the Stars" (1858); articles on the sun and solar system such as "Respecting the Sun" (1865); and several reports on lunar and solar eclipses, such as "My Annular Eclipse" (1858) and "The Eclipse Seen in India" (1869). Students can also work with the letters in which Dickens mentions the controversy between William Whewell and David Brewster over the "polarity of worlds," in Whewell's *Of the Plurality of Worlds* and Brewster's *More Worlds Than One* (*Letters* 7: 454–55, 518). They might consult Whewell's *Astronomy and General Physics Considered with Reference to Natural Theology*, the first of the set of famous *Bridgewater Treatises* that Dickens's library held (Stonehouse 117), written by leading Christian scientists who were bequeathed eight thousand pounds by the eighth earl of Bridgewater to write works "on the Power, Wisdom, and

Goodness of God, as manifested in the Creation," attempting to reconcile science and natural theology. The book explains many astronomical discoveries and ideas but affirms that the advance of science should neither displace God nor disturb the belief in scripture and providence. Students then might consider how *Bleak House* deals with this question of divine order. In describing social circles as planetary systems, does the novel touch on similar concerns or conflicts?

The often quoted metaphor the death of the sun implies a scientific speculation about the eventual extinction of the sun and destruction of earth, as well as an apocalyptic end of the world. In Dickens's time people had long been preoccupied with the invisible and the infinitely great. Astronomers' observations and inquiries showed that all stars were in motion, in evolution and decay; people's common illusion of cosmic permanence had been destroyed, and humankind's place in the universe threatened. Dickens's library held John Pringle Nichol's *Views of the Architecture of the Heavens and Thoughts on Some Important Points Relating to the System of the World* (Stonehouse 84). Nichol, the Glasgow Regius Professor of Astronomy, often referred to the French astronomer Pierre-Simon Laplace's famous nebular hypothesis of planetary origin. The two astronomers suggested that the sun, like all stars in motion, was not permanent. In redefining the scheme of time and space of the universe, astronomy shared the spirit of evolution; both sciences showed human beings' diminished role in relation to the rest of the "creation" and inevitably called into question a literal reading of scripture. In searching for Dickens's views on this dilemma, students may refer back to Dickens's review of *The Poetry of Science*: "the light of yonder planet is diminishing, my lord[,] will shortly die; but the professor of an exact science has arisen in his stead, to prove that a ray of light might occupy a period of six years in traveling to the earth from the nearest of the fixed stars" (132). Such words show that Dickens had been imbued with evolutionary ideas long before reading Darwin's *Origin*, and he favored scientific speculation about origins of all kinds such as Chambers's and the astronomers'. He had already seen the difference that astronomy made to religion, but there is no sign that he was disturbed by it. He was optimistic and liberal about the world's being governed not by providential law but by natural law. He belonged to an age when people's minds had to be free from the past, though he often covered up theoretical disputes by new forms of sentiment.

Physics and Chemistry

Students working on physics and chemistry have to begin with an important caveat. The metaphor the death of the sun, according to many critics and biographers, issues from the scientific idea of entropy, based on the second law of thermodynamics put forward by William Thomson in 1851. Ann Y. Wilkinson in *"Bleak House*: From Faraday to Judgment Day" asserts that Dickens "intuitively apprehended the great laws discovered in his age: of the conservation of energy, with all its results in the dynamics of systems, and in the creation of entropy" (247). Willian Axton comments on the "inevitable fatality" and "increased acceptance of the idea of extinction" as part of the novel's scientific imagery ("Religious and Scientific Imagery" 357, 359), and Gillian Beer and Peter Ackroyd (*Dickens* [1990]) discuss further Dickens's possible understanding of the second law of thermodynamics. It is important, however, for students to know that the fashionable word "entropy" that critics borrow to interpret the decline and inefficiency of Chancery and other moribund systems was in fact coined by the German mathematician and physicist Rudolf Julius Clausius in 1865 and made popular by John Tyndall's lectures at the Royal Institution much later.

The most important figure for students to consider is Faraday, to whom Dickens once wrote to ask permission to use his lecture "On a Candle" in an article in *Household Words.* The article was written by Percival Leigh, who creates a fictional character, nephew Harry, to explain to his uncle Bagges what he had learned from Faraday's lectures at the Royal Institution. Having read this imaginative account of the chemical transformation of candle wax into heat and light, students may speculate that Faraday inspired the episode of Krook's spontaneous combustion. Students should also consider the mention of chemists in the scene of Tom's death, where it is said that "chemists on analysis" will discover one day that Tom's blood is the cause of infection and contagion (710).

Natural History, Geology, and Biology

Students working on natural history, geology, and biology will wish to begin with the opening scene of *Bleak House.* The echo of Genesis here ("as if the waters had but newly retired from the face of the earth" [13]) combines the view of Holborn Hill with the reference to "a Megalosaurus, forty feet long or so, waddling like an elephantine lizard." The mud, the fog, and the megalosaurus represent the world's primordial period in the biblical account of the deluge, but also in the account offered by nineteenth-century science about life and earth from its earliest times. Dickens might have come across William Kirby's account of "a giant lizard calculated to have been forty feet in length" in *On the Power, Wisdom and Goodness of God as Manifested in the Creation of Animals . . .* (1: 372). Three months before Dickens began to compose *Bleak House,* there appeared an article describing the geologist William Buckland's discoveries of parts of a megalosaurus's skeleton (Shatto, *Companion* 23–24). Perhaps it inspired Dickens to compare the obsolescent Court of Chancery to the extinct megalosaurus.

Students should be encouraged to search broadly in the text for allusions to evolutionary thought. For example, Judy Smallweed appears to "date from the remotest periods," having reached "a perfectly geological age" (339). She and her twin Bart "bear a likeness to old monkeys" (333): Bart is "a kind of fossil imp" (318), and Judy "so happily exemplifies the before-mentioned family likeness to the monkey tribe" that she seems "like an animal of another species" (335). Comparison has been made between Dickens and Darwin, but when Dickens began composing *Bleak House* in November 1851, before reading Darwin, he had already been imbued with pre-Darwinian speculation about evolution. Dickens might have read Charles Lyell's *Principles of Geology* (1830–33), as Lyell's discovery is discussed in "Earliest Man" (1861), and his later work *Geological Evidence of the Antiquity of Man* (1863) was held in his library (Stonehouse 75). He certainly knew Chambers's *Vestiges* and was well aware of the conflicts between religion and such scientific discoveries. The *Bridgewater Treatises* and Buckland's reconciliation of faith with science may also have influenced him. His close friend Richard Owen's idea, given in his talk to the British Association in 1858, about creation as a kind of "creative leap" rather than gradual transmutation of species may have influenced him as well (Desmond and Moore 478). K. J. Fielding's and my article "Dickens's Science, Evolution and 'the Death of the Sun'" can be recommended to students. Students working with these materials are challenged to understand how *Bleak House*, beginning with this image of a primordial earth, reflects or comments on these debates.

Classroom Activity 2: Debates and Brainstorming

John Sutherland in "What Kills Lady Dedlock?" offers four probable causes of Lady Dedlock's death, open to debate. Students can be divided into groups, and each group defends one of the following hypotheses, using textual details (time lapses, symptoms, or hints) to support arguments:

> *Smallpox hypothesis*   This group argues that Lady Dedlock might have died of smallpox, contracted from her visit to Nemo's grave with Jo, following F. S. Schwarzbach's points in "The Fever of *Bleak House*" and "Deadly Stains: Lady Dedlock's Death." This theory suggests many symbolic meanings, such as the intimate relationship of apparently unconnected classes in society.
>
> *Exhaustion hypothesis*   This group follows Susan Shatto's "Lady Dedlock and the Plot of *Bleak House*" and defends her idea that "a forty-two mile journey on foot through a snowstorm [is] sufficient reason for a cossetted lady suffering great emotional stress to grow pale, exhausted, hoarse, miserable and, ultimately, to die" (189).
>
> *Melodramatic option*   This group holds that for melodramatic effect, fictional heroines may die of nonpathological conditions such as a broken heart or grief at a critical moment; students can find more such examples to support.
>
> *Suicide hypothesis*   This group will follow Sutherland's argument that Lady Dedlock might have taken opium to kill herself.

Students are encouraged to consider other options. For example, a typhus hypothesis can be deduced from Gillian West's "*Bleak House*: Esther's Illness," in which West argues that Esther and Charley caught from Jo typhus (or a related disease, erysipelas) rather than smallpox, a suggestion that West connects to the Lord Chancellor's custom of carrying a nosegay, perhaps to prevent catching typhus from prisoners. After lively debates, students vote to decide the most convincing hypothesis. Finally, the teacher can ask them to consider why Dickens does not specify the cause of death and what purpose might be served by keeping the ending open.

It is useful to explore Dickens's grasp of science and the way he used science in *Bleak House*. But consider his sentimental short story "A Child's Dream of a Star" and what he says in "A Preliminary Word": "in all familiar things, even in those which are repellant on the surface, there is Romance enough, if we will find it out" (1). Here, as with his *Examiner* review and the allusions and metaphors already discussed, we find Dickens emphasizes the poetic and imaginative side of science. After this course, my students and I feel that we have begun to bridge the divide between science and literature, taking *Bleak House* as an example to demonstrate how the two cultures can possibly be interdependent in a literary text. Here science is not just a sidelight or casual reference Dickens adopts on impulse but an important threshold and resource bearing on the form of fiction, arousing his imagination, and enriching his creation. He transforms scientific allusion into artistic form, while remaining free from any particularly ideological doctrine of science.

The Esther Problem

Timothy Peltason

Is there an Esther problem for teachers of *Bleak House*? I think that there is and that it makes sense to acknowledge the problem early and explicitly to students who will soon be encountering such notorious Estherisms as this one, from the end of chapter 6:

> It was not for me to muse over bygones, but to act with a cheerful spirit and a grateful heart. So I said to myself, "Esther, Esther, Esther! Duty, my dear!" and gave my little basket of housekeeping keys such a shake, that they sounded like little bells, and rang me hopefully to bed.   (103)

Or, in due course, such extremities of self-abnegation as this, immediately after Lady Dedlock's confession of her maternity to the smallpox-scarred Esther:

> [W]hen I saw her at my feet on the bare earth in her great agony of mind, I felt, through all my tumult of emotion, a burst of gratitude to the providence of God that I was so changed as that I never could disgrace her by any trace of likeness; as that nobody could ever now look at me, and look at her, and remotely think of any near tie between us.   (579)

These passages and many others provoke understandable impatience with both Esther and her creator and provoke as well critically relevant questions about the extent to which we are being asked to admire or, worse, to take as girlishly exemplary the sweetness of the first passage or the (near literal) self-effacement of the second. Because these passages likely irk or unsettle us as well, we fall into a damaging disingenuousness if we don't confront directly the critical problems that they raise. Such a strategy has the considerable virtue not just of honesty but also of taking us straight into the deepest moral and psychological concerns of the novel and thus its greatest artistic challenges and achievements.

The weak solution to the Esther problem is just to apologize for Dickens and for Esther, explaining away her peculiarities with a fast account of the angel in the house and asking our students to read Esther symptomatically as another figure in this sexist and sentimental tradition. Students who have encountered Little Nell or Florence Dombey or Agnes Wickfield are only too ready to place Esther in the Dickens branch of the sisterhood.

But this solution is a weak one for two reasons. First, because it invites students to join with us in a collusive condescension to the past that is always, in some measure, morally and intellectually compromising. Second, and more immediately important, because it does so much less than justice to Esther Summerson, who stands out in this female company as one of Dickens's great creations, the only one who is a narrator and thus a fully voiced presence, a worthy sister to David Copperfield and to Pip in that small family of characters whom Dickens both creates and endows with his own extraordinary powers of description and evocation. A gifted narrator, an uncommonly quick observer, a maker of sharp judgments, Esther also mingles surprising strength with her womanly sweetness, unfazed even at the outset by figures of worldly importance ("'You will not be discomposed by the Lord Chancellor, I dare say?' 'No, sir,' I said, 'I don't think I shall.' Really not seeing, on consideration, why I should be" [44]) and emerging in the course of her narrative as a figure of always hesitant but still conspicuous force and power, a figure who finds her way with singular success through the world of the novel.

In my teaching of *Bleak House* and in this essay, I strive to make two chief points about Esther: first, that her many timidities, effusions, and disingenuous disclaimers are brilliantly particular to her, not a portrayal of exemplary girlhood but the moving, plausible, and internally consistent presentation of a particular formation or deformation of character; and, second, that the novel describes in her a gradual process of growth in which she puts herself forward at last as a person capable of declaring and worthy of receiving the love of another. The strong solution, then, is to seize the opportunity presented by Esther's undeniable peculiarities and to teach our students how to hear her voice properly in all its depth and strangeness. And the indispensable means to this end is the careful examination of a sequence of heightened passages throughout the novel, passages in which Esther's voice reveals the full range both of her character and of Dickens's sponsoring genius.

When I ask my students what they're being invited to notice about Esther in her first chapter (3), "A Progress," they readily describe the sorrow and loneliness of her childhood and the cruelty of her godmother and can usually produce a variety of half-formulated observations about her compulsive self-criticisms, accompanied sometimes by complaints about the disingenuousness of these criticisms. It takes some further questioning and answering to make sure that the fact of Esther's illegitimacy has been established and to contextualize the cruelties of Miss Barbary with a quick account of the particular brand of hard and joyless Protestantism of which she is an instance.

With these facts of Esther's life established and from the perspective of the later episodes that students will have read for a first class, they can begin to see that all her anxiety to please has its richly dramatized origins in this opening account of a child whose very right to exist was denied by the adults around her. Confiding in her "dear old doll," Esther illustrates the necessary psychological adjustments that she has made to emotional rejection and isolation:

> My dear old doll! I was such a shy little thing that I seldom dared to open my lips, and never dared to open my heart, to anybody else. It almost makes me cry to think what a relief it used to be to me, when I came home from school of a day, to run upstairs to my room, and say, "O you dear faithful Dolly, I knew you would be expecting me!" and then to sit down on the floor, leaning on the elbow of her great chair, and tell her all I had noticed since we parted. I had always rather a noticing way—not a quick way, O no!—a silent way of noticing what passed before me, and thinking I should like to understand it better. I have not by any means a quick understanding. When I love a person very tenderly indeed, it seems to brighten. But even that may be my vanity.   (28)

Looking at such a paragraph with students, it's helpful to remind them of Dickens's presence and to ask not what Esther is revealing to us about herself but what Dickens is revealing to us about Esther and with what larger implications and purposes. When the discussion is framed in this way, students can work past the tone trouble that they may have with some portions of such a paragraph, arriving instead at a sequence of tentative and usable observations: that Dickens has skillfully established Esther's tenderheartedness as a concomitant of her desperate need for love and approval; that this desperation finds its way into her tone in a variety of ways, making her at once insistently generous in offering love and nervously fearful of presuming to receive it; that this ardency of interest in what she might give to the world and receive from it makes her a special kind of noticing recorder. Once this note of fearful eagerness has been made audible in Esther's voice, a sympathetic reader hears it everywhere and values it more highly for hearing in it the workings of both Esther's touchingly rendered pain and Dickens's larger dramatic purposes.

Esther's struggle to hold herself less cheaply and to act effectively in the world of *Bleak House* is both broadly representative and strikingly successful, for she ends the novel with a fuller share of life's blessings than any other character. And she does so largely through her gradually emergent readiness to figure as both the agent and the object of love, especially of romantic love. As the questions of romantic and sexual love arise for Esther and as her disfigurement comes to complicate and intensify her relation to these questions, Dickens creates for us a distinct and meaningfully particularized subnarrative within the larger story of Esther's progress. To chart with my students the course of Esther's career in love, I pause over a few passages that Dickens and Esther italicize for us by the intensity of her responses.

Relatively early in the novel, Esther receives the first of her several marriage proposals, this one from Mr. Guppy. Although she refuses his proposal with all its comic legalisms, she closes the chapter with this arresting account of her delayed response to it:

> I sat there for another hour or more, finishing my books and payments, and getting through plenty of business. Then, I arranged my desk, and put everything away, and was so composed and cheerful that I thought I had quite dismissed this unexpected incident. But, when I went up-stairs to my own room, I surprised myself by beginning to laugh about it, and then surprised myself still more by beginning to cry about it. In short, I was in a flutter for a little while; and felt as if an old chord had been more coarsely touched than it ever had been since the days of the dear old doll, long buried in the garden. (154)

Asking my students whether they, too, are surprised by this response and whether they can imagine why Esther should think now of the doll on whom she spent her childish love and whom she ritually buried in the garden, I find it possible to deepen their earlier discussions of Esther's longing for love and to notice with them the graduated passage that Esther and Dickens register here from one kind of love to another. Asked to notice Esther's word "coarsely," students can see that Guppy has been securely placed by Esther and that her sudden rushes of feeling in this paragraph in no way signify an interest in him as a romantic partner. Asked to think why Dickens should prepare for Esther's tears with her laughter, they can see the laughter as a fit response to Guppy's absurdity, but also see the emotional instability of the passage as a recognizable symptom of the nervous distress that Esther displays whenever she must consider herself as either the agent or the object of romantic desire.

When Allan Woodcourt enters the narrative, Esther is fluttery and coy in a sequence of passages that are hardly her or the novel's best, but that can be easily adduced in support of the larger argument about the awkwardness and hesitancy that attend any moment in which Esther flirts with the possibility of her own romantic eligibility. Far more worthy of close attention—more rewardingly strange and intense—are two other moments when Esther must confront the question of her lovability.

The first of these is the moment in which Esther reencounters Ada after her face has been scarred by smallpox. Students will have noticed that Esther records at apologetic length her terrible anxiety lest Ada should somehow have changed toward her in response to the change in Esther's appearance. Through the two last pages of chapter 36, from the paragraph beginning "My dear girl was to arrive at five o'clock" (587) until the ecstatic-with-relief concluding sentences of the chapter, Dickens dramatizes through Esther's voice the push and pull of her emotions as she heats herself with waiting, worry, and eagerness. The pitch of Esther's concern, the dance of approach and avoidance as Ada comes nearer, the emphasis on the exchange of gazes, all these things inevitably and appropriately raise a question of categories: what kind of love must this be to be dramatized in this way? That the friendship has a romantic intensity seems clear, and this fact alone produces a salutary complication of categories.

Yet there are other currents flowing through the passage, and it's hard to know exactly what we'd be asserting if we named Esther's feelings for Ada as sexual, given the drift of these other currents and given the ways that the rest of the narrative redirects our attention. Another thing to notice about this encounter is that it comes just a few pages after Esther's equally charged if quite different encounter with Lady Dedlock. Looking back to that encounter, the conclusion of Esther's meeting with Ada acquires special meaning:

> O how happy I was, down upon the floor, with my sweet beautiful girl down upon the floor too, holding my scarred face to her lovely cheek, bathing it with tears and kisses, rocking me to and fro like a child, calling me by every tender name that she could think of, and pressing me to her faithful heart.   (588)

"Like a child": coming so soon after Esther's first and only encounter with her mother, these words ask to be noticed, and they alert us to another source of the powerful feelings that Esther displays here. For this is precisely the loving comfort that Lady Dedlock did not offer to Esther, filled and thrilled as she was by the knowledge of her own sinfulness. A comparison between these two closely connected scenes of close encounter provides an excellent paper topic or a rich class discussion, exfoliating into a variety of other discussions about theme, tone, and treatment. For me, there is no contest between the soap operatics of Esther's meeting with her mother and the heated and affecting tenderness of her meeting with Ada. But other judgments will differ, and the thematic richness of each passage survives critique and sponsors further analysis.

Still another way to think about the power of this episode is to note the variety of ways in which Esther makes use of Ada throughout the novel as a kind of licensed emissary in the world of romantic desire. Because Ada functions as an alter ego for Esther, Esther's concern with what she will see in Ada's face when Ada first encounters her makes for a point of comparison with the scene in which Esther first encounters herself in the mirror after her illness (572). To encounter Ada is to encounter a beloved other but also, for Esther, to encounter another version of herself, the beautiful self who lives and moves freely in the world of acknowledged romantic desire. "One morning," begins a later chapter, ". . . as my beauty and I were walking round and round the garden" (695), and the disoriented reader requires a moment to understand that it's Ada with whom Esther walks, Ada to whom Esther can assign the beauty that she has never dared to claim, and that she has now traumatically lost.

Esther assigns Ada a similar and oddly central role in another crisis of feeling, when she receives her proposal of marriage from John Jarndyce, a proposal so scrupulously disinterested that it hardly merits the name. For Esther, this proposal offers a timely answer to her question about Jarndyce, "[H]ow could I ever be good enough, how in my little way could I ever hope to be forgetful enough of myself . . . to show him how I blessed and honored him" (686). And the self that she must forget is the self of romantic possibility, the self that she identifies instinctively with Ada, a fact that renders slightly less mysterious the lovely and uncanny moment when she seals her decision to accept Jarndyce's proposal by ritually disposing of the dried remains of flowers that Woodcourt had once given her:

> They were in a book, and it happened to be in the next room—our sitting-room, dividing Ada's chamber from mine. I took a candle, and went softly in to fetch it from its shelf. After I had it in my hand, I saw my beautiful darling, through the open door, lying asleep, and I stole in to kiss her.
>
> It was weak in me, I know, and I could have no reason for crying; but I dropped a tear upon her dear face, and another, and another. Weaker than that, I took the withered flowers out, and put them for a moment to her lips. I thought about her love for Richard; though, indeed, the flowers had nothing to do with that. Then I took them into my own room, and burned them at the candle, and they were dust in an instant.   (693)

Renouncing forever—or so she thinks—the object of romantic and sexual love, Esther acts through Ada, naming that love only by invoking Ada's love for Richard and bidding it farewell by having Ada kiss the flowers goodbye. The passage is an extraordinary one, vibrant with Esther's complications of feeling and with the many currents of meaning that Dickens channels through it.

At other points in the course of her engagement to Jarndyce, Esther again deploys Ada as an alternate self to whom her own unacceptable feelings can be attributed. Thinking a few chapters later that she detects "some hidden regret" in Ada, she speculates "that she was a little grieved—for me—by what I had told her about Bleak House" (774–75). What Esther has told is the engagement to Jarndyce and what she detects in Ada is actually the shadow of Ada's secret marriage to Richard. But she uses Ada instead to express her own inexpressible grief for the loss of Woodcourt. That Esther simultaneously grieves for Woodcourt and turns openly toward Jarndyce suggests the continuity, but also the strength and the flexibility, of her character, as she surrenders her desires, regrets their loss, and then strives to renew them in the only way that she can.

That she does strive for such a renewal—even before Woodcourt is reinstated as her romantic partner—is quietly but firmly established. Read aloud, the entire last page of chapter 44, in which Jarndyce has sent his marriage proposal, dramatizes Esther's sad and near-comic efforts to offer her positive response to a maddeningly recessive Jarndyce. She concludes the account with this unmistakable, if also muted and frustrated, gesture of romantic forwardness:

> I put my two arms round his neck and kissed him; and he said was this the mistress of Bleak House; and I said yes; and it made no difference presently, and we all went out together, and I said nothing to my precious pet about it. (694)

That it makes no difference is vexing to Esther, as she makes clear in subsequent passages such as this one, when she offers to "do all she can to make [Bleak House] happy":

> The letter had made no difference between us, except that the seat by his side had come to be mine; it made none now. He turned his old bright fatherly look upon me, laid his hand on my hand in his old way, and said again, "She will succeed, my dear. Nevertheless, Bleak House is thinning fast, O little woman!"
>
> I was sorry presently that this was all we said about that. I was rather disappointed. I feared I might not quite have been all I had meant to be, since the letter and the answer. (790–91)

The verbal echoes closely link this passage to the earlier one. In both cases it is Jarndyce (with his "fatherly look") who refuses to acknowledge these timidly sexual signals and Esther who is "rather disappointed." Esther's romantic readiness on these occasions is both a discreet evidence of her sexual nature and a crucial sign that she is now, increasingly and movingly, ready to assert her right to the place in the world that her godmother would have denied her.

I hope that it will seem open-minded rather than evasive if I decline to untangle this last knot of conflicting feelings in Esther and the novel, all of which must be revisited in the light of the final entanglement—or is it a disentanglement?—that reunites her with Woodcourt. For those students who have been successfully engaged by Esther's voice and character, the conclusion of the novel offers not just the vicarious gratification of Esther's romantic fulfillment but a last occasion to encounter the meaningful strangeness of her character. She remains at the conclusion of the novel a character who has offered herself to Jarndyce but then been offered to Woodcourt ("a willing gift" [966] in Jarndyce's ambiguous formulation, since we don't know whose willingness is meant); a character who can hardly acknowledge her own deserts and yet who claims them nevertheless; who leaves unvoiced but reached for, in the closing words of the novel, the reclamation of the never-before-acknowledged beauty that is the outward sign of those deserts. With the small exception of the Bagnets, the only flourishing households and families in the novel are those of Esther's making, and she survives as the single character in the novel who successfully executes her will. That the full discussion of her character can hardly go forward without discussing John Jarndyce's character and half a dozen others and without tracing outward the thematic connections to the larger questions of successful self-assertion in the world of the novel—all this only confirms the centrality and the richness of the Esther problem.[1]

NOTE

[1] For an extended account of the historical plausibility of Dickens's handling of Esther's illegitimacy, see Leavis, especially the section "Case-Histories of Life in Chancery." For a more skeptical account of Esther's motives and particularly of her relationship with Ada, see Welsh, chapters 2 and 3. For a fuller and recentered version of the argument of this essay, see Peltason.

What Esther Knew

Lisa Sternlieb

In my Victorian novel class we begin the semester with Charlotte Brontë's *Jane Eyre*, Emily Brontës *Wuthering Heights*, and Wilkie Collins's *The Woman in White*. My primary concern with these novels is to have students consider how and why each is being narrated. We discuss why Jane's narrative is retrospective and why she has waited ten years to tell it. We examine the secretive Charlotte Brontë who wrote her novel in the presence of, but without the knowledge of, her blind father and ask why Jane needs a blind husband to be able to write her autobiography. I ask why Nelly Dean has chosen Lockwood as her confidant and to what extent Nelly and Lockwood are significant characters as well as narrators in *Wuthering Heights*. We challenge Walter Hartright's reading of his own work and consider how the various narratives he has compiled undermine the stated purpose of his project. In particular, we question Marian's retrospective re-creation of the contents of her diary and her reasons for omitting those passages "relating to [Walter] which she thought it best that [he] should not see" (Collins 456).

By the time we get to *Bleak House*, then, students should be ready to take on the most anomalous of Victorian narratives. In both *Wuthering Heights* and *The Woman in White* the relationship between and among narrators is explicit. Lockwood leaves off his account in *Wuthering Heights* when it makes sense for Nelly Dean to pick up the story. Walter Hartright knows each of *The Woman in White*'s disparate narrators and compiles and organizes all the testimony. There is no intermediary figure in *Bleak House* to explain to us the relationship between its two narratives or, as in *The Woman in White*, to explain to the narrators themselves what information is required of them.

By the first class on *Bleak House* students need to have read the first ten chapters. They should then be ready to notice and consider the differences between the two narratives. Our initial classes on the novel focus on its structure. During the first class, I ask students to consider the following questions: Why does *Bleak House* have two narrators? Why do they write in different tenses? Why do they scarcely acknowledge each other? Why is a skilled narrator paired with a hesitant one? In particular, I help the students think about the novel's structure by asking them to consider how each of the two narratives begins and ends. Do the narratives rely on each other? Are they independent of each other? Are they aware of each other? Why are certain characters introduced in both narratives? Why do some characters appear only in one narrative and not the other? With few exceptions students won't find answers to these questions in the critical literature on the novel.[1]

We read *The Woman in White* before *Bleak House* (although Collins's novel was published seven years later) because I want students to be prepared to grapple with the more complex narrative structure. It is helpful while reading

Bleak House to consider Walter Hartright's preface: Hartright purports "to trace the course of one complete series of events, by making the persons who have been most closely connected with them, at each successive stage, relate their own experience, word for word" (Collins 1). After reading a novel in which the author makes a painstaking effort both to explain the narrative structure and to avoid overlap, we move to a novel in which information is often repeated and in which characters are introduced and reintroduced to us. Our primary experience of reading *Bleak House*'s double narrative is of living in the present and past simultaneously. The novel's characters routinely experience this as déjà vu. But as Robert Newsom writes:

> It is finally we, the readers, for whom the experience of déjà vu is most persistent. . . . There are in *Bleak House* about a hundred characters. . . . Of these, thirty or so . . . figure in both narratives. Now what this means is that we are introduced to all of these characters, as though for the first time twice. . . . We are continually being led to believe that we are meeting people, or entering places, or witnessing events, that are new and unfamiliar to us, only to discover that what we are seeing as though for the first time is nothing new at all, but something old and familiar.
>
> (*Dickens on the Romantic Side* 54–56)

I ask students to try to account for this doubleness. They are to pay careful attention to the transitions between narratives and to the information that appears first in Esther's narrative only to be repeated by the omniscient narrator and vice versa. Students notice examples like the following:

> Esther visits Krook's shop with Miss Flite, his female tenant, in chapter 5. Six chapters later her companion narrator writes, "'Run, Flite, run! The nearest doctor! Run!' So Mr Krook addresses a crazy little woman, who is his female lodger" (166).
> Just after Esther finishes telling Gridley's tale of woe in exhaustive detail, the narrator off-handedly describes Gridley as "a disappointed suitor, [who] has been here to-day, and has been alarming" (259).
> After we have witnessed Nemo's death and Miss Flite's reaction to it, Esther must be told three chapters later that "there had been a sudden death there, and an inquest; and that our little friend had been ill of the fright" (232).
> Many chapters after we have met Sir Leicester, he is still a stranger to Esther who feels compelled to introduce us to him again.

Students also notice that both the nameless narrator and Esther allude to companion narrators: "While Esther sleeps, and while Esther wakes, it is still wet weather down at the place in Lincolnshire" (103). "I have a great deal of difficulty in beginning to write my portion of these pages" (27), but Esther never seems to have any notion of the contents of her fellow narrator's narrative. Each of her sections picks up where the last ended. So when chapter 6 ends with her going to bed, chapter 8 opens with her waking before daylight. Chapter 15 ends with her visiting London, and chapter 17 begins with Richard visiting them often in London. Chapter 18 ends with a visit to Mr. Boythorn's; chapter 23 begins with their coming home after six weeks at Mr. Boythorn's. The other narrator is not burdened by Esther's concern for continuity. Chapters 7 and 16 end with the sound of footsteps on the Ghost's Walk at Chesney Wold, and chapters 10 and 19 open in Chancery Lane. As an omniscient narrator, he is free to rely on—or ignore—Esther's narrative. Since Esther, however, is (apparently) unaware of her conarrator, she does not share this freedom.

While reading the novel for the first time, students often struggle just to follow the plot. Once we have finished reading *Bleak House,* it is time to look back over the text and consider the necessity of retrospection to Esther's narrative. In our first reading we are led to believe over and over that Esther is the ignorant narrator, that she is uninformed or misinformed, that the present-tense narrator is far more aware of events and of the existence of Esther's narrative. But my students have already considered at great length why the accounts of Jane Eyre and Marian Halcombe are retrospective. Retrospection, we have discovered, is designed to achieve self-protection, not self-exposure. We read Jane and Marian as trustworthy because of the elaborate defenses created and allowed by retrospection. They are neither naive nor unaware of the plots in which they are involved, but deeply invested in portraying themselves as lacking agency, as amanuenses, as artless scribblers. The tension we explore all semester is between unconscious and conscious, lived and narrated experience. Of course, as in actual lived experience fictional characters may be unaware or uninformed. But when these characters come to tell of their experience, they have insight and understanding.

What we try to do, then, as we go back over *Bleak House* is to consider both the difference and the distance between Esther's lived experience of the events she relates and the way in which that experience is narrated. Throughout most of the book, Esther does not appear to rely on her companion narrator. It is only as we come to the end of *Bleak House* that we question whether this is a conscious choice because (as we finally come to realize) she actually does know the content of his narrative.

Although Esther never broaches the subject of her father, Jarndyce hands her over to Woodcourt saying, he "stood beside your father when he lay dead—stood beside your mother" (965). How would Esther's readers understand Jarndyce's reference to her father without having read the other half of the novel? And how would we make any sense of this exchange between Bucket and Mrs. Snagsby?

> "[Y]ou recollect where you saw me last, and what was talked of in that circle. Don't you? Yes! Very well. This young lady is that young lady."
> Mrs Snagsby appeared to understand the reference better than I did at the time.

"And Toughey—him as you call Jo—was mixed up in the same business, and no other; and the law-writer that you know of, was mixed up in the same business, and no other; and your husband, with no more knowledge of it than your great grandfather, was mixed up (by Mr Tulkinghorn deceased, his best customer) in the same business, and no other; and the whole bileing of people was mixed up in the same business, and no other."   (908)

Everything that Esther writes here would be pure gibberish to us if we had been reading only her narrative. We would have no idea what business has connected Tulkinghorn, Jo, the Snagsbys, and others. We would have no sense of why Bucket has discussed Esther with Mrs. Snagsby earlier. Esther has never presented us with such impenetrable dialogue before, but although she hears this conversation as nothing but gibberish—"Mrs Snagsby appeared to understand the reference better than I did at the time"—she records it conscientiously for her readers knowing that it makes sense to us. Esther knows that she is helping to piece together the various strands of the narrator's massive, disjointed account because she has known all along the contents of the other narrative. We see here a brilliant illustration of the difference between Esther the character and Esther the retrospective narrator. The neglected child is often in the dark; the beloved wife knows a great deal but chooses a naive narrative persona.

Now that we have spent all this time analyzing the novel's design, it is time to consider why Dickens has chosen such an anomalous structure. I ask students to think about the multiple examples of family life in *Bleak House*. They should notice that the dreadful parents and surrogate parents include the Jellybys, Pardiggles, Skimpoles, and Smallweeds; Mr. Turveydrop, Miss Barbary, and Mrs. Chadband. The neglected, abused, orphaned, or abandoned children (some now grown) include Jo, Charley, Tom, Emma, Prince, Richard, Ada, Guster, Judy, Bart, and Phil; and the Jellybys, Pardiggles, and Skimpoles. George is estranged from the Rouncewell family, Krook from the Smallweeds, Miss Barbary from her sister, and, of course, in the main plot of the novel Esther discovers that neither of her parents knows of her existence. *Bleak House*, in my reading, is first and foremost about bad parenting and familial estrangement, and the novel's structure mirrors its content. The strange, awkward relationship between the two narrators and two narratives echoes the strange, awkward relationships between parents and children in the novel. Just as Mrs. Pardiggle overlooks her children, Skimpole neglects his, and Mrs. Jellyby exploits hers, the omniscient narrator overlooks, neglects, and exploits Esther's narrative. I read the novel's third-person account as the parent narrative, Esther's as its offspring. I do not argue that the third-person narrator is a character in the novel or that he is, in fact, Esther's father; rather, I contend that her relationship to this unidentifiable figure is modeled on the relationships between parents and children in the novel. In particular I stress that the omniscient (parent) narrator relies on his child's narrative but that the child cannot in turn depend on the parent narrative.

While Dickens maintains this relationship for most of the novel, he allows it to change dramatically the night of Lady Dedlock's death. As Esther discovers her parents' dead bodies, she is finally given the opportunity to move forward with her life. She and her conarrator are finally working with the same set of circumstances, the same group of characters. Esther takes over six of the last eight chapters, and the parent narrator moves farther into the background. The new, dominant narrative voice changes markedly at this moment. In the last line of the eighteenth number Esther writes, "And it was my mother, cold and dead" (915). We are accustomed to watching Esther double back and reverse course. But in a bold move she begins the nineteenth number in the present tense: "I proceed to other passages of my narrative" (916). In a few words she tells of her sorrow and illness, but never again does she mention either of her parents. We are seeing a new Esther. While it is Esther who has attempted to redeem Lady Dedlock, Esther who has pursued Lady Dedlock, it is Esther's prerogative to drop Lady Dedlock. The mother is never again mentioned by her daughter after her dead body is found at the end of the eighteenth book.

Students can easily see that *Bleak House* is about a damaged young woman struggling for self-acceptance and reconciliation with her parents. By carefully studying the novel's narrative structure, they come to realize that this struggle continues even through the process of retrospective narration. Esther is allowed to marry happily. She is allowed to take over most of the narrative by the end of the novel. But, if the narrative structure tells us anything about her psychological development, she will never be a fully healthy woman because she is never allowed a "normal" parent-child relationship. She is never able to rely openly on the parent narrative. She is never able to learn from and become like the parent narrator – even at its strongest, hers will always be the weaker narrative voice. Just as she is never able to embrace her parents, she is never able to embrace the parent narrative. Her relationship to it is always tentative. She can never be fully independent from it, nor can she ever be fully dependent on it.

What is harder for students to recognize is that Esther's is, nonetheless, an extraordinary narrative achievement. Although terribly neglected, Esther is, against all odds (like Dickens himself), amazingly literate. Like Charlotte Brontë before him, Dickens uses feminine virtue as a narrative strategy. It is only as an innocuous angel in the house that Esther can perform the complicated narrative maneuver of complaining without bitterness, of critiquing while staying loyal. None of Dickens's first-person narrators accuse their parents directly. We may recognize Mrs. Copperfield's weakness and disloyalty, we may regret Joe's implicit countenancing of abuse, and we may shudder at Jarndyce's flirtation with incest, but Dickens's narrators forgive. Esther's narrative style lacks David's confidence or Pip's humor, but its complex relationship to that of the companion narrator allows Esther to use retrospection for entirely different ends. For her narrative is not motivated by regret—and Dickens need not pretend it is. David Copperfield and Pip use their more popular narratives to grapple with their own past wrongs. While remaining sentimental, "good," and apparently faithful, Esther is able to use retrospection to grapple with her parents' instead.[2]

I am not interested in imposing my particular reading on my students. I hope that my studying the novel's structure with them closely will lead them to come up with their own readings of *Bleak House*. Although Chancery does not play a large role in my reading, I encourage them to consider how they would construct an argument that explores the relation between the novel's structure and Dickens's view of the English legal system. As one of my brighter students noted, Jarndyce and Jarndyce is the quintessence of familial estrangement, doubling, and competing narrative accounts. The novel's design, he argues, may lead us to revisit our judgments more effectively than any legal case ever does. I ask students to consider other structural and narrative questions that my reading only touches on. What other implications are there for the emphasis on doubling and the preponderance of doubles? While I take it for granted that the parent narrator is male, how can this position be proven or undermined? Is the dual narration intended to cast doubt on the veracity of Esther's account or to add color to it? Surprisingly, few of my students have ever read any Dickens before taking my class. By helping them develop their own theories of first-person narration, I also hope to awaken their interest in *David Copperfield* and *Great Expectations*.

NOTES

[1] There are, however, important readings of the double narrative. These include Hornback; Newsom, *Dickens on the Romantic Side*; and Gaughan. For a lengthier discussion of the questions I pose here, see my essay "Esther Summerson: Looking Twice."

[2] Many other critics have powerfully defended Esther's narrative. See especially Jaffe, *Vanishing Points*; Peltason; Wilt; Dever; Graver; and Zwerdling.

Mr. Tulkinghorn's Chambers

Barbara Leckie

In an early review of *Bleak House* George Brimley famously commented on the novel's "absolute want of construction." The "centre of the arch [the Chancery proceedings]," he said, "has nothing to do with keeping the arch together" (934). In *Bleak House* itself Dickens employs the arch metaphor to somewhat different ends: "What was his [Mr. Tulkinghorn's] death but the key-stone of a gloomy arch removed, and now the arch begins to fall in a thousand fragments, each crushing and mangling piecemeal!" (855). In both examples it is the arch that connects, or fails to connect, disparate aspects of the novel's plot, and in a novel that insistently poses the question of connection, it makes sense to consider the keystone—Mr. Tulkinghorn—that the novel itself proposes.[1] As Alexander Welsh has noted, the complexity of the novel's construction frustrates the ability of "any architectural critic" to "know where to enter" (18). Mr. Tulkinghorn's chambers provide one point of entry that illuminates the novel's architecture in Brimley's sense and in terms of its broader dialogue with social and architectural issues.[2]

The greatest difficulty my students have with *Bleak House* is its length. It is not just architectural critics, after all, who have a hard time knowing how to approach this novel. I address this difficulty through teaching paired close readings; because the focus of the course I teach is architecture and the novel, the readings I select relate to some aspect of architecture flexibly defined (the architecture of the text, the architecture of the house, the haunted house, the uncanny, the doll's house, the angel in the house, the country house, tours of country houses, visits to poor houses, working-class housing, slum housing, homelessness, philanthropy and housing, and so on). My goal is to provide students with a manageable section of the text, to emphasize the insights that can be gained from close reading, to compare passages with others we have examined in the novel (to compare Mr. Tulkinghorn's chambers, for example, with Tom-all-Alone's), to consider the internal structure of the passages and their place in the novel (What comes before the passage selected? What comes after? Why? What is the effect of these alignments?), and to explore how these passages relate to the novel's social and political concerns. Dickens's political commitments are clear. In a letter to a friend, he stresses that when he writes novels he hopes to "interest and affect the general mind in behalf of anything that is clearly wrong—to stimulate and arouse the public soul to a compassionate or indignant feeling that *it must not be*" (*Letters* 7: 405). In a novel entitled *Bleak House*, it is not surprising that architecture—a "distinctively political art," in Ruskin's words (*Seven Lamps* 2)—captures issues related to the architecture of the text, architecture in the text, and the text's role in architectural and social reform.

At the outset, I illustrate the range of Dickens's architectural interests at the time he was writing *Bleak House*. With the wealthy philanthropist Angela

Burdett-Coutts, Dickens devoted a great deal of time and energy to the planning and administration of Urania Cottage, a residence for homeless women. He was also involved in a model housing project funded by Burdett-Coutts. Through his brother-in-law, Henry Austin, he knew Edwin Chadwick, one of the most prominent social reformers of the time, and followed his work closely. While most critics are familiar with Chadwick's lengthy documents outlining recommended social improvements, they are often unaware of the numerous architectural drawings Chadwick draws on there or of his descriptions of working-class interiors. On a more personal level, Dickens was moving house through the first year of *Bleak House*'s composition and was intimately involved in plans for his new house as well as profoundly sensitive to the impact of place on his writing and his work.[3] His interest in architecture and interior design extended to his active involvement in the set designs and theater spaces of amateur theatricals. His earlier novel *Martin Chuzzlewit* illustrates his extensive knowledge of architectural practice in the 1840s (see Tambling, *Martin Chuzzlewit*). Finally, in the summer of 1851, while he was first thinking about *Bleak House*, Dickens was reading John Ruskin's *Lamps of Architecture* (Forster 2: 57).

After I discuss this background information with my students, we proceed to a close analysis of two passages involving Mr. Tulkinghorn in his chambers. The first (158–59) provides an extended description of the solicitor's chambers and shows Tulkinghorn in a moment of indecision as he attempts to determine how to conduct his inquiry into Lady Dedlock's secret. The second passage (747–52) describes the action preceding and following the murder of Tulkinghorn in his chambers. In this essay I discuss only a section of the first passage in detail, but I indicate the direction a close reading of the second passage might take throughout.

We begin with the question, what do we know thus far about Tulkinghorn in the novel? We recall the first description of him in chapter 2 at the Dedlocks' country home; he is said to be "old-fashioned," an owner of "many cast-iron boxes" with the Dedlock name on the outside, "rusty," a "silent depository" of family confidences with secrets "shut up" in his breast; he is of the "old school"; he is "[m]ute, close, irresponsive" (23) and "retainer-like" (24). The result of a focus on secrecy, Laura Mulvey notes, is to generate "the divided topography of inside and outside" (58). Such a topography is linked not only to the inside and the outside but also to the private and the public, the visible and the invisible, the legible and illegible on which much of the novel's narrative economy relies, even as the novel questions the durability of such oppositions. And Tulkinghorn clearly participates in—indeed epitomizes—this economy, in a description of character that is architectural from the outset: Tulkinghorn is a space (a "depository," "retainer-like") in which secrets are hidden.

After his introduction in chapter 2, Tulkinghorn exits from the novel until chapter 10, "The Law-Writer," in which we encounter the first close-reading passage. The first sentence of the passage is as follows: "The day is closing in

and the gas is lighted, but is not yet fully effected, for it is not quite dark" (158).
We note that Tulkinghorn almost always enters the text at twilight, a liminal
time that draws our attention to the liminal spaces of the text: the focus on the
Ghost's Walk, the leads, balconies, hallways, enclosed gardens, and the "stair-
cases, passages, and antechambers" in the passage below. These liminal spaces
disrupt the integrity of the opposition between the inside and outside associated
with Tulkinghorn above. Reference to twilight refers us back to the beginning of
the text (the *arche*)—with its lighting of the gas lamps and its stress on the not
quite dark afternoon—in one of the many doubling movements of this text. The
phrase "closing in" also carries us forward in the novel to the next description
of Tulkinghorn's chambers in chapter 16—"A wretched evening is beginning to
close in. In his chambers, Mr Tulkinghorn sits . . ." (259)—and to the second
close-reading passage, in chapter 48, which is itself entitled "Closing In."
    The narrator then adopts the conceit of the crow to carry us from the Snags-
bys in Cook's Court to Tulkinghorn in Lincoln's Inn Fields. The paragraph introducing Tulkinghorn's chambers reads as follows:

> Here, in a large house, formerly a house of state, lives Mr Tulkinghorn. It
> is let off in chambers now; and in those shrunken fragments of its great-
> ness, lawyers lie like maggots in nuts. But its roomy staircases, passages,
> and antechambers, still remain; and even its painted ceilings, where Alle-
> gory, in Roman helmet and celestial linen, sprawls among balustrades and
> pillars, flowers, clouds, and big-legged boys, and makes the head ache—as
> would seem to be Allegory's object always, more or less. Here, among
> his many boxes labelled with transcendant names, lives Mr Tulkinghorn,
> when not speechlessly at home in country-houses where the great ones
> of the earth are bored to death. Here he is to-day, quiet at his table. An
> Oyster of the old school, whom nobody can open.   (158)

Students are quick to notice echoes of the earlier description of Tulkinghorn
in this passage: there are the "many boxes labelled with transcendant names,"
the "quiet" man, his association with "the old school," and the general emphasis
on secrecy and enclosure (maggots in nuts, boxes, oysters in shells). And yet
Tulkinghorn's antiquity is contrasted to the repeated stress on the here and now:
"here," "now," here," "here," "to-day." Indeed, three of the six sentences in this
passage begin with the word "here." We discuss how this stress on the here
and now lends urgency to the passage and consider whether it is valid to read a
"hear" in "here." Just as Tulkinghorn does not draw attention to himself (in the
earlier passage we were told that his clothing "never shine[s]" [23]), this passage seems to call out—"Hear, hear"—and perhaps invites us to be suspicious
of Tulkinghorn's apparent quiet and reserved personality.
    If enclosure is emphasized in the metaphors in this passage, the most striking
example of it is, of course, Tulkinghorn in his room. The architecture here is
important: Tulkinghorn's large house was "formerly a house of state," but now

the rooms are only "shrunken fragments" of its former "greatness." The painted ceiling is interesting not only as a relic of a former period (the house of state) but also as a reference to a period before even houses of state existed (the reference to the "Roman helmet" and implicitly the Roman empire). We pause here to define *allegory* etymologically (*allos* = other + *ēgorein* = speaking in a public place) and rhetorically (a metaphor moving through time). We note that allegory famously moves in two directions: toward absolutely legible interpretations (Frye's prescribed reading [90]) and toward an instability of meaning following from the fact that it speaks through a veiled language (literally, speaking otherwise) that may always fail to signify, or may signify errantly.[4] We further note that allegory can be a form of private speaking (the other text) in a public place (the *agora*) that accordingly destabilizes the opposition between the private and the public, the inside and the outside.

The painting is on the ceiling—it is inside the room—and yet, as a ceiling, it is also a liminal space that poses a challenge to the sharp opposition between the inside and outside on which Tulkinghorn relies. Unlike Tulkinghorn's encrypted secrets, allegory's secrets are strikingly visible—allegory does not hide—but they are not self-evident. The painting of Allegory is described in extravagant terms: in contrast to Tulkinghorn in his proper black clothes, Allegory sprawls across the ceiling in what is almost a display of display—or an allegory of allegory—with images that bespeak phallic power ("balustrades and pillars") as well as a certain effeminacy ("flowers, clouds, and big-legged boys"). If allegory is speaking otherwise, what exactly is being communicated here? Students often note the homoerotic imagery, and we speculate on the possibility of a queer subtext in the context of the very closeted Tulkinghorn. Usually, we defer our extended discussion of allegory for the second close-reading passage, in which we note the introduction of Allegory pointing (259), the excessiveness of the pointing in the second passage (750), the link between Phiz's illustration of Jo pointing and his illustration of Allegory pointing (discussed by Steig 152), and the indeterminacy of the pointing and its implications for signification and meaning in general (in one passage Allegory points out the window [259], in the other at the floor [750]). Since our attention has been drawn to the room and details of the room—the ceiling and the painting—we pause to consider some extratextual sources.

Charles Dickens the younger notes that Tulkinghorn's chambers are modeled after John Forster's rooms at 58 Lincoln's Inn Fields (cited in Shatto, *Companion* 101–02). What is not noted, however, is that the architect John Soane lived kitty-corner to Forster at 17-18 Lincoln's Inn Fields; indeed, Soane designed the porch of Forster's house (Hardwick and Hardwick 110). While there is no evidence that Dickens knew of Soane's work, several aspects of Soane's house, which he turned into a museum in 1810, resonate with Dickens's novel. Robin Middleton stresses Soane's fascination with "antique fragments" and "ruined fragments" (27) and summarizes his work as an "architecture of fragments" (31). These descriptions echo not only the "shrunken fragments" of Tulkinghorn's current living space but also the repeated emphasis on his antiqueness. The painting of Allegory, moreover, is consistent with Soane's interest in antiquity, in plaster casts and bronzes of allegorical figures. (He had a copy of John Flaxman's *Victory* in his breakfast room, for example [Middleton 27].) Soane's work draws our attention to the role of the ruin and the fragment in the novel that Dickens imagined entitling "The Ruined House" before settling on *Bleak House*.

We conclude our discussion of this paragraph with a consideration of its last sentence: "An oyster of the old school, whom nobody can open" (158). It is a sentence fragment and so recalls both the room as fragment and Soane's interest in building with fragments. We note the extraordinary repetition of *o*'s in this sentence and speculate on their impact (as a closed circle, as a series of screams, as holes in the text). And then we pause on the double meaning of the phrase "whom nobody can open": either Tulkinghorn cannot be opened, or "nobody," if such a person were to exist, can open him.[5] This description of Tulkinghorn's chambers immediately precedes the discovery of Nemo's body (alone in his room), and since Nemo translates as "no one," we consider reading this sentence through the prism of Nemo's role in the novel. In what way could Nemo be said to open Tulkinghorn? Does the pursuit of Lady Dedlock and the discovery of Nemo make Tulkinghorn vulnerable in a way that he was not before? Or is it the pseudonym—the possibility for names to mislead (common to both Nemo and allegory in general)—that disturbs the quiet efficiency of Tulkinghorn's carefully named boxes? With a close reading I like to pose questions to keep alive several threads to our argument—the role of enclosure in the novel, the opposition between the inside and the outside and its relation to the novel's secrecy and its architecture, allegory and the painting of Allegory, the study of the home, and the focus on liminal places. I have focused thus far on the opposition between the inside and the outside in particular; what interests me here, and in my teaching, is not so much the challenge that that novel poses to this opposition as the fact that this challenge is articulated through architectural imagery: Tulkinghorn as a sort of locked room and Tulkinghorn in his room by contrast to the painting of Allegory displayed on the ceiling.

If the architectural imagery in the Tulkinghorn passages at once asserts and challenges the topography of inside and outside, it also produces connections in unexpected places. I return to the arch as an architectural figure; it is here that the architectural engagements of the text are most closely aligned with Dickens's commitment to social reform. To illustrate this point, I offer an abbreviated reading of Tulkinghorn's chambers and Jo's slum housing at Tom-all-Alone's. While this connection between Tulkinghorn is made through the maggot metaphor—"lawyers lie like maggots" and people are drawn to Tom-all-Alone's in "maggot numbers" (257)—and in the generic reference to "any crossing-sweeper in Holborn" (159) in the first close-reading passage, it is most forceful in the passages that depict Tulkinghorn's murder.

In these passages Tulkinghorn and Jo are bound together through shared language; as Jo is "moved on" (e.g., 731), Tulkinghorn is "pitilessly urged upon his way," with "the crowd pressing him on" (748). The two are linked as well by an embedded focus on ruins (Soane's interest in ruins and the "ruinous place," Tom-all-Alone's [256], where Jo lives), by the architectural alignments that the structure of the text itself enforces (both Jo and Tulkinghorn die at exactly the same time in the evening, and in the chapter entitled "Tom-all-Alone's" [16] the narrative shifts from Jo's slum life to Tulkinghorn's luxurious life), and by the fact that for both characters the home is not a safe shelter. As several critics have noted, moreover, Phiz's illustration (751) of Allegory pointing at the floor in Tulkinghorn's chambers deliberately echoes his illustration (263) of Jo pointing at the burial grounds (J. H. Miller, "Interpretation" 184; Steig 146; Welsh 65). Further, Tulkinghorn's failure to read the significance of Allegory recalls Jo's illiteracy, and the question of meaning, legibility, signification, is posed explicitly in the context of both characters (257, 750).

These links are made through the architecture of the text (the reference to both Jo's and Tulkinghorn's death is made at the end of a chapter and invites comparison accordingly), architecture in the text (the architecture of Tulkinghorn's room, the description of painted Allegory on the ceiling, the failure of architecture in Tom-all-Alone's), and the novel's link with extratextual issues related to architecture (the debate on working-class housing and slum reform, which Dickens participated in himself [see Dickens's "Home," "Health," and "Speech"], and Soane's "architecture of fragments"). When we read about Tulkinghorn's chambers, then, we are simultaneously reading the superimposed text of Jo's slum housing.

It is difficult, in the context of the extraordinary care and attentiveness to form exhibited in these linked passages, to endorse Brimley's description of *Bleak House*'s "absolute want of construction." In Dickens we encounter a novelist for whom the architecture of the novel is inseparable from the very architectural reform that the novel itself promotes. Tulkinghorn's chambers indicate the pitfalls of focusing too intently on the inside-outside topography of the secret and the advantage—indeed the necessity—of drawing connections where we least expect to see them. For Tulkinghorn, Jo is inconsequential and Tom-all-Alone's is invisible, but for him to fail to make connections between himself and Jo, to fail to calculate the consequences of Jo's being inside his room and Tom-all-Alone's inside London, is literally a matter of life and death. When Tulkinghorn dies, "the arch begins to fall in a thousand fragments, each crushing and mangling piecemeal!" (855). In Tom-all-Alone's the arches are already falling. "Twice, lately, there has been a crash and a cloud of dust, like the springing of a mine, in Tom-all-Alone's; and, each time, a house has fallen" (257). It is through the allegory of an old lawyer in his room that Dickens draws his reader's attention to the pressing need for housing reform in the slums, slums that are at once distant from and very much inside, and connected to, Mr. Tulkinghorn's chambers.

NOTES

¹ In *The Stones of Venice* Ruskin discusses the role of the arch as a form of connection (65).

² There are several extended interpretations of Tulkinghorn's character that I encourage students to consult (P. Morris, *"Bleak House"*; White; Welsh; J. H. Miller, "Interpretation").

³ See the following letters, for example: 28 September 1851 and 9 October 1851 (*Letters* 6: 498–99, 513–14).

⁴ See Saunders for a good discussion of allegory in these terms (216–25). See also Greenblatt (vii).

⁵ It is interesting to note that this sentence was corrected in the proofs from "whom no man can open" to "whom nobody can open" (*Bleak House* [ed. Ford and Monod] 829).

Plot and the Plot of *Bleak House*

Robert L. Patten

Students frequently say that *Bleak House* has either too much plot or too little. If plot includes the activity of minor characters scurrying around on their special business—like the brickmakers and Mrs. Snagsby—then their small dramas multiply almost to the point where no one except Dickens could possibly keep track of them. If, on the other hand, plot means the principal actions of the book, Esther Summerson's finding her place in the world and the Jarndyce case finding an heir, then the plots seem unresolved: Esther passes her father in the street but never knows him, meets her mother but cannot be publicly acknowledged by her, and accepts two different offers to be mistress of two different "Bleak House"s. The Jarndyce case implodes, leaving no assets at the very moment when an apparently definitive will turns up. Understandably students wonder if it is worth reading almost a thousand pages to reach these dead ends.

For Victorians, and for Dickens, it was worth it. Dickens plotted his monthly serials very precisely. Before he began to write, he determined the title, principal characters, chief events, and central themes of the story. These decisions are allusively illustrated in the design of the parts' paper wrappers, reproduced in some modern editions. During composition, Dickens jotted reminders about what he was putting in and leaving out of each installment. Those number plans still exist. Close study of them reveals that Dickens did construct each number as part of an imagined whole. The midpoint of any twenty-part novel is number 10; there are subsidiary midpoints in the two halves, at numbers 5 and 15, and, as classes can discover for themselves, identifying these structural "keystones" (Axton) can lead to other discoveries.

It might be helpful for students lost in the maze of Dickens's convoluted prose and plotting to apply simple Aristotelian notions about artistic structure. Despite the differences between sixth-century Attic drama and nineteenth-century British fiction, Dickens shared with Aristotle several crucial presumptions: that art might serve civic purposes by modeling human possibilities and their consequences; that artistic works have beginnings, middles, and ends; and that a well-wrought work economically structures its characters, rhetoric, and story to elicit a powerful response from its audience. Victorians, including Dickens, believed that fiction could disclose the fundamental principles and operations of the world and that when readers understood those principles rightly, they would be moved to correct injustice and improve society.

Dickens also shared with Aristotle a preference for plots wherein protagonists do not progress straight from beginning to end, but rather have their course interrupted by an unexpected recognition of some sort, followed by a reversal of fortune. In his *Poetics*, Aristotle maintained that the best kind of plot is one in which fundamentally good persons, through ignorance or overconfidence, commit (or are about to commit) terrible deeds (Halliwell, *Poetics*, ch. 13; commentary, pp. 122–31). Oedipus does everything he can to avoid murdering his father, but still does; Iphigeneia recognizes a prisoner as her brother just in time to avoid sacrificing him to the gods. Discovery of the true identity of persons is crucial either to the horror evoked by the deed done or to the pity and terror evoked by the deed intended. In either case, the audience sees the fateful consequences of deeds committed by honorable and well-meaning persons and may learn from these instances how difficult and essential it is to fully know oneself and the identities of others (Halliwell, *Poetics*, ch. 6; commentary, pp. 88–98).

If students apply this pattern of recognition and reversal to *Bleak House*, the repetitive pattern can help them sort out the multiplicity of plots, characters, and themes. Dickens structures his novel to illustrate the ways that characters have misconstrued and misconducted their relationships as a result of the distorting fictions of the law that have infiltrated and corrupted those relationships at every social and spiritual level. Aristotle construes character not as spiritual disposition, constitutional temperament, eccentricity, or psychological battleground but rather as ethos, a person's values as they are acted out (Halliwell, *Poetics*, ch. 15; commentary, pp. 139–43). In Dickens's novel so many characters' values have been warped by Chancery that their choices and deeds often harm those close by and injure the larger social world. While sometimes the damage done is deliberate, many times good people commit bad acts because they do not know who they are or in what relationship they stand to others.

In *Bleak House*, as in classic drama, identity is therefore understood as being connected to ethos and to society, to ethical standards, class and family structures, and a person's "station in life" (35). Most of the characters seem to be engaged in discovering their identity and station, defining the place of others (Mrs. Woodcourt and Mrs. Jellyby, for instance), or spying on another to learn about hidden relationships (Mrs. Snagsby, Tulkinghorn). Although the connection between "the world of fashion and the Court of Chancery" is only asserted at the beginning of chapter 2, by the end of the novel students may understand better how every one of the characters is shaped by and positioned in both worlds. At one end of the social spectrum, standing in the center of Tom-all-Alone's, a precinct controlled by Chancery, is the orphan Jo, a crossing sweeper. He is so ignorant he cannot fathom anything about his relation to earthly society ("Never know'd nothink" [732]) or heaven, although the physician Allan Woodcourt tries at least to teach Jo on his deathbed that he does have a celestial father. At the other end of the spectrum, apparently, stands Honoria Dedlock, "at the centre of the fashionable intelligence, and at the top of the fashionable tree" (22), though her intelligence has left her ignorant about the fate of her lover and her child and she will end up not at the top of the tree but at its foot, dying at the gate of a pauper's burying-ground.

Discovering identity does not suffice; characters need also to find their relationship to family and others and then to decide what their responsibility toward society might be. Identity, relationship, and responsibility are managed in this novel in every conceivable combination and sequence: Harold Skimpole creates his identity as a "child" by denying relationship and responsibility (101); Esther tries to create an identity as the one responsible for everyone, regardless of their relationship to her; Lady Dedlock and Captain Hawdon have created their positive and negative ("Nemo") identities out of concealing their relationship.

Thus *Bleak House* conceives personal identity in social terms: who one is is ratified—in some senses determined—by how one is understood by others. While individuals may feel connected to an inner and continuous life, they get read and labeled in terms of how they are classified by others. But if identity is so dependent on externals, then altering those externals can alter identity in ways that become almost determinative. Jo, in his supreme confusion crying out, "Is there *three* of 'em then?," gets it about right: an orphan, a "forrenner" (493), and an aristocrat may all seem to be alike when they appear in public garbed similarly. (Indeed, a lady may also be a brickmaker's wife, and one child, living or dead, may substitute for another.)

In this novel characters don't even have a clearly defined relationship to blood kin. So many are orphans, bachelors, absent or selfish parents, or lost children that the fundamental social organization of the family seems to have deteriorated into multigenerational cousinship. John Jarndyce, Ada, and Richard are all distant cousins, as are Volumnia and other Dedlock relatives. Characters may also be related through being wards of an improvident and careless legal system, cousins in Chancery, so to speak. Identity is further confused because the novel insistently doubles and triples characters with the same name: Jarndyce and Jarndyce, two Misses Donny, two Lord Chancellors; three husbands for Mrs. Badger (whose third is cousin to Kenge), three Necketts, three Vholes daughters (repellent thought!); and two indistinguishable threesomes involving Esther—herself, Hortense, and Lady Dedlock and herself, Jenny, and Liz. Having students chart and sort out these plural identities might provide a useful way into issues of identity and how it is constituted in particular cases in the novel.

Bleak House articulates mid-nineteenth-century beliefs that identity is composed of external relations as well as interiority. The novel is not naive about the connections between upbringing and psyche: many critics have demonstrated how Esther's childhood with her godmother conditioned her psychology and voice. Esther's crippled, compensating psyche leads her to vow, on her "birth" day (she is reborn often), to "do some good to some one, and win some love" to herself (31); she is at once self-effacing and competitive.

But the novel also inquires into the sociological and ethical components of character. Somehow, *Bleak House* must establish the reciprocal relations between Chancery and Esther, connections that go beyond any formal or informal testament that might write her among the Jarndyce heirs. Esther's familial and social identities need to be overtly confirmed for them to be consolidated and recognized. Some agents, such as Guppy, hope to prove that she is an heir and thus belongs to a higher place in the social hierarchy; others, most passionately Lady Dedlock herself, want Esther to know that she is loved despite the bleakness of her life; still others dismiss her as an insignificant element of the body politic, largely because their pride (in the case of Mrs. Woodcourt, for example) blinds them to any connection with ordinary people. Miss Flite asserts two essential connections. She calls Esther "Fitz-Jarndyce" (399), signifying Esther's illegitimate membership in the suit and the patronym (the "Fitz" was attached to the names of royal bastards). And she insists on an apocalyptic spiritual connection between the wards in Chancery and the last coming. In some ways she is right, for only when the graves give forth their dead can Esther's fullness of identity, relationship, and responsibility be manifested. The novel pushes ever forward along the track toward that end, of establishing Esther within the social station and families withheld from her at her first birth, and situating her within all human settings, from birthday to Bleak House to graveyard.

So a class that has become acquainted with the stakes of finding identity in *Bleak House* might very well approach the midpoint anticipating some kind of clarification or a change in situation that will raise expectations for an eventual happy ending. Every element in number 10, chapters 30–32, however, tends toward parodying Aristotle's "recognition and reversal" moments, producing not discoveries that either disclose and purge or foreclose terrible deeds but, rather, more baffling concealments. Repeatedly, Esther's identity is erased, not declared; her connections to any level of society, from Jo to the Dedlocks, appear to be canceled, written off or out.

Appropriately, the tenth number harkens back to the end of the fifth (ch. 16), where Jo shows Lady Dedlock her lover's polluted gravesite. That moment, for Lady Dedlock and the reader (if not for Jo), connects her past to her present, the dead to the living, and the depths of poverty and social invisibility to the heights of wealth and renown, reversing her public reputation and rank. Those connections have been insistently refused by society. According to some aristocratic toadies and industrialists like Ironmaster Rouncewell, the present destroys rather than builds on the past. Chancery, refusing to enact the provisions of testators or remediate the misfortunes of heirs, demonstrates that the dead may not exercise any beneficial power over the living. And no connection between Tom-all-Alone's and Chesney Wold can possibly be discerned by anyone except Inspector Bucket. So Lady Dedlock's discovery does not connect the world of fashion to Chancery, and identity, when discovered, discloses only the burial place of "no man."

Chapter 30 of number 10, "Esther's Narrative," relates two episodes detecting identity. Mrs. Woodcourt proses on about the royal forefathers of her son Allan, insinuating that Esther should look elsewhere for a suitor. Caddy, following Esther's advice, acts properly to bring her and her betrothed's families together and publicly instantiate her marriage. In chapter 30 we have identities revealed (Allan's ancestry), interrogated (foreclosing Esther's eligibility), and enacted, in Caddy's wedding. Chapter 31, "Nurse and Patient," destroys identity. Esther's illness apparently defaces any similarity to her mother that Guppy or anyone else might notice. Aristotle considers physical marks the least artistic way of establishing identity (Halliwell, *Poetics*, ch. 16; commentary, pp. 143–44). Dickens reverses and inverts Aristotelian recognition and reversal, by so marking Esther's face that she no longer resembles her mother. (*Bleak House* assumes that illegitimacy disfigures the daughter with the mother's stain, rather than the father's, as in law at the time it did.) While Charley (patient, then nurse) has round eyes, even though she can't inscribe circles, and while she is vigilant and quick to learn housekeeping, her mistress and teacher Esther (nurse, then patient) holds the keys to all the household closets. At the end of the chapter, she who sees most, Esther, the one who is most insightful and secretive and writes the horizons of her world, is blind and hidden behind a locked door, the greatest secret of all.

In the third chapter of this midpoint, "The Appointed Time" (ch. 32), readers reach the most apocalyptic of the many "appointed times" that have organized the temporal progression of the narrative. This time was appointed not by the Lord Chancellor but by his double, Krook, for midnight on his birth-, and as it turns out death-, day. Tony Jobling, concealing his identity under the appropriate alias Weevle, and Guppy wait in Nemo's old room for Krook to provide them with what Guppy believes will be Honoria Barbary's love letters to Captain Hawdon, papers that Krook took from Nemo's portmanteau just after Nemo died. When the clocks of London strike midnight, the coconspirators walk downstairs but cannot discern Krook's whereabouts in the apparently occupantless room.

At this point the narrative does something quite strange. A paragraph that begins in the third person—"They advance slowly"—suddenly engages the reader as a participant in the investigation: "What is it? Hold up the light?" (519). The succeeding paragraph inserts the reader into the time, place, and action of the scene, erasing all distances that have hitherto rhetorically and imaginatively maintained the identity of the readers as spectators, not actors:

> Here is a small burnt patch of flooring; here is the tinder from a little bundle of burnt paper . . . and here is—is it the cinder of a small charred and broken log of wood sprinkled with white ashes, or is it coal? O Horror, he IS here!   (519)

At this moment, the structure of the text at every level, from the disposal of incidents over the twenty monthly parts to the minutest lexical details, enacts an Aristotelian recognition ("he IS here") and reversal ("a little bundle of burnt paper") connected to the discovery of identity (Krook's, Hawdon's, Esther's), relationship, and responsibility. It also eradicates the distance between spectator and participant, temporarily turning readers into detectives like all those others who misread or read too late what the signs really mean—if they mean anything more than the water, fog, smoke, ashes, and mud into which all the material world and its social distinctions are devolving. At this moment characters, narrator, and readers read together the marks on the floor and on the page and learn that by whatever name terminal dissolution has hitherto been called, it is now identified by its timeless ("eternal") name, "Spontaneous Combustion"—"inborn, inbred, engendered in the corrupted humours of the vicious body itself" (519).

Halfway through the novel, at a climactic moment of recognition and reversal, one certainty is named, and all other certainties appear canceled. No more external marks, on skin or parchment or paper, of Esther's identity and relationship; no more manifest connections (apparently) between her and Chancery or Chesney Wold; no more discoveries for Charley or Guppy, who, when he next meets Esther, is quite repelled by her altered face. This spontaneous combustion is but the most fundamental erasure of identity; it has been anticipated by the death of Nemo in that same mock Chancery—but in the earlier death enough traces of identity remain, in handwritten documents and human memories, for some to reconstruct his name, station, and legacy. Far from dramatizing a recognition and reversal that will bring Esther from the shade of her past into the light of society, the central moments in *Bleak House*, number 10, eradicate those signs of her connection to the world. Esther does later meet her mother and exchange mutual recognition. But instead of producing a reversal and a manifesting of relationship and responsibility, that recognition only suppresses the identity of mother and daughter further. Lady Dedlock, "bored to death" (27) and locked within her errant earlier self, continues down her "dark road alone" (579).

Thus at the heart of *Bleak House* are Aristotelian moments of recognition and reversal apparently operating in the opposite direction from Greek tragedy. The marks of identity are canceled, not discovered. There is nothing to see, and most are blind in any case. What, one could ask a class, might *Bleak House* offer as possible outcomes for characters living in a world in which

> social identity has been obscured;
>
> "the universe . . . makes rather an indifferent parent," as John Jarndyce observes (93);
>
> the will of the father (Jarndyce, and possibly the Father as well) cannot be interpreted and his legacy is used up;
>
> those with the power of secular healing cannot eradicate the contagious disease at the very heart of the world; and
>
> those like Miss Flite who act in the belief that destiny will be fulfilled as prophesied are deemed mad and—even more alarming, since prophets in the biblical past were connected to cosmic power—are thought harmless?

It may not be easy for students to imagine, after the midpoint of *Bleak House*, how the world could be righted. If the action of this novel involves discovering identity, relationship, and responsibility and if at its midpoint readers and characters encounter the spontaneous combustion of the fundamental markers of civil society, what kind of ending, of second half, of second chance, can Dickens provide? The remaining numbers contain multiple, startling new recognitions and reversals, in numbers 15 (chs. 47–49, ending when George is identified as a murderer) and 18 (chs. 57–59, ending when Esther first misrecognizes and then in horror sees, in the body lying outside the pauper's graveyard, her "mother, cold and dead" [915]).

By the end, *Bleak House* seems to assert that genealogy matters much less than what one does with one's own gifts and life. It posits that fundamental connections extend beyond the nexus of family, so violently configured here as in Greek mythology. The ground of being, the graveyard shows, is the unfathomable bond between the living and the dead; connections derive not only from recognizing the physical inscriptions of kinship within society but also from acknowledging, without perhaps understanding, that all are part of the family. Human beings are related by universal need. All are debtors, and beyond Joshua Smallweed ("a leech in his dispositions . . . and a lobster in his claws" [538]) and Tulkinghorn, who makes "good thrift" out of "family confidences" (23), the narrator insists there is a greater creditor who requires that all persons discover their identity within the universal community, not just within the circles of fashion or Chancery. And the novel, through its multiplication of characters and incidents that portray detection and discovery of identity in every guise, on every level, with every possible degree of misinterpretation, enacts with the reader the same impulses the characters display to find out who is what and the same costs the characters pay for denying their shared relationships and common responsibility. In such ways *Bleak House*, like Greek drama, structures its plot to educate and reform the reader.

The Reader as Detective:
Investigating *Bleak House* in Class

Robert Tracy

Whether Harvard freshmen in 1954, senior citizens in 2004, or generations of Berkeley students in between, they always begin discussing *Bleak House* by commenting about length and prolixity. The students are right, of course. An instructor's job is to help them realize that *Bleak House* is worth their time and attention. We must help them see that reading *Bleak House* can be an exhilarating experience and that *Bleak House* is about reading: reading character, reading situations, reading texts, and reading Phiz's illustrations. Every word—400,000 of them—every character and episode, is integral to the total effect and an essential part of Dickens's response to this novel's central question: what do these disparate people, classes, and localities have to do with one another?

One way to confront the issues of length and prolixity is to involve the class in rewriting the opening paragraphs, removing whatever is not essential to bringing us into Chancery on that foggy November day. So out go the megalosaurus and the ill-tempered foot passengers, the banking metaphors about deposits and interest, the Greenwich pensioners and the shivering apprentice boy. What's left is brief, flat, and uninteresting. Most students come to see that something precious has been lost, that Dickens's dynamic and extravagant use of language, his piling up of incidents and metaphors, is a way of infusing even brief passages with the lively variety on which the entire novel depends.

Eventually, after the students are well into the novel, I always return to those opening paragraphs and suggest thinking of them as an overture to Dickens's symphony, touching on various themes to come. Is the clumsy megalosaurus a metaphor for the outmoded machinery of Chancery? Is the emphasis on mud an anticipation of Jo, who lives by clearing mud away at street crossings? What other kinds of fog pervade Dickens's England? How do you write—or read—an encyclopedic novel?

Students are also apt to see certain minor characters as expendable. There is Mr. Grubble, for example, in chapter 37. He exists for half a page, together with a description of his inn parlor, perhaps only so Dickens can show how readily he could invent him for a walk-on part and make his heterogeneous parlor another metaphor for the novel's variety. Could he be removed? Probably. How would the novel be altered if he were? I find that asking students to suggest characters who may be unnecessary makes them aware that Dickens enjoyed the richness and randomness of life, including its irrelevancies. They sometimes hotly defend a minor character's presence.

I usually stipulate that students are to read *Bleak House* in parts and not read ahead. This offers them some approximation of how Dickens's first readers experienced his novels. Meeting three times a week for fifteen weeks, students can read *Bleak House* serially if I assign two serial numbers for only five of those weeks; we discuss the current number(s) of *Bleak House* on Mondays. In a small (about 20 students) class I can assign teams of two or three students to work together and report on the story as it develops, noting the introduction of new themes and issues and the probable role of striking incidents and new characters. Does Jo's appearance at Nemo's inquest (ch. 11) suggest that he will be an important character? Or is he only there because Dickens likes to portray waifs as part of his social agenda? Why is Little Swills there? As students work their way further into the novel, they become aware of some of Dickens's methods and begin to recognize the signals he uses to underline important episodes.

Read in serial form, *Bleak House* works well as the core of a course in nineteenth-century British fiction, offering a marvelous opportunity to introduce students to some of the major types of Victorian novels. On Wednesday and Friday, I supplement *Bleak House* with, say, Charlotte Brontë's *Jane Eyre*, Mary Elizabeth Braddon's *Lady Audley's Secret*, Elizabeth Gaskell's *North and South* or *Mary Barton*, and Wilkie Collins's *The Moonstone* or *The Woman in White*. Students can see for themselves how Dickens incorporated different types of novel into a single narrative. Reading serially is possible even in a large lecture course, combining it with more rapid coverage of other assigned works. I can still reserve Mondays for *Bleak House* and discuss other assigned novels in the remaining two class meetings.

Combining *Bleak House* with *Jane Eyre* invites discussions about self-made heroines and first-person narration and about the gothic tradition. To add *The Woman in White* or *The Moonstone* is to compare plots treated as criminal investigations. *Lady Audley's Secret* is a more melodramatic version of Lady Dedlock's secret, a contrast to Dickens's treatment of a woman with a past. William Makepeace Thackeray's *Vanity Fair* glances obliquely at the determination that Lady Dedlock must have needed to achieve her high position.

Senior citizens are an increasing presence in our classrooms, as more and more universities institute programs of continuing education. The questions about motivation and behavior that they raise are often unexpected and invariably acute. Like the general readers encountered at the University of California's Dickens Universe (an annual week-long summer school focusing on a single Dickens novel), they are often already familiar with the novel under discussion and want a fuller exploration of background—Chancery, topography, London graveyards, Victorian politics. At San Francisco's pioneering Fromm Institute for Lifelong Learning I usually supply this material in lectures and leave plenty of time for questions.

The reader is the real protagonist of *Bleak House*. As we read, we experience many events through Esther Summerson, at once a mask for Dickens and the first reader of the actions and mysteries she records. Esther's dual role as reader and narrator must have been evident when each monthly part was read aloud to eager Victorian listeners. Sometimes I have tried just that, using an entire class session to read as much as possible of a *Bleak House* number aloud. While no Emlyn Williams, I can report that students listen attentively and seem to be enjoying themselves. Once I have done it, I can ask students to do the same. I assign each student to a section of about ten minutes. I ask them to read through their sections beforehand at least once and check on the pronunciation of unfamiliar words. This exercise helps them appreciate the different voices that we hear in *Bleak House*.

Esther is supplemented by that other narrative voice, male, worldly wise, sardonic, at times angry at what he must describe. But it is Esther who, as it were, gives him his opportunities to speak, who steps aside for him. It is important to emphasize her skill as narrator, her ability, as Dickens's representative within the text, to control the novel's many plots and characters. Students often dislike Esther's insistent cheerfulness and industry, but as early as chapter 4 we can begin to discuss how shrewdly she selects details that condemn Mrs. Jellyby as a representative—like Chancery, like Parliament—of the self-satisfied indifference toward England's problems that is Dickens's subject. Then Esther becomes housekeeper at Bleak House, where she organizes the household to run smoothly; as chief narrator she organizes *Bleak House*; she would organize England if she were let.

For many students Esther's role as housekeeper seems demeaning, subordinate. Things get more interesting when the relevant feminist issues invariably arise, especially the complaint that Jarndyce educated her primarily to be his servant, then decided to make her his wife, and eventually handed her over, like a parcel, to be the housekeeper of Bleak House Lite. Why did she passively allow Jarndyce to dispose of her?

There is never enough time to explore adequately the restrictions imposed on Victorian women and many of their descendants, but students can at least be persuaded that Esther is no doormat. She shows a great deal of courage in her handling of her mother and her mother's confession and in her nocturnal ride in pursuit of Lady Dedlock. She is more than a match for Guppy's romantic approaches and Mrs. Woodcourt's efforts to discourage her interest in Allan. And, whether we respect it or not, she has a sense of duty that governs most of her actions.

By encouraging students to voice their objections to Esther often and early, I have gradually been able to persuade at least some of them that she is a superb narrator. Emphasizing her narrator role opens up opportunities to discuss the role of narrators in fiction generally and some of the technical problems involved in determining what they knew and when they knew it. This discussion offers a chance to examine a novelist's control over his or her characters and the way Esther takes, or seems to take, some of that control into her own hands. She accepts Jarndyce's proposal of marriage, but with so little enthusiasm that he abandons the idea; she tries to direct Richard Carstone away from the fate Dickens plans for him; she suppresses Lady Dedlock's confessional letter, which would have made a lively chapter indeed. She works deliberately against the grain of the sensational novel that is the matrix of *Bleak House*, continually reminding us of the values she represents: decency, domestic normality, and tranquility. These values can be criticized, but we should understand how effectively Esther represents them. By encouraging students to talk about her role as narrator, the instructor can help them see her as Dickens's surrogate in controlling his complex plot, even when she steps aside and lets the novel's other narrative voice take over.

Like Esther, the student-reader must assess the meaning of each plot development, the authenticity of behavior. Dickens challenges our skills as readers by altering narrators, letting his characters change, shifting fictional genres. *Bleak House* is by turns a love story, a gothic romance, a sensation novel, a novel about high society, a "condition of England" novel, and a detective story. There are even three opening chapters, as if Dickens was unsure what novel he would write. Is the reader facing a polemic novel about the Court of Chancery? a "silver fork" novel about the doings of the fashionable world? or a novel about a young woman and her life as a kind of governess?

I always assign a *Bleak House* text that contains Phiz's illustrations, reproduced clearly enough to avoid eyestrain. Once students have been encouraged to "read" the illustrations, they are intrigued by the possibilities. Inviting them to share what they can see in "Attorney and Client"(627) can produce a competitive excitement as they find spider webs, a maze, a cat at a mouse hole, a butterfly net, and a hunting rifle and relate them to Richard Carstone's entrapment in *Jarndyce and Jarndyce*. When they connect pairs of illustrations with the numbers in which they appeared together, they can see how Phiz's "dark" plates worked to signal ominous developments in the story. "The Little Church in the Park" (291) gives us the social panorama that Dickens portrays and emphasizes the barriers between classes: Sir Leicester and Lady Dedlock enclosed in one box pew, the Boythorn party in another. The Dedlock servants are curtained off from their master despite the Christianity they share. Above the Dedlocks a biblical text reminds us that it is easier for a camel to pass through the eye of a needle than for a rich man to enter heaven. Respectable pew holders are fenced off from their inferiors. Students delight in discovering and pointing out these visual ironies. From the illustrations we go to the cover used for every monthly part, where they can speculate at its hints about the progress and meaning of the story.

My general approach to *Bleak House* is to treat it as a mystery story. I encourage undergraduates, probably reading Dickens for the first time, to uncover the mysteries that the plot conceals, to become investigators themselves. Like several characters in the story, they are to follow clues about Lady Dedlock's past and Esther's origins. But with this transparent mystery solved, Dickens adds a murder mystery and a disappearance: Who killed Mr. Tulkinghorn? Where is Lady Dedlock? Inspector Bucket's investigation, along with his pursuit of Lady Dedlock, demonstrates for students the techniques the successful reader of *Bleak House* must employ: attention to detail, empathy, suspicion, imagination, a readiness to consider the implausible and challenge the probable. Pursuing Lady Dedlock, Bucket even misreads at one point, then realizes where he has gone wrong.

As would become traditional in mystery stories, we participate by recognizing clues as the author supplies them and by anticipating solutions to the mysteries. To do this the reader must pay close attention to hints and intimations and connect one with another as they appear. The nature of serial publication, with a month between parts, was ideal for encouraging Dickens's readers to speculate about the "connexion . . . between many people . . . who, from opposite sides of great gulfs, have nevertheless, been very curiously brought together"(256)—the central theme of the book, as well as an instruction for reading it. Once students start wondering how the three apparently autonomous opening chapters are connected and why Lady Dedlock is agitated at a page of handwriting, they begin to investigate. Eventually they learn to connect overcrowded graveyards with disease, slums with illiteracy, the tedious cruelties of Chancery with injustice and so to question the way things are.

Most readers of *Bleak House* soon guess Lady Dedlock's secret, but the real mystery is what might happen when her secret is revealed. Dickens is interested in how people behave in the presence of a mystery, not in tantalizing us by withholding the solution to the mystery. What he does with his mysteries is to multiply the detectives who try to solve them. By watching these competing detectives, students learn how to read his novel. Bucket is a professional solver of mysteries. But Mr. Tulkinghorn, Lady Dedlock herself, "the young man of the name of Guppy" (460), and Mrs. Snagsby all become investigators. They all grope to solve the plot's mysteries, now advancing, now thwarted, now advancing again, slipping and sliding along dark ways, a process metaphorically expressed by the pedestrians groping through mud and fog on the novel's opening page. We must grope with them through Dickens's evasions, distractions, and complications.

Tulkinghorn and Guppy work with wills and contracts, written texts that determine actions. They are trained to be close readers, to test meanings and authenticity. The central mystery of *Bleak House* begins in chapter 2 when Lady Dedlock asks Tulkinghorn, who is reading a legal document to her, "Who copied that? . . . Is it what you people call law-hand?" (26). When the lawyer opines that the writer did not always write law-hand, she faints, and Tulkinghorn determines to find out why. Guppy meets Esther for the first time in chapter 3; by chapter 7 he sees her resemblance to Lady Dedlock's portrait. Tulkinghorn begins to investigate Lady Dedlock's past, Guppy to investigate Esther's. Students can participate in both investigations.

By chapter 40, Tulkinghorn knows that the legal copyist was once Lady Dedlock's lover and Esther is her illegitimate child. He acts in the novel as a surrogate for the reader, reading events as we read the novel's pages and directing the reader's curiosity and eagerness to connect the various strands of the plot. Class discussion usually develops around Tulkinghorn's obsession with Lady Dedlock and the power over her that possessing her secret gives him. In this mystery novel his motivations remain, if not mysterious, at least uncertain and so intriguing. Discussing the mystery of Lady Dedlock's past gives way to discussing the mystery of Tulkinghorn's intentions. Is he only interested in possessing, as he thinks, the power to destroy her? in cherishing that power and the knowledge that he could use it? Does he see himself as an objective agent of justice, or does he hate Lady Dedlock? Is he revenging himself on all those lords and ladies who have patronized him for so many years?

Guppy is a quicker and luckier surrogate for the reader than Tulkinghorn. He is in possession of most of Lady Dedlock's secret by chapter 29 and clearly explains to her that Esther is her child. "O my child, my child," she wails, in a wild transport of grief; "Not dead in the first hours of her life, as my cruel sister told me; but sternly nurtured by her, after she had renounced me and my name! O my child, O my child!" (469). In chapter 36 Lady Dedlock reveals herself to Esther as her mother and gives her a letter, a kind of confessional autobiography. Esther reads and then destroys this letter; we never get to read it. Esther will keep her parentage a secret.

By thinking of themselves as investigators, students come to see Tulkinghorn's and Guppy's investigations as Dickens's device for gradually revealing his plot. Readers of the novel's secrets, Tulkinghorn and Guppy both assist the reader by discovering essential information. Like Dickens himself, Tulkinghorn's power lies in his ability to tell a story. He even tells Lady Dedlock's story, with names omitted, in chapter 40, where one critical listener finds it implausible. Tulkinghorn and Guppy read the story of Esther's origin with the eagerness that often motivates the reader of fiction: to know what happened, to penetrate secrets, to pursue a story.

Tulkinghorn and Guppy, as Dickens's agents and the reader's surrogates, read the story with us. Mrs. Snagsby, the third investigator, misreads it. She has clearly read novels—*Oliver Twist*, perhaps—in which a beggar child turns out to be the heir to a fortune. She misreads incidents, creating, as naive readers sometimes do, extravagant and implausible hypotheses. She responds to the investigators around her by becoming, like them, a spy, and she parodies the mystery about Esther's parentage by persuading herself that Jo is Mr. Snagsby's illegitimate son. Her jealousy and her melodramatic imagination coincide with Tulkinghorn's methodical investigation to bring together evidence that establishes Lady Dedlock's long-ago transgression. "That little pickled cowcumber of a Mrs Snagsby," Bucket explains, ". . . has done a deal more harm in bringing odds and ends together than if she had meant it" (829).

By focusing on these readers and misreaders in the novel, we can enlarge our classroom discussions of *Bleak House* to discuss how to read a literary text. Without losing sight of the plot or the language or parallels with other Victorian novels, we can explore the ways in which a student reader might be misled or relax into the belief that he or she has read *Bleak House* by simply mastering the plot. Those who complain about the novel's length might well complain if, after almost a thousand pages, they come away with little more than the secret of Esther's parentage and the idea that Chancery suits were a bad thing. *Bleak House* offers the student much more: a chance to understand what a novel can be, how Victorian novels function, a rehearsal for any serious reading that is to come.

Dickens's narrative method internalizes the process of reading the novel by comparing it with investigating a mystery. He represents the reader in the text by characters who try to read the story of Lady Dedlock and Esther, gradually gathering the facts that will enable them—and so the reader—to penetrate that story's mysteries. As for Mrs. Snagsby, she reads intuitively and so admits into the investigation a series of fortuitous coincidences, Dickens's favorite device for surprising the reader into recognizing the interdependency of high and low, rich and poor, the mutuality of social responsibility. Reading in search of solutions to the novel's interrelated mysteries educates the student-reader to understand the novel's larger issues, those failures of reason and compassion that tolerate things as they are.[1]

NOTE

[1] I have borrowed a few sentences from my own earlier "Lighthousekeeping: *Bleak House* and the Crystal Palace" and "Reading and Misreading *Bleak House*."

Bleak House and Illustration: Learning to Look

Richard L. Stein

In the age of the Internet, it is both more and less difficult to approach the illustrations in any Dickens novel, more and less difficult to approach the novels
themselves. Less difficult because now (as our students say) so much can be
found on the Web, including complete texts of many of the novels and high-
resolution images of many original illustrations. More difficult precisely because
of that ease of access and the tendency of electronic reproduction to blend
books and images into a virtual, digital sameness. As texts become more accessible, volumes seem more distant. And the very idea of the illustrated nineteenth-
century book—lengthy, weighty, with a feel and odor of its own, letterpress
set off by separate pages of illustration (on different paper stock) sewn in—
becomes, literally, harder to grasp.

The challenge of reading a Dickens novel in relation to its illustrations begins
here, with the challenge of recovering—or discovering—the book as material
artifact. Perhaps it is more accurate to refer to it as a series of material artifacts,
since most Dickens novels begin with serial publication in monthly parts, or
numbers. To consider Dickens novels this way gives illustration a prominence
that tends to be lost in book format. This was the consensus of a seminar cen-
tered on *Bleak House* I recently taught. We spent one meeting in the University
of Oregon's Special Collections reading room, each of us holding one original part and discussing what could be learned from it. The conclusion was, a
great deal—beginning with the wrapper (fig. 3, p. 9), the blue-green folded
and printed sheet in which each number was bound, its front page illustrated
with drawings by Hablot K. Browne (Phiz) that (in keeping with his practice
as designer of most of Dickens's wrappers) anticipate some of the novel's main
themes and incidents.

Few courses have the luxury of using original parts. But it's worth trying (and
asking students to try) to imagine the look of one, if only to emphasize the extent
to which the first publication of *Bleak House* (the same could be said for most
Dickens novels) draws attention to the relation of text and illustration, or (as Victorians might have put it) pen and pencil. Each part displays this in at least three
ways. First is that wrapper, the title surrounded by a dense circuit of images on
the front, the back reserved for advertisements.[1] Next and harder to recover for
classroom use comes the *Bleak House Advertiser*, a multipage commercial supplement inside the wrapper, sandwiching the narrative (see, e.g., fig. 4, p. 10).[2] A
recent *Bleak House* exhibit at the University of Glasgow Library explained that
these advertisements (some illustrated) cumulatively amount to over three hundred pages, "constituting over half of the physical form" of the monthly parts.[3]
Some ads directly refer to the novel, like one for winter clothing headlined "Anti-
Bleak House": "Woe to the inhabitant of Bleak House if he is not armed with the
weapons of an Overcoat and a Suit of Fashionable and substantial clothing, such

as can only be obtained at E. Moses & Son's Establishments. . . ."[4] Finally, after the first section of the *Advertiser*, printed on heavy paper, we find the illustrations (normally two, four in the final double number) bound in before Dickens's text.[5] Originally, then, the novel appeared within a diverse array of cultural material that shaped readers' sense of the narrative and their own interpretive roles.[6]

Our students come to *Bleak House* through a similar field of cultural markers, including the canonical status of the novel and assorted dramatic adaptations. I find it useful to discuss these markers as a prologue to illustration: What "outside" interpretations of Dickens shape our responses? Can we relate them to this novel's emphasis on interpretive activity? J. Hillis Miller begins a famous essay declaring that "*Bleak House* is a document about the interpretation of documents" ("Interpretation" 179). In fact, it concerns interpretation of many kinds, as the work of Inspector Bucket (to mention only one of the novel's interpretive figures) attests. And the material frame of each number reminds us of the novel's reference to a world where there is much more to interpret than documents alone. Each part requires reading of several different sorts, situating the novel among the proliferating forms of texts, images, and objects. The ads place it (literally) in the world of commerce.[7] The illustrations locate it alongside Victorian visual culture. Robert L. Patten explains that booksellers sometimes displayed illustrations of current numbers in their windows "as an inducement to buy the installment" ("Illustrators" 290). Lynda Nead shows how such images "create the visual environment of the streets," constituting an audience "around the shop windows where they are displayed" (155). These remarks suggest that Dickens novels enter culture before and apart from their textual reading, reading that is in turn inflected by a larger cultural environment. Patten adds that "readers sometimes studied the pictures closely as clues to the contents of the installment" (290). Indeed, they approached the novel through various "outside" clues and contexts. So do twenty-first-century readers who associate Dickens with Olde English Tea Shoppes, holiday apparel, or kitsch memorabilia. Once students recognize Dickens's ubiquity as an object of cultural reference, the project of illustration will seem less strange.

How do we open that project to discussion or link it to discussion of *Bleak House*? We do it first by treating Browne's illustrations as complex objects requiring critical exploration. Some, of course, seem simpler, more straightforward. Yet it is clear from the start that Browne aims for more than pictorial "realization"—to use Martin Meisel's term—more than a visual summary of scenes or characters or textual detail (29–30). The very choice of incidents (in which Dickens assisted) draws attention to particular narrative elements—not just certain scenes but certain kinds of scenes, certain kinds of passages. This is where discussion might begin: Which subjects are chosen or excluded? What dimensions of the narrative does Browne depict? Many of my students notice that he draws material almost equally from "Esther's Narrative" and the third-person chapters. Indeed, he often pictures situations expressing those viewpoints— registering how incidents are perceived, narrated, or understood. The illustrations for the first number, for instance, "The little old Lady" (Miss Flite) (fig. 5, p. 11) and "Miss Jellyby," include the figure of Esther; in both, she is seen from behind—her face hidden, once by her bonnet and once by her hair. How can we read this? Students sometimes suggest that she is represented as an observer, her features invisible to us just as they are excluded from her own gaze. This inaccessibility may associate her with the mystery that is central to her character and the novel's development; it may even allude to the fog described in the opening paragraphs, more explicitly indicated by a heavily wrapped coachman (with steaming breath) and shadowy hatchings in the background of the first illustration. But Browne isn't just accumulating textual information. What makes these images interesting is something more elusive—tone, nuance, interpretation.

No wonder Browne takes such interest in the novel's interpretive moments, its scenes of seeing, especially those involving Esther. She appears, as we'd expect, in illustrations of "her" narrative, and they often suggest some aspect of her narrative consciousness. Her face is averted in seven of the seventeen where Browne depicts her, including the first three, perhaps to portray that invisible third-person observer, perhaps to suggest her unpicturable process of thought. If these images help us see the novel's world, they also record Esther's "progress" (to cite the title of chapter 3) in assessing it. The first that show her face fully—starting midway through the second number, in "Coavinses"—illustrate scenes exhibiting her growing insight. Chapter 6, "Quite at Home," where "Coavinses" appears, ends with Esther reflecting on what she has learned: "Any seeming inconsistency in Mr Skimpole, or in Mrs Jellyby, I could not expect to be able to reconcile; having so little experience or practical knowledge" (102). As students frequently note, the disavowal of knowledge reveals how much she already understands. The next illustration, "The visit at the Brickmaker's," depicts an incident that confirms her moral development. Browne even manages to represent her deepening consciousness in an image where she doesn't appear at all (although it comes from "her" narrative), "The Ghost's Walk," which doesn't picture a place as much as her sense of place:

> Stopping to look at nothing, but seeing all I did see as I went, I was passing quickly on, and in a few moments should have passed the lighted window, when my echoing footsteps brought it suddenly into my mind that there was a dreadful truth in the legend of the Ghost's Walk; that it was I, who was to bring calamity upon the stately house; and that my warning feet were haunting it even then. Seized with an augmented terror of myself which turned me cold, I ran from myself and everything, retraced the way by which I had come, and never paused until I had gained the lodge-gate, and the park lay sullen and black behind me.   (586)

Browne's interest in the novel's self-consciousness is anticipated in the wrapper design. It makes a useful case study of the functions of illustration and our own interpretive choices, not just because of how much imagery can be explicated but partly because of how much cannot. We see, for instance, a version of Esther's obscured features: a woman whose hair hides her face and whose back is turned to a man whose back is turned to her, the two separated by a puzzled Cupid. Part of the novel's mystery, the image suggests, involves romantic love, but initially we can't know what this will mean, to whom it will refer. Michael Steig identifies the couple as Lady Dedlock and Captain Hawdon, who only could have been included here if Dickens explained his plans to Browne in detail (132). Steig refers to the hidden face as "a motif—one might almost say an emblem—which continues through the novel and links Esther visually with her mother" (136). But (as Steig grants) such identifications must be made in retrospect, at later stages of reading. As we attempt to decipher the imagery earlier, this group alludes more vaguely to unknown events. It marks our uncertainty as we begin to read.

The complete wrapper design supports similar readings. Its iconography is both specific and open, precise and suggestive, enough to stimulate discussion that often leads back to narrative issues. Some scenes (like the woman releasing birds midway down the left-hand side of the framing series of images) are comprehensible early in our reading, since we encounter Miss Flite's aviary in the second number. Some (like the left-side figure Steig associates with Esther, looking at a young man carrying a globe on his head with a fox at her side) may remain permanently opaque. The resistance of some images to explication teaches us something about illustration and text. Do obscure illustrations allude to narrative uncertainties? Consider those to the penultimate number: "The Night" and "The Morning." First-time readers (like Esther, in the blur of pursuing her mother out of and back into London) may identify one or both of the dark figures of women as Jenny, the brickmaker's wife, whose clothing Lady Dedlock assumes to escape detection. In this sense these dark drawings are "about" the process of visual interpretation (of appearances rather than documents); both contribute to narrative (that is, our) suspense.

Illustration can be more precise. I invite students to see how much information they can find. Some of Browne's drawings supply what Jane R. Cohen calls "unsolicited details" to elaborate on textual themes. In the illustration "Attorney and Client, fortitude and impatience," the Hogarthian title signals a profusion of symbolic features:

> the legend of the fox and grapes carved in [Vholes's] mantle, the portrait of a nearsighted judge above, the wolves' heads below, the ironically labeled cartons stacked to the right, the butterfly net leaning against the wall, the spider web with trapped flies on the ceiling corner, the cat watching for the mouse behind the desk, the overturned wastebasket disclosing an advertisement for "fool's cap," the book opened to the plan of a maze, and the mass of tangled legal string next to it.   (Cohen 108)

But the distinguishing feature of the complete suite of illustrations is the group of "dark plates" (primarily in the novel's last half), where Browne seems less interested in depicting emblematic detail than in representing the narrative's atmosphere and moral tone, finding visual equivalents for the gravity of Dickens's concerns. Interestingly (as John Harvey observes), six of the ten dark plates contain no human figures, reflecting the "insignificance" of people in "a society whose institutions dwarf, isolate, and too often destroy [its] members" (Harvey 152; the quotation is from Cohen 109).

We can arrive at readings of this kind only when we consider the illustrations as a group, published serially in pairs. I encourage students to compile illustration logs, recording the chapter locations and monthly pairings of all Browne's images as a way to reconstruct a cumulative visual narrative and see if any patterns emerge. Few are surprised to learn that Esther appears more often than any other character or that Lady Dedlock is depicted next most often (nine illustrations—plus two where she appears symbolically, in her portrait and her tomb), although her identity in some dark plates is recognizable only after reading the associated text. More unexpectedly, Guppy is third in pictorial frequency, in keeping with his centrality to the novel's plot of visual recognition. In four of the five illustrations that include him, he is shown with Esther or Lady Dedlock, mostly with their features, so often obscured, fully visible. His first four appearances (numbers 3, 4, 8, and 9) progressively depict his discovery of their relation, culminating in the illustration "The Young Man of the name of Guppy," where he is ushered into the presence of the Dedlocks with his dangerous secret (fig. 6, p. 12). If his access to this exclusive space demonstrates the power he is about to assert, his open-mouthed expression suggests astonishment at the strategy's success. It also (as some students argue) registers visual confirmation of the connection he has established by "interpretation of documents," the crucial relation he now sees directly. To emphasize its ominousness, Browne paired this scene with "Visitors at the Shooting Gallery" (or tried to—that second image was postponed to the next number [see note 5]) and echoed it later (number 11, in "The old man of the name of Tulkinghorn") where Lady Dedlock is visited by the lawyer.

Illustration logs help students explore the dynamic relation of paired illustrations, a visual dialogue that deepens as new images enter the list. My students note when monthly pairings underscore the novel's social range, as in the fifth number, illustrated by a drawing of the Turveydrops at "The Dancing School" and another of Jo in "Consecrated ground" pointing out the place of Nemo's burial—a motif that first appears in "The Lord Chancellor copies from memory" and culminates in the pointing finger of the allegorical Roman (an image paired significantly with "Friendly behaviour of Mr Bucket"). I ask students to explore the relation between "Lady Dedlock in the Wood" and its accompanying image, "The Ghost's Walk," the familial site that announces her fall. We also consider the very different contrast between the first image of Lady Dedlock's flight from home, "The lonely figure," and the illustration that accompanies it (in number 17), the reunion in "Mrs Bagnet returns from her expedition." And students find much to say about the pairs of images contrasting Guppy's comic behavior with graver incidents. The fourth part was intended to combine "The visit to the Brickmaker's" with "In Re Guppy. Extraordinary proceedings"; the final part links "Magnanimous conduct of Mr Guppy" with "The Mausoleum at Chesney Wold." That final pair, some students argue, frames the last chapters more moralistically than Dickens does, depicting a dimension of experience this self-centered character cannot imagine: Browne shows that for all Guppy's ability to "see" the truth about Esther and Lady Dedlock, his moral vision is limited.

"Magnanimous conduct" and "The Mausoleum" represent only half the illustrations in the final double number. The others—a drawing of Jo the crossing sweeper for the title page of the first edition in book form (fig. 7, p. 13, and on the cover of the paperback edition of this Approaches volume), and one of Bleak House itself, labeled as the volume's frontispiece—seem more perfunctory. Yet here, too, Browne interprets Dickens, creating a pair of final images that will assume a more important role as introductory plates for the book. As concluding illustrations they sum up the novel's social vision and the mood of Browne's dark plates; introducing the novel in book form, they alert us to these qualities in advance, providing a visual framework within which reading can take place. The wrapper design is open-ended, picturing events that cannot be understood until later, emphasizing the balance of comic and serious incidents. The initial illustrations for the book focus attention on Dickens's public concerns; the dark drawing of Bleak House now characterizes the novel that bears its name.[8] And the shift illuminates other differences: the wrapper illustrates multiple facets of serial narration; the book's initial images picture its unity, its cumulative achievement. For classes, the two positions of this final pair create another opportunity for discussion—not about which location is better but about how each shapes interpretation, textual as well as visual. For that matter, it is worth calling attention to the letterpress associated with each: even the word "frontispiece" appears in a different font from the other captions, as if (but this, too, is debatable) illustration here as on the title page is assuming a more official status. In a sense, in their new position—perhaps echoing the fact that the final *Bleak House Advertiser* begins with ads for Dickens's own work—these introductory illustrations provide one last (only now it is first) advertisement, not just to accompany but to sell the novel itself, repackaging it for its next audience, materializing it in new, compact, and perhaps more accessible form.[9] But that question, too, may best be left for our students to decide.

NOTES

[1] For an electronic image of the wrapper design, see the University of California, Santa Cruz, Dickens Project Web site: http://humwww.ucsc.edu/dickens/bibliographies/bleakhousebiblio/Wrapper.Design.jpg. The relation of text and image is also developed in the novel's many references to the visual arts.

² The *Advertiser* thus appears at both the beginning and the end of each monthly part. I include one illustrated ad for *Lloyd's Weekly Newspaper* in my essay "Dickens and Illustration" (Stein 185).

³ Some materials appear on the library's Web site: http://special.lib.gla.ac.uk/exhibns/month/nov2004.html.

⁴ Compare the ad in number 4, headlined "A Suit in Chancery and a Suit out of Chancery."

⁵ More precisely, publication was planned so that every number before the final one would contain two illustrations. Number 9 includes only "The Young Man of the name of Guppy" and the following note: "An accident having happened to the Plate, it has been necessary to cancel one of the Illustrations to the present Number. It will be supplied in the next Monthly Part." Part 10 thus has three illustrations: "Nurse and Patient," "The appointed time," and "Visitors at the Shooting Gallery" (the last actually illustrating text from the previous installment; the Penguin edition puts it in the place originally planned).

⁶ Jennifer Wicke argues that "modern 'reading' can only arise in the dialectical space opened up between novel and advertisement" (2; see also Curtis's brilliant account "The Art of Seeing: Dickens in the Visual Market" in his *Visual Words* 103–42).

⁷ I discuss one example in "Dickens and Illustration" (185–86).

⁸ It is worth noting that in its introductory position, the dark plate of Bleak House seems very much at odds with Esther's first response to the place in "Quite at Home" (85–87). This discrepancy provides an interesting visual-textual homework assignment that requires students to look back at a section of the novel they had finished and see whether it takes on new significance in view of the completed novel's framing images.

⁹ The last part also included the novel's preface, table of contents, and a list of illustrations.

Teaching *Bleak House* and Victorian Prose

Robert Newsom

I have regularly taught *Bleak House* in conjunction with both undergraduate and graduate courses on the canonical Victorian prose writers, whom I call the Prosers—chiefly Thomas Carlyle, John Stuart Mill, John Henry Newman, John Ruskin, and Matthew Arnold.[1] The formal novelty of the course is that we read the novel in parts alongside the prose works. Since my university is on the quarter system and our quarters are ten weeks long, this conveniently breaks down into reading two monthly numbers a week. Graduate seminars consist of ten weekly three-hour meetings, and in this format we devote approximately the first two hours to the prose writers and the third to the novel, following a break. Undergraduate classes meet two or three times a week, and the division of attention we give there to the prosers and the novel is more flexible, sometimes spending two meetings in a week to prose and the third to the novel, sometimes alternating classes between prose and novel, but often devoting at least ten minutes to the novel in any given class. In any event, discussions that cross over and connect the concerns of the Prosers with *Bleak House* are integral to the course.

Why do this? The simplest explanation is that it has, for me at least, made the teaching of canonical Victorian prose a lot easier and more coherent. The Prosers often offer what can seem to today's students a very dry if varied meal, one that benefits enormously from being accompanied by a juicy novel. But this begs the question of why read the Prosers at all?

I offer my graduate students the following explanation in the course description:

English literature as a discipline (in Britain and its colonies and in the United States) has been from its founding fundamentally informed by the ethos of the classic Victorian prose writers: especially Carlyle, J. S. Mill, Newman, Ruskin and Arnold; so to read these writers is necessarily to study not only a very important part of British intellectual history, but also to study the beginnings of what it is we do—whether we end up as medievalists, modernists, Americanists, theorists, whatever. We will be reading books, portions of books, and essays by these writers (including some earlier writing by Bentham), and will supplement this mostly non-fictional diet with a reading of one of the richest and most resonant of nineteenth-century novels, Dickens's *Bleak House*, which will extend throughout the quarter (reading two of what originally were its twenty monthly numbers each week). We shall follow our writers in attending to questions about authority, identity, sexuality, literature and culture more broadly, especially as these are worked out in philosophical and political debates that struggle ambivalently with various materialisms (sometimes identified with political economy, sometimes with "liberalism," sometimes with science). We shall watch the notion of the "intellectual" (especially the urban, literary, public intellectual) aborning, and we shall often be surprised to encounter ourselves.

Behind my broad thinking about the course is the more pedagogically minded consideration that *Bleak House* is a peculiarly—perhaps uniquely—large and fluid text in the range of its interests, more so even than such other massive and comparable Victorian novels as *Little Dorrit*, *Our Mutual Friend*, *Vanity Fair*, *The Way We Live* Now, or *Middlemarch*—novels that all offer the illusion, at least, of encompassing the whole of society. *Bleak House*, as its opening chapter famously demonstrates, seems to encompass the universe as well as all of time, both cosmological and mythical, even as it is precisely located in Victorian England (Newsom, *Dickens on the Romantic Side* 11-45). And because of its thematic obsession with "connexion" (*Bleak House* 256), or rather because it realizes that obsession formally so well, almost any page provides an entry into almost any of those "questions about authority, identity, sexuality, literature and culture more broadly" mentioned in the course description. The practical consequence of this for the purposes of the classroom is that it rarely calls for much ingenuity to start an interesting conversation quite randomly juxtaposing any page of Victorian prose and any page of *Bleak House*. While I mean this literally (and I often ask students to bring in for discussion a passage from the week's reading in the novel and hope to connect these with the week's reading in the Prosers), I am not seriously advocating a random teaching plan; rather I mean to point to the happy fact that teaching Victorian prose and *Bleak House* alongside each other does not require a huge amount of what we might call interpreparation and that I have come to expect happy accidents and coincidences from this format.

I would like to believe that the match between *Bleak House* and Victorian prose is a good one no matter how variously scholars interpret the novel and Victorian intellectual history, but I recognize that the fit likely depends on the interpretations. So here are mine.

I see both canonical Victorian prose and *Bleak House* as centrally concerned with questions of authority—political, social, ethical, scientific, and religious. This of course fits well with accounts of the Victorians most generally that give major roles to political reform and the rise of the middle class, the separate spheres of gender, utilitarianism versus traditional ethical systems, and the rise of science and its corrosive effects on religious belief. It also fits well with my understanding of *Bleak House* as deeply informed by the death of Dickens's father in March 1851 and the very difficult and conflicted period of mourning for him that followed and that saw "the first shadows of a new story hovering in a ghostly way" about him, as Dickens had noted the month before in a letter to Mary Boyle (Dickens, *Letters* 6: 298). For the deaths of fathers as important in the growing up of their sons as John Dickens had been to Charles shake their very foundations and lead to radical reexaminations of religious, social, and intellectual assumptions about authority. (See my *Dickens on the Romantic Side* 105–13.)

I begin the prose portion of the course with Carlyle's essays "Signs of the Times" and "Characteristics," which introduce the large themes of the "Mechanical" and Carlyle's sense of his period as morbidly self-conscious. (All the Carlyle readings appear in *A Carlyle Reader*.) We follow these up in the second week with a reading of Carlyle's *Sartor Resartus*, emphasizing book 1, chapters 5, 8–11; book 2, chapters 1–3, 7–9; and book 3, chapters 3, 7–8. I spend a lot of time on Carlyle's account of his spiritual crisis (fictionalized through the character Diogenes Teufelsdröckh) and his reworking there of the problem of the origin of evil, trying to show that despite his diatribe against the utilitarians and "happiness," he is unable to escape either the good of happiness or a logic that is essentially mathematical:

> But the whim we have of Happiness is somewhat thus. By certain valuations, and averages, of our own striking, we come upon some sort of average terrestrial lot; this we fancy belongs to us by nature, and of indefeasible right. . . . I tell thee, Blockhead, it all comes of thy Vanity; of what thou *fanciest* those same deserts of thine to be. Fancy that thou deservest to be hanged (as is most likely), thou wilt feel it happiness to be only shot: fancy that thou deservest to be hanged in a hair-halter, it will be a luxury to die in hemp.
>
> So true is it, what I then said, that *the Fraction of Life can be increased in value not so much by increasing your Numerator as by lessening your Denominator.* Nay, unless my Algebra deceive me, *Unity* itself divided by *Zero* will give *Infinity*. Make thy claim of wages a zero, then; thou hast the world under thy feet. (203–04)

Thus I use Carlyle to set up one of the main conflicts I see in Victorian thought, between an antipathy to the kind of "Mechanical" thinking associated chiefly with Jeremy Bentham and the utilitarians on the one hand and attempts (almost never entirely successful) to escape such rational and skeptical thinking on the other.

Carlyle appears to renounce happiness: "Foolish soul! What Act of Legislature was there that *thou* shouldst be Happy? A little while ago thou hadst no right to *be* at all" (204). There is a higher good than happiness: "Love not Pleasure; love God. This is the EVERLASTING YEA, wherein all contradiction is solved: wherein whoso walks and works, it is well with him" (205).

But Carlyle cannot give up the logic of happiness altogether. The road to happiness involves lowering one's expectations and putting the needs of others before one's own. His "God" is, moreover, hardly the God of scripture, and the question of what exactly one needs to do in order to do one's duty to such a god turns out to be problematic in the extreme—especially because Carlyle scrupulously insists that the real content of the "Blessedness" that is higher than "Happiness" is necessarily intangible. His answer to the question of duty is secular and practical: "*Do the Duty which lies nearest thee*, which thou knowest to be a Duty! Thy second Duty will already have become clearer" (207). The universe may not be the dead steam engine he had imagined in his crisis (188, 202), and soul may not be exactly synonymous with stomach, as he says the utilitarians would have it (185), but because spirit is invisible and unnameable, it is approachable only through the humble particularities of the material and actual.

While we are reading about Carlyle's notion of duty, we are also reading Esther Summerson's statement of her notion of duty against the intrusive and insistently religious philanthropy of Mrs. Pardiggle in *Bleak House*:

> I thought it best to be as useful as I could, and to render what kind services I could, to those immediately about me; and to try to let that circle of duty gradually and naturally expand itself.   (128)

Esther's "circle of duty" is clearly a homely rendering of Carlyle's injunction to do the secular duty nearest to hand and let that be the guide to the next and the next.

Having looked at Carlyle's account of the origin of evil and, in the opening number of *Bleak House*, the third-person narrator's mournful account of the worlds of Chancery and fashion, as well as Esther's account of her brutally religious upbringing, we turn to John Stuart Mill's rigorously utilitarian upbringing and subsequent crisis as recorded in his *Autobiography* and then take a step back into the philosophical underpinnings of the Victorians by reading Jeremy Bentham's *An Introduction to the Principles of Morals and Legislation* (chs. 1–3), Mill's essay on Bentham (originally published in the *London and Westminster*

Review in 1838), and the first four chapters of his *Utilitarianism* (all the readings in Bentham and Mill are in Mill and Bentham, Utilitarianism *and Other Essays*, except for Mill's *Autobiography*). I compare Mill's identity crisis with Carlyle's and argue that in both cases the postcrisis person actually resembles his precrisis self a lot more than he realizes and that both men have in the end more of Bentham's devotion to the greatest happiness of the greatest number than they realize. I take my students through some of the classic problems that classic utilitarian ethics pose and try to make them aware of the extent to which Bentham has won—the extent, that is, to which happiness and the greatest happiness of the greatest number have become the consensus "good" in social and political spheres nowadays (as well, by the way, as the extent to which we have come to accept the quantification of value through economics and the quantification of ourselves through not only economics but also statistics and the whole technology of identity).

As the exception that proves the rule of our having become largely utilitarianized, we read John Henry Newman's account of his conversion to Roman Catholicism, the definitive account for me of a search for authority that denies the authority of self and of pleasure, and I point especially to the famous passage in which Newman writes:

> The Catholic Church holds it better for the sun and moon to drop from heaven, for the earth to fail, and for all the many millions on it to die of starvation in extremest agony, as far as temporal affliction goes, than that one soul . . . should commit one single venial sin, should tell one willful untruth, or should steal one poor farthing without excuse.   (190)

Now this is a genuinely antiutilitarian thought, and it helps underscore that, even at their most conservative and authoritarian, the Victorian Prosers are nevertheless working, however ambivalently or confusedly, within the terrain that Newman identifies with some cogency as "Liberalism" (see, e.g., his note on that topic, 216–25). Even as Carlyle extols the virtues of obedience, he remains nevertheless a good Protestant, fiercely independent and confident in his own judgment, and, for all his railing against pleasure, he does not in fact escape a logic that strives for the general happiness. Similar cases can be made for Ruskin and Arnold.[2]

How does this relate to *Bleak House*? I have argued elsewhere that Chancery embodies evils Dickens associates especially with Roman Catholicism ("Authorizing Women," esp. 64-68), but perhaps more important is that while Miss Barbary's evangelical religion gives "submission" and "self-denial" as its primary goods (30), Esther modestly but significantly transposes these into personal goals that have as their end pleasure, including her own: "I . . . would strive as I grew up to be industrious, contented and kind-hearted, and to do some good to some one, and win some love to myself if I could" (31). Esther's progress, therefore, can be read as a struggle between what Dickens saw as Old Testament, evangelical, and Roman Catholic authoritarianism, on the one hand, and the liberal, domestic, and New Testament goods of pleasure, on the other, as well of course as a struggle against the evils of Chancery at the most literal and topical level. (It's worth mentioning that Chancery reform had been a passionate goal for Bentham from late childhood; indeed, it was the first among all his reformist ambitions [Mack 36-40].) Esther's own crisis of identity, which plays out through the delirium of fever that accompanies her smallpox, provides lots of material to relate to and compare with Carlyle's and Mill's crises and like theirs involves a profound ambivalence about her duty to others and her duty to herself.[3]

I would love to be able to say that I wrap the course up with a neat conclusion and thesis, but just as *Bleak House* ends inconclusively with its famous final sentence fragment, "—even supposing—" (989), I end my accounts of both the novel and the Prosers somewhat inconclusively. Or rather I might say that my conclusion is that the story of Victorian intellectual history as played out both in Victorian prose and in Dickens is largely about an unresolved questioning of ethical and social authority. The figures of Bentham and Newman provide exceptional examples of thinkers who are clear and unambivalent about where they locate authority (pleasure and pain for Bentham, God and the Roman Catholic Church for Newman) and clear about the absoluteness of its force, while Carlyle, Mill, Arnold, Ruskin, Dickens—and most of us—struggle to find viable middle ways.

NOTES

[1] I have also taught an undergraduate variation that is lighter on the canonical Prosers and includes several women writers: for example, Mary Wollstonecraft, Anna Laetitia Barbauld, and Barbara Bodichon. These allow us to take up quite directly questions of gender and female authority raised by Esther's narrative.

[2] Consider the following bit of crypto-utilitarianism from the final chapter of Ruskin's "*Unto This Last*": "THERE IS NO WEALTH BUT LIFE. Life, including all its powers of love, of joy, and of admiration. That country is richest which nourishes the greatest number of noble and happy human beings; that man is richest who, having perfected the functions of his own life to the utmost, has also the widest helpful influence, both personal, and by means of his possessions, over the lives of others" (222).

Ruskin no doubt intended this to be a striking turn on the Greatest Happiness Principle, and yet there is nothing here to which Mill or Bentham could have objected as ethically misguided, especially inasmuch as Ruskin himself quickly elides "life" with the "happy."

[3] She writes, "Dare I hint at that worse time when, strung together somewhere in great black space, there was a flaming necklace, or ring, or starry circle of some kind, of which *I* was one of the beads! And when my only prayer was to be taken off from the rest and when it was such inexplicable agony and misery to be a part of the dreadful thing?"

(556). The visionary circle surely refers back to the "circle of duty" we have discussed as the core of Esther's ethics. I suspect Dickens also had in mind the image of a total solar eclipse. There was an eclipse that would have been visible in London had the weather been fine on 28 July 1851, the first such eclipse to be photographed and widely covered in the press, including illustrations of the phenomenon known as "Baily's Beads."

Bleak House and Uncle Tom's Cabin: Teaching Victorian Fiction in a Transatlantic Context

Jennifer Phegley

Bleak House is without a doubt a challenging novel to teach. It is extremely long, has a complex plot, and contains an overwhelming array of minor characters. American students often find it difficult to relate to Dickens's critique of the unfamiliar and seemingly irrelevant Court of Chancery. In this essay, I focus on how teaching the novel in a transatlantic context helped my students relate what is arguably one of Dickens's most complex works to the field of American literature with which they were already familiar. My urban university caters to a large number of older, commuting students who often hold down full-time jobs and sometimes shoulder the responsibility of providing for their families. Among this population there are many students whose background in American literature is much stronger than their training in British literature. Having taught both the American literature and British literature surveys, I saw this disparity over and over again. Students who were engaged and active in my introductory American literature classes clammed up in the British literature surveys; lack of exposure to the writers and the context led to a lack of confidence in their reading skills and interpretative abilities. As a result of these teaching experiences, I had long planned to teach a transatlantic nineteenth-century literature course as a way of reducing the gap between the two national literatures and easing students into the British literary works by pairing those works with more familiar writers and themes.

I first thought about teaching Dickens's novel in a transatlantic context while researching the serialization of *Bleak House* in the American *Harper's New Monthly Magazine*. I noticed that the novel was published in the magazine alongside several editorial discussions of Harriet Beecher Stowe's *Uncle Tom's Cabin*. *Bleak House* was serialized in *Harper's* from April 1852 until October 1853 (lagging one month behind the British part issues). It began in the same month that Stowe's novel completed its serial run in the *National Era* (where it ran from June 1851 until April 1852). The more I thought about the two works, the more I was struck by the parallels between them. Both were highly sentimental, both were social protest novels, both were being serialized in 1852, and both were central to *Harper's* attempts to define good literature. In addition, both were wildly popular across the Atlantic; Stowe may well have been more popular in England than in America and Dickens more widely embraced as one of the greatest writers of the day in America than he was in his own country. Indeed, Dickens's novel was highly praised in the pages of *Harper's* while Stowe's was mildly disparaged. In a periodical that profited both financially and culturally by publishing primarily British fiction (at first pirated and later paid for), it is not surprising to see the competition between Dickens and Stowe, representatives of the British and American national literary identities, played out to Dickens's advantage.[1] I decided that teaching the two novels together, in a course that explored these international publishing relationships, would provide an excellent way to encourage students to see British and American literary culture as more interconnected and mutually constitutive than they had previously imagined. This idea was also spurred on by Harry Stone's "Charles Dickens and Harriet Beecher Stowe," which reprints Dickens's correspondence about Stowe and recounts their meeting and Dickens's growing sense of rivalry with the phenomenally popular American writer. Stone quotes Thomas Noon Talfourd, who toasted the two authors at their first meeting by declaring that each had "employed fiction as a means of awakening the attention of the respective countries to the condition of the oppressed and suffering classes" (198). This particular connection between the two authors served as the organizing principle for my course.

I constructed a 400/500-level Victorian literature course, Transatlantic Social Issues and the Victorian Novel, in which *Bleak House* and *Uncle Tom's Cabin* were the central texts. The class, which included about fifteen advanced undergraduates (both majors and nonmajors) and five graduate students, met three days a week for fifty minutes. Unfortunately this schedule was not very conducive to intense reading assignments and in-depth discussions. During the weeks we devoted to Dickens and Stowe, however, it allowed us to spend Mondays reading several installments of *Bleak House*, Wednesdays reading several installments of *Uncle Tom's Cabin*, and Fridays discussing the relation between the two works. In a sixteen-week course, I devoted five weeks to these two novels. Because these weeks were reading intensive, I spread them out over the semester, devoting weeks 4, 6, 8, 10, and 12 to Dickens and Stowe while assigning in alternate weeks shorter works that involved discussions of social issues in a transatlantic context. For example, in the intervening weeks we read Harriet Martineau's periodical writings on slavery and the Civil War (assessing her outsider's perspective on America's peculiar institution), *The History of Mary Prince* (comparing Prince's representation of slavery with American slave narratives), Arthur Conan Doyle's *A Study in Scarlet* (examining his depictions of both London and the American West), and Bram Stoker's *Dracula* (focusing on imperialism and the role of the American "cowboy" Quincy Carter).

The weeks devoted to Dickens and Stowe were organized around transatlantic publishing practices, common social issues, and various critical approaches to the novels. With each of these themes, I assigned two scholarly articles that groups of students would collaboratively present to the class on Fridays, when we were to compare the two novels. These pairings worked particularly well as discussion starters and got students involved as "experts" who taught the class about what they had learned. The themes and articles were "The Transatlantic Literary Scene" (Fisch; Phegley), "The Function of Sentimentality" (Lenard; Tompkins), "Narrative Strategies" (Belasco Smith; Salotto), "The Genre of the Social Protest Novel" (Yellin; Fasick), and "Dickens and Stowe in Popular Culture" (Gossett, chs. 12 and 14; Schlicke, "Dickens's Public Readings").

In addition to comparing these pairs of articles, I set up the transatlantic framework for reading the books by providing an overview of the American reception of Dickens before the serialization of *Bleak House* in *Harper's*, beginning with E. P. Whipple's article "Novels and Novelists: Charles Dickens."[2] Whipple draws clear distinctions between the sentimentality of American novelists (like Stowe) and Dickens's supposedly more sophisticated "pathos" (402) as well as between the caricature presented in the American romance and Dickens's ability to excel "in the exhibition of those minor traits [of character] which the eye of genius alone can detect" (402). Whipple outlines the stereotypical rivalry between British (masculine) and American (feminine) literature, claiming that "we cannot refrain from expressing a regret that we have not a class of novels illustrative of American life and character, which does some justice to both. Novelists we have in perilous abundance . . . some of them unexcelled in the art of preparing a dish of fiction by a liberal admixture of the horrible and the sentimental" (405–06). By framing the gendered terms of debate about the value of British versus American writing, Whipple allows students to understand the context in which *Bleak House* was presented in *Harper's*.

Students also mapped the mid-century debate over literary nationalism by examining discussions of Dickens and Stowe in *Harper's* during the serial run of *Bleak House*. (*Harper's* is easily accessible on the *Making of America* Web site at http://cdl.library.cornell.edu/moa/.) I asked them to read selections from the magazine and to consider why Dickens's class-based protest novel is championed by a periodical that is generally apolitical and strictly avoids mentioning slavery or the Civil War. Students concluded that the magazine heartily champions Dickens's focus on class relations in large part because class was an issue deemed irrelevant to a nation based on the myth of class mobility. Just as the British could easily embrace Stowe's critique of an institution that their nation had outlawed decades earlier, Americans could divert their attention away from the painful divisions wrought by slavery and instead focus on Dickens's critique of a classist society supposedly foreign to the United States. The transatlantic critical responses to these novels enabled students to explore how the British obsession with Stowe elevated her to the status of a hero fighting against the barbaric American institution of slavery, while the American promotion of Dickens, in *Harper's* at least, celebrated him as an outraged critic of class inequality, thus sidestepping the deeply divisive slavery debate. In this framework, students recognized how Dickens provided not only an acceptable social reformist agenda but also a high cultural model for Americans to follow.

Harper's "Editor's Easy Chair" for June 1854 exemplifies the magazine's protection of Dickens as an effective social reform writer whose ideas can be comfortably embraced in a politically neutral venue intended to appeal to a broad range of Americans. In response to "sharp criticisms upon Mr. Dickens's Mrs. Jellyby" raised by the British press, *Harper's* proclaims:

As usual, whenever Dickens is censured, we do not agree. We believe that the satire was the result of very shrewd observation and wise consideration. . . . The Borrioboola-Gha style of philanthropy is the most fatal blow to real charity. Fictitious feeling exhales in a fancied sympathy, which not only tends to bring actual sympathy into disrepute, but dissipates the action and the charity of those who are truly, but not wisely, generous. (119–20)

The focus on Mrs. Jellyby and her "false" charity is interesting given that she attempts to fix a problem that exists far from home while her home itself is in disarray. Students considered whether this argument belittled Stowe's antislavery novel by equating Stowe's efforts to Mrs. Jellyby's or supported Stowe's efforts as appropriately nationalistic and domestic. By comparing Stowe to Jellyby as well as to Esther Summerson, the more successful reformer in the novel, students began to think about what kind of public response each writer was advocating. In contrast to Mrs. Jellyby, with her alienating ministrations, Esther Summerson becomes the ideal reformer who listens to the poor, feels true compassion for their plight, and helps each sufferer she meets on an individual basis. Esther is able to balance fulfilling her household duties and participating in the reformation of society. As a result, she embodies the model woman reformer, who works from within the private sphere to affect the public sphere but does not move from one sphere to the other as the more dangerous women activists do. Students debated Stowe's position within this continuum to determine why Dickens may have had both admiration for and frustration with her success, as well as why *Harper's* itself was conflicted in its reception of her work.

More specifically, it was interesting for students to consider why Dickens's use of pathos is embraced, while Stowe's sentimentality is disparaged in *Harper's*. The December 1853 "Editor's Easy Chair" provides a way to engage in this conversation. In this essay, the editor laments that such a practical people as Americans could also be "the most sentimental people in the world. . . . There is a kind of literature and art grown up among us, which is weak and unhealthy, and yet the most popular of all." *Harper's* rejects women's fiction as a rising form of American literature and discourages readers from wasting their time on the sentimentality of "alliterative ladies" like "Tabithy Toadstool," when "Scott, Fielding, Dickens, and Thackeray are easy to obtain, and are of an incomparable superiority." The magazine ridicules the pseudonyms used by many American women writers as distasteful, and it characterizes women readers enchanted with such sentimentality as unhealthy. This characterization, however, prompted students to ask how different Stowe's and Dickens's use of sentiment really is. In addressing this question, students explored the ways in which debates about literary value are caught up in debates about gender and nationality.

While *Harper's* esteemed Dickens more highly, the editors show signs of conflict that complicate the place of male British writers in America. Even in

Harper's, the enthusiastic promotion of Dickens is sometimes tempered with national pride over Stowe's success. The February 1853 "Editor's Easy Chair" laments that "New York ladies are certainly literary the present season. . . . We do not know but old English literature is absolutely driving out of the market Uncle Tom's Cabin, and that fervor, and passion, and strong expression, will yield to the quiet simplicity of [English authors]" (419). The sense of remorse over the perceived loss in popularity of Stowe's American classic is emphasized even more directly in a mock literary stock report, included in the column, that refers to literary taste as "spasmodic and whimsical" and charts a strong growth in shares of Thackeray and Addison and a decline in "Domestics" such as Stowe (419–20). In these statements, the use of the terms "domestics" and "literary women" emphasizes the implicit connections being made between women and national literary productivity. Women's power in the domestic realm, a power *Harper's* characterizes as literary as much as moral, is also constructed as a vital power to be seized by the nation. Discussing *Harper's* responses to a feminized audience also opened up spaces for students to consider the effects of gender and readership on emerging divisions between high and low culture.

As the culminating experience for the course, students wrote research papers on some aspect of the publication of, or cultural response to, Dickens, Stowe, *Bleak House*, or *Uncle Tom's Cabin*, paying special attention to the transatlantic context. The purpose of this paper was to immerse students in primary (perhaps archival) materials so that they could draw conclusions about the significance of those literary artifacts to society. Students were inspired by the class discussions and readings to write papers on topics such as American reviews of *Bleak House* and British reviews of *Uncle Tom's Cabin*, on *Bleak House* in its serial context in *Harper's* as well as in *Frederick Douglass's Paper*, and on the marketing and sales of "Tomitudes," cultural and commercial products based on Stowe's novel, on both sides of the Atlantic (many examples of Tomitudes can be found in the "Uncle Tom's Cabin and American Culture" multimedia archive at http://www.iath.virginia.edu/utc/). These projects allowed students to broaden their understanding of Dickens and Stowe in the context of an interdependent international publishing arena. In evaluating the course, one student noted that after "examining [British and American novels] together, it was easy to visualize America's connection/relationship with Victorian England, and by viewing British literature through this lens I was able to make a relationship between myself and . . . the past. . . . It was nice to be able to contextualize the readings of the Victorian era with America and its social issues." Another class member stated that she or he "liked studying authors from both sides of the Atlantic" because the connections between the two cultures became more significant than the disconnections. Yet another student found that British and American works "were actually quite similar with regards to . . . social protest . . . slavery being the most significant [issue in] America . . . and the court [and class] systems being most specific to England." Studying Dickens within a transatlantic context helped students understand the similarities between British and American cultures and to see connections between present-day and Victorian media. I found that this approach made *Bleak House* relevant to the national and cultural arenas with which students were familiar and encouraged them to reconsider those arenas from an international perspective.

NOTES

[1] For more on *Harper's* practice of reprinting British literature, see Phegley.

[2] For other American reviews of the novel see *North American Review* Oct. 1853: 409–39; *Knickerbocker* 39 (1852): 421–31; and *Harper's New Monthly Magazine* June 1854: 119–20. For British reviews see P. Collins, *Critical Heritage*, as well as *Illustrated London News* 24 Sept. 1853: 247; and [Lewes], "Dickens in Relation to Criticism."

Transatlantic Transformation: Teaching
Bleak House and *The Bondwoman's Narrative*

Daniel Hack

The Bondwoman's Narrative, by Hannah Crafts, is an antebellum fictional slave narrative that borrows liberally from Charles Dickens's *Bleak House*. Or, one might say, an antebellum fictional slave narrative that appropriates parts of *Bleak House*. Or rewrites *Bleak House*. Or plagiarizes it. The lack of an agreed-on or even a strictly neutral term with which to characterize the relation between these two texts testifies to how fraught and complex this relation is and to its pedagogical value. The effort to understand what *The Bondwoman's Narrative* does to or with *Bleak House* requires close attention to the formal patterns and verbal particularities of both texts while raising historical and theoretical questions concerning transatlantic and interracial literary relations, the significance of authorial identity, practices of referential reading, and the politics of literary form. This pairing of texts is therefore ideal for courses on Dickens, nineteenth-century British and American fiction, subaltern rewritings of canonical literature, and critical methods.

The unpublished manuscript of *The Bondwoman's Narrative* was purchased at auction in 2001 by the leading African Americanist Henry Louis Gates, Jr., who had its authenticity as a mid-nineteenth-century physical artifact confirmed and who arranged for its publication the following year. Gates's discovery was widely publicized, thanks partly to his fame but also to the work's potential status as "the earliest known novel by a female African-American slave," "the earliest known novel by a black woman anywhere," and the sole "surviving handwritten manuscript of a book by an escaped slave" (to quote the front-page *New York Times* article that first reported the discovery [Kirkpatrick]).[1] The work was only potentially these things because its authorship was a mystery, as it remains to this day: research by Gates and others has established that Hannah Crafts is probably a pseudonym, and various candidates have been proposed, but as of this writing the author's identity—including the person's race—has not been established (although there is physical evidence to suggest that the author was in fact a woman [Crafts 330]). From a pedagogical perspective, this uncertainty is wonderfully useful, since it encourages students to think about whether and how our understanding of the text—including its use of Dickens—hinges on our sense of the author's motives and identity. On the one hand, *The Bondwoman's Narrative* offers a strong challenge to stringently antibiographical or anti-identity-based approaches, since Crafts's appropriations would seem to signify differently if the text is by an escaped slave rather than, say, a white abolitionist. On the other hand, the novel illustrates the pitfalls of overly hasty referential or biographical readings, because passages that were initially seen to reflect the author's firsthand experience turn out also or instead to reflect her reading. (See, e.g., Gates, "Fugitive.") This is fertile ground for discussion.

When addressing questions of authorship, identity, reference, and authenticity, the instructor might incorporate attention to *The Bondwoman's Narrative*'s paratexts, from its cover illustration of a dog-eared manuscript wrapped in twine to Gates's long introduction to the inclusion of crossed-out passages from the manuscript. Bringing into the discussion both the original monthly numbers of *Bleak House* and the edition of the novel that has been assigned, one might consider the different messages conveyed by the packaging of each novel. When discussing authenticity and authority, one might also compare the truth claims made in Dickens's and Crafts's prefaces, both of which situate their work in relation to "romance" (Crafts 3) or "the romantic" (Dickens 7).

Students who have just read *Bleak House* have no trouble recognizing that novel's presence in *The Bondwoman's Narrative*. Crafts's borrowing begins at the beginning, textually and perhaps conceptually: her narrator and protagonist, a light-skinned slave named Hannah, is plainly modeled on Esther Summerson. Just as Esther begins the part of *Bleak House* labeled "Esther's Narrative" by stating, "I have a great deal of difficulty in beginning to write my portion of these pages, for I know I am not clever" (27), Hannah begins the first chapter of *The Bondwoman's Narrative* by stating, "It may be that I assume to[o] much responsibility in attempting to write these pages. . . . I am neither clever, nor learned, nor talented" (5). Throughout the novel Crafts mines *Bleak House* for scene-setting and descriptive passages, plot elements, characters, and dialogue. Thus, after Hannah is injured in a carriage crash, her illness and recovery are described in language recalling Esther's epochal illness, and the mansion where she recovers closely resembles Bleak House as Esther first describes it. The novel features a blackmailer, Mr. Trappe, who is based on *Bleak House*'s Mr. Tulkinghorn, and some of his conversations with his victim, Hannah's mistress, are drawn word for word from those of Tulkinghorn and Lady Dedlock. Hannah's move to Washington produces a long pastiche of the opening paragraphs of *Bleak House* ("Gloom everywhere. Gloom up the Potomac; where it rolls among meadows no longer green, and by splendid country seats. Gloom down the Potomac where it washes the sides of huge war-ships. Gloom on the marshes, the fields, and heights," and so on [162]). Dickens's evocation of the street-crossing sweeper Jo's subjectivity is adapted to evoke that of field slaves in North Carolina, and his description of the London slum Tom-all-Alone's is reproduced virtually verbatim as a description of their quarters. The last chapter of *The Bondwoman's Narrative* tracks the last chapter of *Bleak House*, as Hannah brings her story up to the time of writing, when she is living as a free woman in New Jersey, happily married to a minister and running a school.

Crafts draws on other works as well—for example, a description of a prison comes from Walter Scott's *Rob Roy*, and the last sentence of the novel recalls that of Charlotte Brontë's *Villette*—but none nearly as extensively as *Bleak House*. Many though not all of these debts are identified in the annotations to the 2003 paperback edition of the novel. While students should certainly be directed to this resource, they should also be warned that these annotations are incomplete and sometimes inadequate in their description of the nature and

scope of Crafts's appropriations. I have students use the annotations as the basis
for forming their own list or table, with the relevant passages from the two texts
arranged side by side. I then produce a shared table that collates and if necessary supplements their findings and forms the basis for discussion.

After compiling this table, students often accuse Crafts of plagiarism and
wonder why such behavior is any more acceptable on her part than it is on theirs.
I address this concern in several ways. First, I note that students who plagiarize
are trying to get credit for someone else's work. What, I ask, is Crafts trying to
do? This question hangs over all further discussion, as it admits of no simple
solution (not least because we do not even know if Crafts sought to publish her
work). Second, I explain that notions of authorship and literary property were in
flux and highly contested in the nineteenth century. Literary borrowing in various forms was not uncommon, and while Crafts's technique is atypical, it is not
as aberrant as it seems to modern readers. I mention the lack of international
copyright protection and the circulation of both pirated editions of and unau-
thorized sequels to Dickens's work. Dickens himself, I suggest, was well aware
of his work's appropriability, and I ask how this awareness is inscribed in *Bleak
House* itself. Here I call on James Buzard's argument concerning the novel's interest in the refunctioning of cultural artifacts (see Buzard), and I point out that
the novel allegorizes its own reproduction, ending as it does with Esther living
in a second house modeled on (and also named) Bleak House. Crafts's authorial
practice itself thus becomes visible as a form of engagement with the concerns
of Dickens's novel.

I also describe a racial context for Crafts's method (without forgetting that
Crafts's race is unknown). *The Bondwoman's Narrative* bears comparison with
William Wells Brown's *Clotel* (1853), the first published novel by an African
American, which borrows extensively and at times verbatim from a range of
sources. Bringing in the example of Alexandre Dumas, whose controversial
views of authorship were as widely publicized as his part-African ancestry, I
have my class read a contemporary defense of the prolific Dumas in the *Anglo-
African Magazine* that exclaims, "Take from Shakespeare, all his borrowed stories, and what of invention have we left?" ("Alexandre Dumas" 4). Citing the
case of Phillis Wheatley, I also discuss the history of denying claims of creative
agency by African Americans. These examples call attention to ways in which
notions of authorship are historically shifting and attributions of authorial origi-
nality are racially charged. However, rather than claim that the nature and circumstances of the examples I offer are identical, I encourage students to think
(or write) about the differences among them. For instance, Brown does not rely
as heavily on any single work as does Crafts, he acknowledges his indebtedness
in his novel's final chapter, and he borrows mainly from American texts explicitly
concerned with slavery.

This contrast between Crafts's and Brown's choice and use of their sources
is one way to broach one of the most intriguing questions raised by *The Bondwoman's Narrative*: why *Bleak House*? Why, that is, would someone wanting

to write a fictional slave narrative (whether partly autobiographical or not) turn to *Bleak House*—which is, after all, an English novel set entirely in England? To begin to answer this question, I discuss the circulation and reception of Dickens's work in America, emphasizing his popularity, his reputation as a reformer and champion of the downtrodden, and his well-known criticism of slavery in *American Notes*. In my nineteenth-century transatlantic fiction class, these matters will have been broached already when discussing Dickens's influence on *Uncle Tom's Cabin*. Building on this background, I call attention to the existence of a precedent of sorts for Crafts's relocation of *Bleak House* itself to an African American context: the serial publication of Dickens's novel in its entirety in *Frederick Douglass' Paper* in 1852–53 (hard on the heels of its original publication in London and New York). Whether or not Crafts knew of Frederick Douglass's reprinting of the novel, this reprinting indicates that the social criticism and humanitarianism on display in *Bleak House* were seen by some antislavery activists as continuous with their own agenda.[2]

This context helps make sense of Crafts's decision to transfer Dickens's story to the United States. However, before turning to examine some of the specific elements of *Bleak House* Crafts incorporates, I have the class consider the question of whether *Bleak House* itself encourages or discourages this sense of transatlantic solidarity. This question leads us to focus on the novel's brief references to race, slavery, and Africa. The most prominent of these references come in Dickens's famous satire of "telescopic philanthropy" (49) through his depiction of Mrs. Jellyby and her "African project" (53)—a satire that led the abolitionist Lord Denman to accuse Dickens of giving aid and comfort to defenders of slavery (see Denman). Two other moments in the novel similarly suggest that attention to the needs of people in England does not model but instead competes with, and deserves to take precedence over, concern for distant people of color: the novel's moving depiction of Jo is used to indict those who concern themselves instead with "the spiritual destitution of a coral reef in the Pacific" (258), and in the novel's one direct reference to American slavery, Esther contrasts the pleasure Harold Skimpole purports to take in thinking of the "enterprise and effort . . . of the Slaves on American plantations" with his neglect of his own family (294–95).

This localist, arguably antiabolitionist and even racist, strand of *Bleak House* lends no small irony to Crafts's appropriation and reworking of elements of the novel (as well as Douglass's publication of it). Yet even as *The Bondwoman's Narrative* calls attention to this strand of *Bleak House*, it also raises the possibility that this strand is not intrinsic to the novel's humanitarianism. To what extent, the instructor might ask, does Dickens's cultivation of sympathy for a character such as Jo appeal to the reader's imagined geographical proximity or shared racial (or national) identity? To what extent does our own sympathy as readers seem to depend on or instead transcend such factors? For vivid evidence that Dickens's localism was sometimes viewed as neither problematic nor expendable but instead portable and therefore universal, we read an anonymous poem titled "Borroboola Gha: A Poem for the Times," which was published in *Frederick Douglass' Paper* 2 February 1855 (see app. 2, p. 201). This poem adopts—or should one say coopts?—the novel's antitelescopic stance and imagery while simply ignoring its geographical and racial specificity.

Pursuing this line of inquiry further, I ask the class to consider whether *The Bondwoman's Narrative* critiques *Bleak House*'s localism or installs a version of its own—or does both, just as *Bleak House* itself may be said both to celebrate an Esther-like dedication to a "gradually and naturally" expanding "circle of duty" (128) and to reveal the limitations of such a stance. Key passages to examine in this context include Crafts's rewriting of Dickens's imagining of Jo's subjectivity as that of brutalized field slaves (257–58; Crafts 206–07) and her rewriting of the peroration following Jo's death as a speech occasioned by an enslaved mother's murder of her child to keep it from being returned to slavery (734; Crafts 183). Noting that Crafts's narrator exhibits greater revulsion from the field slaves than does Dickens's narrator from Jo, we ask whether Crafts's cultivation of sympathy for some slaves entails the denial of sympathy to others? When discussing the speech at the end of Crafts's version of the story of Margaret Garner (familiar to many students from Toni Morrison's *Beloved*), we focus on Crafts's replacement of Dickens's dramatic appeal to spatial proximity ("And dying thus around us, every day" [734]) with a condemnation of "laws that occasion such scenes as this" (Crafts 183). Consideration of this revision can easily expand into a comparison of the play of individual and systemic responsibility—or, put differently, ethics and politics—in the two novels. (On this aspect of *Bleak House*, see Robbins.)

This scene can also serve to bring forward a pair of concerns central to both novels: the control of women's sexuality and the forced separation of mothers and children. The crucial loci here are *Bleak House*'s blackmail and mother-daughter plots, both of which Crafts transforms into stories about slavery. Whereas Lady Dedlock's secret is her scandalous liaison with Captain Hawdon, the secret of the woman similarly blackmailed in *The Bondwoman's Narrative*, Hannah's mistress, is her race: as her blackmailer has discovered, she was removed from her slave mother as a baby to take the place of her owner's dead child. Threatened with exposure, Hannah's mistress flees and dies. Even as she thus relives the experience of Lady Dedlock, then, she more closely resembles Esther Summerson—that is, not the unmarried mother but the illegitimate daughter separated from her mother at birth, not a sexual transgressor but an innocent victim of an unjust society. Hannah too is separated from her mother as a baby, simply because they are slaves. Thus, even as Crafts models her story on Dickens's, she presents her characters as victims of their society's defining injustice. By contrast, *Bleak House*'s treatment of illicit sexuality and illegitimacy seems separate from its attack on Britain's legal system and ruling class. (See Schor for an analysis that connects these topics.) This restructuring demonstrates Crafts's creative agency while also illuminating the structure of *Bleak House* itself.

Similarly revealing for both novels is Crafts's dramatic revision of the ending of *Bleak House*'s mother-daughter plot. Like Esther, Hannah grows up without contact with her mother, but whereas Esther has only one meaningful encounter with her mother before the latter's death, Hannah announces in her final chapter that she now lives with her mother in freedom and happiness. Questions to be asked here include the following: Does the blatant implausibility of this turn of events undermine the text's apparent truth claims? Does it instead underscore the ending's utopianism and thereby sharpen the novel's criticism of existing conditions? Why is Esther denied a similar happy ending with her mother? Noting *The Bondwoman's Narrative*'s lack of a final call for political action—a typical gesture in slave narratives and abolitionist fiction—one might also ask if the closing emphasis on domesticity carries a similar charge in the two works or instead signifies differently.

The Bondwoman's Narrative returns us to *Bleak House* with fresh eyes and fresh questions. It renders concrete and inescapable theoretical and methodological questions that might otherwise seem abstract or arcane and opens a window onto a vibrant transatlantic dialogue. To continue studying this dialogue, the instructor might well turn next to *The Garies and Their Friends* (1857), by Frank J. Webb. Only the second novel published by an African American, it features various Dickensian tropes, an illiterate shopkeeper clearly based on *Bleak House*'s Krook, and several borrowed character names (Esther, Caddy, Charlie).[3] Given how much less indebted Webb is to Dickens than is Crafts, one wonders why he does not cover his tracks better by changing these names. Is he in fact alluding to *Bleak House*, inviting the reader to make the connection? Why? The discussion continues.

NOTES

[1]For criticism of *The Bondwoman's Narrative*, see the essays collected in Gates and Robbins. Two of these essays focus on *Bleak House*: "Blackening *Bleak House*: Hannah Crafts's *The Bondwoman's Narrative*," by Hollis Robbins (this essay builds on Robbins's contributions to the textual annotations in the paperback edition of the novel), and "'I Dwell Now in a Neat Little Cottage': Architecture, Race, and Desire in *The Bondwoman's Narrative*," by William Gleason.

[2] I discuss the relations among *Bleak House*, *The Bondwoman's Narrative*, and *Frederick Douglass' Paper* at greater length in "Close Reading at a Distance: The African Americanization of *Bleak House*," on which the present essay draws.

[3]I am grateful to my student Russell Sbriglia for calling these echoes to my attention.

Bleak House and Neoliberalism

Lauren M. E. Goodlad

Teaching *Bleak House* today offers an exciting if somewhat challenging opportunity to any instructor who wishes to emphasize the novel's political meanings in the light of present-day contexts. The term *liberalism*, though indispensable to such an endeavor, is multivalent—for it is used to describe the left-leaning collectivist mode of governance that took off in the United States with the New Deal[1] and, more broadly, a wide-ranging political philosophy that, for several hundred years, has articulated concepts of individualism that are integral to stances on both the left and right.[2] Distinct from these meanings is the *neoliberal* economic doctrine that has dominated contemporary political discourse since the 1980s, touting so-called free market forces as the arbiter of all human affairs.[3] Classical political economy was only one facet of the mid-Victorian worldview on display in *Bleak House*. But under neoliberalism, the revival of classical notions has resulted in an economistic political rationality or governmentality that, as Wendy Brown has argued, "involves *extending and disseminating market values to all institutions and social action*" (par. 3; cf. Gagnier 5 and Frank). The result is that the project of building human and social capacities—a challenge that also concerned the author of *Bleak House*—is, in today's climate, often entrusted to market forces (which in practice often means that such capacities are simply taken for granted). In contrast to a mid-twentieth-century era that stressed Keynesian social policies in the West and "development" in industrializing nations, under neoliberalism low-income people, especially women, are constructed "as already or potentially able-bodied workers" (Kingfisher, "Introduction" 3). To contrast the liberalism of Dickens's time to today's neoliberalism is thus to attend differences in prevailing notions of *pastorship*.[4]

In what follows I do not articulate a specific set of classroom strategies so much as provide a guide to reading *Bleak House* as a novel that both anticipates present-day problems and, in a way, talks back to them.[5] Mid-Victorian governmentality—a fervidly individualist and antistatist political culture that extolled self-help, laissez faire, and free trade—bears comparison with a neoliberal agenda bent on rolling back welfare provisions in the West and eliminating subsidies in other parts of the world.[6] *Bleak House* can thus be read in dialogue with any number of present-day policies including welfare reform, trade agreements, and the "transitioning" of postcolonial or post-Soviet economies. Yet to apprehend the limits of such comparison, one needs to remember that classical political economy was, for a long time, discredited (hence the "neo" in neoliberalism). In the late-Victorian and Edwardian years, socialists and New Liberals mounted successful campaigns to overturn moralistic understandings of poverty, regulate capitalist excesses, and adopt collectivist notions of social agency—transformations that intensified under the full-blown welfarism of later decades.[7] At the vanguard of such developments were John Stuart Mill and T. H. Green, mid-Victorian intellectuals whose articulation of a positive conception of liberty marked a crucial turning point in the shift toward statist forms of liberalism. Whereas classical liberalism had stressed a negative view, in which freedom was defined as the absence of interference, liberals like Mill and Green saw liberty as consisting in the positive ability to realize potential—a more complicated conception anchored to collective quests for equalitarian social democracy (see, e.g., Nicholson 485; Bellamy, "T. H. Green"; Simhony; cf. Foucault, "Social Security" 161).

Teaching *Bleak House* alongside Mill's *On Liberty* (esp. chs. 3 and 5) thus provides the occasion to pose searching questions. For example, what social and political conditions enable the individuality Mill wants to build? Does Dickens's interest in promoting pastoral care tally with a Millean ideal of individuality? What kinds of positive and negative liberty does each text endorse and what are the tensions between them?

As such questions imply, the idea that freedom entails the ability to develop human and social capacities is important to understanding Victorian notions of character. In the early 1850s Britain was a deeply stratified society with an expanding colonial regime and a political constitution that excluded the great majority of working-class males.[8] Yet many earnest liberals held to an Enlightenment-era notion of the limitless improvability of human character regardless of descriptive features such as class, race, or nationality. Although such a view of character posited eventual democratization, during the Victorian period it was bound up in existing hierarchies. Character building was portrayed as requiring intimate pastoral relations between rich and poor, educated and uneducated, colonizer and colonized. Such ideas legitimated the Victorian exercise of power—underwriting the charitable "civilizing mission" of the urban middle classes and the Anglicist imperial policies deployed in British India.[9] Governing practices that entailed vast inequalities of wealth and power were thus construed through a liberal rhetoric—as if they created mutual relations between potential equals.

At the time of *Bleak House*'s serialization, this civilizing project was, within Britain's metropolitan borders, located largely in the voluntary sphere of philanthropic, religious, and civic institutions. In the years after the 1834 Poor Law Amendment Act, the British state began to oversee local governance and became especially active in centralizing and producing social knowledge. Nonetheless, this distinct Victorian governmentality should not be conflated with the intrusive disciplinary institutions that Michel Foucault describes in *Discipline and Punish*, based largely on the history of nineteenth-century France. As Foucault himself realized, nineteenth-century British liberalism involved the perception "that if one governed too much, one did not govern at all" ("Space" 242; cf. "Social Security" 167). Modernization and expansion of the state was necessary to promoting capitalism, trade, and empire, but such goals could be achieved without politically unpopular interventions in domestic affairs. Thus the New Poor Law, one of the most influential social policies of the century,

had been purposely designed as a negative measure that would curtail indis-
criminate dispensation of poor relief and leave moral guidance to voluntary and
local agencies (Senior, Chadwick, et al. II.4.59).[10] Such formidable investment
in the voluntary provision of pastoral guidance—arguably the hallmark of Victorian liberalism—created a distinctive governmentality, a "dense network of
self-governing institutions" (Harris 68). It was also a chief means of constituting
middle-class social authority.

It is, therefore, a common Victorian boast that self-governance was the key to
England's robust national identity; Samuel Smiles's radically individualist notion
of character as a "self-originating force" had, likewise, broad appeal (27–28).
Nonetheless, a diverse range of literary intellectuals—not only Dickens but also
Mill, Thomas Carlyle, Elizabeth Gaskell, and John Ruskin—were among those
to promulgate more critical views of the liberal social order.

As figured in *Bleak House*, Victorian governance variously consists in antiquated institutions such as Chancery, economizing innovations such as the New
Poor Law, and philanthropic enterprises that smack of bourgeois hypocrisy and
self-aggrandizement—governing practices that manifestly serve existing class
interests at the expense of popular needs. The novel thus enunciates an impassioned cry for humane and efficacious pastoral care. Yet, in doing so, *Bleak
House* offers a complicated but, in many respects, typical example of ingrained
liberal resistance toward collectivist forms of governance. Although Dickens
was not himself a dogmatic antistatist (a type that he gleefully caricatured in
Mr. Podsnap in *Our Mutual Friend*), his fiction tends, on the whole, to recoil
from modern governing strategies. *Bleak House* thus dramatizes a paradox that
runs deep in liberalism: it figures the desire for an impossible pastoral authority
that is rational but unbureaucratic, omnipresent but personal, authoritative but
liberatory, efficient but English. This is a topic that resonates with students who
may look to government for solutions to a range of problems (global warming,
national security, disaster relief) even as they witness government's repeated
failures and hear much of the inherent superiority of the market.

Teaching D. A. Miller's still-important reading of *Bleak House* is an excellent way to highlight liberalism's deep-seated paradoxes ("Discipline"). Miller's
chapter, which is indebted to Foucault's *Discipline and Punish*, offers a dazzling but ultimately anachronistic interpretation of Dickens's novel. Nonetheless, it remains a stimulating classroom tool. Miller reads Chancery as the
symbol of a fully fledged tutelary state that had yet to emerge.[11] In actuality,
what *Bleak House* figures are not the docile objects of panoptical discipline
but, rather, the same dangerously neglected social body that was depicted
in contemporaneous debates over sanitary reform (see Brundage; Childers;
Finer; Lewis; Logan; and Poovey). With the exception of the uniformed police,
praised by Esther for its efficiency (867), the novel declines to present modern
institutions as offering suitable aid for the nation's ills. Thus, though Inspector
Bucket possesses the skills necessary to solving Mr. Tulkinghorn's murder, his

impressive detective agency is undone by the entrenched social quandaries at the novel's heart.

Such limitations are made glaringly apparent in the famous scene in which Bucket shines his "lighted bull's eye" on the "stinking ruins" of Tom-all-Alone's, a must-read for in-class discussion. Questioning the brickmakers' wives, he indifferently surveys the same "undrained" streets and raging "fever-houses" that recent sanitary reforms (still unfolding as the novel was serialized) had publicized but not redressed (358). As he advises the battered Liz to raise her infant "respectable," his high-handed treatment recalls Mrs. Pardiggle, another "inexorable moral policeman," "pouncing upon the poor" (361, 132, 483). The novel thus makes clear that the detective polices for the status quo, his new-fangled agency ultimately being channeled back into deadlock. This is not a Foucauldian paradox but an exploitative deployment of disciplinary power with material foundations in the mid-century alliance between middle-class and landed interests. Thus the underside of Bucket's masterful allure is his being, on the one hand, the hired tool of Sir Leicester and, on the other, the official of a post–New Poor Law order that requires the impoverished to "move on" at the convenience of those who thrive off their exploitation (308). Students might wish to discuss the difference between this "neoliberal" reading of *Bleak House*, inspired by Foucault's later essays on governmentality, and the disciplinary reading that, in Miller's essay, took *Discipline and Punish* for its cue. Though neoliberalism requires the exercise of state power, both within and across national borders, its advent calls for nuanced distinctions between the market's discipline and that of the state—distinctions already apparent in the pages of *Bleak House*.

In 1852, while writing the first number of *Bleak House*, Dickens was helping the wealthy Angela Burdett-Coutts choose a real-life Tom-all-Alone's to be cleared: a classic example of Victorian voluntarism. Significantly, Dickens rejected the expert advice of Mr. Field—the detective on whom Bucket is modeled—in favor of Dr. Southwood Smith, a member of the recently instituted General Board of Health (see Butt and Tillotson 197–98). Yet while Dickens's preference for the doctor's well-rounded social knowledge suggests a model pastoral agency, *Bleak House* almost entirely refrains from representing it. Whereas Bucket is an obvious tribute to Field, there is no comparable attempt to portray Southwood Smith's role as physician-reformer—no picture of the charismatic, middle-class professional expert, appointed to an embattled board but determined to push through deadlock to provide much-needed pastoral care.[12] What Dickens represents instead is Allan Woodcourt, one of the least well developed characters in *Bleak House*. The doctor's role in addressing Britain's multifarious social ills is displaced in an episode that occurs thousands of miles from Tom-all-Alone's. Following a shipwreck in the East Indian seas, Esther's "dear physician" "[s]aved many lives, never complained in hunger and thirst, wrapped naked people in his spare clothes, took the lead, showed them what to do, governed them, tended the sick, buried the dead, and brought the poor survivors safely off at last!" (568–69).

Here is precisely the comprehensive pastoral agency necessary to implementing effective social reform. It is all the more significant, then, that Dickens neither installs Woodcourt in the civil service nor depicts him as an activist for local or voluntary sanitary improvements. For all his symbolic potential, Woodcourt is no more (or less) than an exemplary neighborhood doctor. Hence, like the revitalization of Sir Leicester's noblesse oblige and the stress on Esther's feminine domesticity, Woodcourt's private paternalism—representing what is least modern in middle-class reformers such as Southwood Smith—is conservative. In this respect, the conclusion of *Bleak House* favors the normative self-reliance, local autonomy, and ardent voluntarism of the Gladstonean liberal era to come—even though the novel depicts that very mode of governmentality as mired in class interest, political inertia, institutional archaism, and pastoral neglect.

Of course, Dickens's ambivalent support for state authority is not surprising. Although the public speaker mocked the Englishman's provincial fear of "centralization" (*Speeches* 107), the novelist created works that "as a whole [are] not centralized" (Arac 183). On the one hand, *Bleak House* implies that reforming antiquated institutions such as Chancery is crucial to the nation's well-being. On the other, the novel's implicit wish for an England resembling the interior of Bleak House—"pleasantly irregular" and "old-fashioned rather than old" (86)—recalls William Blackstone's well-known defense of the English law as "an old gothic castle": "venerable," "cheerful and commodious" despite its "winding and difficult" approaches (qtd. in M. Stone 128–29).[13] Dickens's inability imaginatively to render a modern pastoral agency like Southwood Smith's thus suggests a consciousness trapped between incompatible worldviews.

Like so much antistatist discourse today, *Bleak House* cannot visualize a collective foundation on which safely to ground the deployment of modern expertise. That is especially evident in the novel's terrifying depiction of Mr. Tulkinghorn. Lady Dedlock's chilling description suggests the very type of bureaucratic impersonality: he is "mechanically faithful without attachment" and "indifferent to everything but his calling" (581). Yet it is worth emphasizing that Tulkinghorn is more a prototype for privatization than a government official, and his expertise is even more unaccountable than the do-nothing aristocratic regime it aims to supplant. Jeremy Bentham had believed that official power could be safely monitored by public vigilance. But Dickens's novel, much like the contemporaneous writings of Mill, evokes the diminished agency of average citizens such as the "puzzle[d]" Mr. Snagsby (406). Indeed, from his foggy vantage the novel's most signal governing failure is the disabled civic agency of the ordinary middle classes. Much like Mill's analyses of bourgeois modernity, the novel shows that though mid-century Britain lacked the centralized state apparatuses of the Continent, it did not lack the tendency to render individuals dependent on and enmeshed in social forces beyond their control.[14] Here is another aspect of *Bleak House* likely to resonate for students who are often called on to exert their agency as consumers rather than citizens, only to discover that neither position is especially empowering.

Bleak House's gloomy social prognosis is, however, partly offset by the uncompromised pastoral care attributed to selfless feminine domesticity (exemplified by Esther, the working-class Mrs. Bagnet, and the domesticated professional Woodcourt). The novel thus strives to defend the home along with the gender mythologies on which the home's exceptional qualities rely. Since such defense involves an antifeminist satire on female philanthropists such as Mrs. Jellyby and Mrs. Pardiggle, Dickens's novel is pitted against an important movement to organize charity—a project that many contemporaries believed would provide the efficient but personal pastorship so ardently looked for in *Bleak House*.[15] It is therefore crucial to recognize that the notion of Mrs. Pardiggle as an "inexorable moral policeman" was far less absurd to contemporaries than the novel's burlesque treatment implies. Rather, Mrs. Pardiggle's activities illustrated a venerated civic tradition: as it expanded throughout the century, the practice of home visiting became increasingly influential and identified with the authority of social science. An unmistakably British blend of voluntarism and professionalism, private and public agency, collectivism and self-help, the figure of the mid-Victorian visitor cum social worker—including the iconic lady visitor—provided an important ideological synthesis around which alternatively statist, localist, or voluntarist versions of modern pastoral agency might flourish. Thus, although proponents of organized charity were determined to obviate state intervention, their activities ultimately led "to the development of the professional, and eventually state-employed, social worker" (Perkin 24).[16]

Dickens's recoil from Mrs. Pardiggle, like the absence of a fictional Southwood Smith, is symptomatic of the paradoxes of a self-consciously liberal society. Victorian society manifestly lacked the kind of order, method, and efficiency that makes the Bagnet family thrive. But neither Dickens nor many of his contemporaries were prepared to vest such comprehensive powers in any but the most homely and charismatic of agencies. In the relatively prosperous years that followed the publication of *Bleak House*, Britain's liberal social order was stabilized and strengthened. It was not until the very different circumstances of the fin de siècle that the quest for efficiency became sufficiently broad to weaken the culture of antistatism (see Searle). In its impassioned critique of inadequate governance, Dickens's mid-century fiction can be likened to the stymied efforts of ambitious reformers such as Sir James Kay-Shuttleworth and Edwin Chadwick. Yet, though Dickens publicly supported the state's limited involvement in education and public health, his novels perpetuated the liberal mindset that helped retard such efforts. The creator of the ominous Tulkinghorn and the officious Pardiggle had done his share to solidify the Victorian predisposition to favor the "pleasantly irregular" over the rational and bureaucratic.

Despite many significant differences between Dickens's time and our own, *Bleak House* thus tells a very timely story. Ironically, neoliberalism's tendency to cast government as inefficient and outmoded has made the archaic Chancery a resonant metaphor for the twenty-first century's perception of big government. Yet in a way that Dickens might not have predicted, Tulkinghorn seems to figure the kind of unaccountable expertise that students may associate more with the power of the private sector. Students may thus contrast mid-Victorian perceptions of governing dilemmas to those of our own day. Although it would be wrong to suggest that neoliberalism has simply turned back the clock, asking students to decide what has changed—to describe how *Bleak House* might have been different were it written today—is the kind of exercise that might make them more alive to government as well as more attentive to Dickens's writing.

Of course, the rights of citizenship are no longer limited to middle-class males such as Mr. Snagsby. In this sense the democratization promised by Victorian notions of character has formally materialized. But formal equality often functions to mask the impact of socioeconomic differences that continue to persist along lines of class, gender, and race (see Young). In fact, under neoliberalism inequality has dramatically increased: in Britain "overall income inequality was greater in the mid-1990s than at any time in the forty years from the late 1940s" (John Hills, qtd. in Lister 112), and in the United States (the country that provided many ideological resources for the Thatcher revolution), inequality has, since the Reagan years, climbed steadily under Republican and Democratic administrations (see Duggan). Such regressive economic trends, coincident with declining voter participation, have prompted commentators to describe the return to a "Victorian pattern of income distribution" (Edward Luttwak, qtd. in Frank 13). At the same time, conservative critics of the welfare state laud self-help in the manner of Samuel Smiles and embrace "Victorian values" by way of promoting the merits of a rigorous individualism (see Hadley). Does a reading of *Bleak House* support this conservative vision of neoliberalism as neo-Victorianism?

For me, the answer is no. Victorians such as Dickens and Mill were, to be sure, anxious about the modern state; for Mill the question of the state's pastoral role was "one of the most difficult and complicated questions in the art of government" (*On Liberty* 164). Nonetheless, both Victorians regarded the building of human potential as a social project of the highest importance. Both therefore rejected the notion that the more just, humane, and intellectually vital world they hoped for would emerge through laissez-faire orthodoxy—and still less that the market authorized such political "slumber" (Mill, "Civilization" 136).[17] My point is not that we today would choose to visualize social democracy through the class and gender strategies that Dickens employs in *Bleak House*: the novelist was hardly a consistently equalitarian thinker. But we can help our students understand Dickens's profound recognition that positive liberty, along with the kind of individuality it might foster, is inevitably a collective enterprise—not a self-interested pursuit, a negative ideal of noninterference, or the narrow expression of consumer choices. Students will not find any simple answers in *Bleak House*. Instead they will find a work that, for all its foggy puzzlement, insists that prevailing modes of governance be discussed and not simply accepted as the divinely or naturally sanctioned expression of the so-called free market.

NOTES

[1] This United States–derived usage of liberalism is not found in Europe, where more avowedly socialist and labor-oriented forms of democratic politics took the place of a left-leaning liberalism so-called. But New Deal liberalism can be roughly equated to the Keynesian economic policies that exerted a dominant influence over British governance from the interwar period until the Margaret Thatcher years.

[2] As a political philosophy, liberalism signifies an order in which the state's perceived function is "to secure the freedom of individuals on a formally egalitarian basis" (Brown, par. 7). Although left and right interpretations of political liberalism differ considerably, especially insofar as left liberals regard such freedom as a collective project that requires the state's intervention, leftists of a more radical stripe tend to critique liberalism of either cast—sometimes without distinguishing between the two.

[3] Such ideologies are neoliberal because they reject the welfare and regulatory state in favor of the laissez-faire tenets of classical political economy. Yet, as Regenia Gagnier argues, few classical political economists "were prepared to say, as free marketers have been boasting" in the post-Soviet era, that the market "was the highest form of society" (9; cf. 61–89). The economist Joseph Stiglitz concisely describes neoliberalism as a "simplistic model of the market economy" in which "Adam Smith's invisible hand works, and works perfectly" (74). But the so-called free market of today is, in fact, heavily subsidized by government, and industrializing economies have historically relied, and continue to rely, on concerted state activity. For detailed discussions of neoliberalism's impact on Western welfare states, see Clarke and the essays collected in Kingfisher. On United States cultural contexts see Duggan.

[4] I use "pastorship" and "pastoral care" to describe modes of governance located inside and outside the state. As in the study from which the present essay partly derives (see Goodlad, *Victorian Literature*), my usage is inspired by Michel Foucault, who, in his later essays on "governmentality," developed notions of pastorship by way of analyzing the kinds of governing practices that tend to develop in self-consciously liberal societies (e.g., "Governmentality," "Social Security," "Space," and "Subject"). As Brown explains, governmentality "moves away from sovereign and state-centered notions of political power (though it does not eschew the state as a site of governmentality)" (17n2).

[5] In my own teaching I find that using current events—something from the day's paper, a recently aired episode of a popular television program, a song in the charts, or a recent movie—is often a more effective way of introducing present-day political contexts into the literature classroom than is a more concerted approach (not least because it enables students to draw their own conclusions). That said, a course designed to teach such contexts more substantively might use excerpts from Brown; Duggan; Frank; Gagnier; or Stiglitz to provide a rich (if more polemical) understanding of neoliberalism today.

[6] As Catherine Kingfisher shows, the neoliberal restructuring of welfare states in the West corresponds to the structural adjustments imposed on the non-West ("Introduction" 5).

[7] On the New Liberalism of the late-Victorian and Edwardian era see Freeden; Searle; and Simhony and Weinstein.

[8] For a reading of *Bleak House* that emphasizes such exclusion, see Vanden Bossche.

[9] On middle-class character building see, e.g., Gunn; Behlmer, "Character" and *Friends*. On Anglicist colonial policy, which purported to "anglicize" Indians through English education, see Stokes; Viswanathan.

[10] Under the principles of 1834, pauperism would be discouraged by the administering of poor relief for the able-bodied only within the confines of the workhouse. But the history of the New Poor Law is complicated for three main reasons: first, local officials often ignored such centralized recommendations; second, relief of the able-bodied unemployed in workhouses was economically impracticable as well as politically untenable; and, third, many of the destitute poor were not, in fact, able-bodied. For teachers of *Bleak House* what is important to bear in mind is that though the New Poor Law was unpopular (Dickens critiqued it in novels such as *Oliver Twist*, *Little Dorrit*, and *Our Mutual Friend*), it was successful in rendering the idea of dependence on poor relief shameful and stigmatic (e.g., Betty Higden in *Our Mutual Friend*). For general historical accounts of the New Poor Law, see the essays by Rose and Mandler and the studies by Crowther; Thompson; and Wood.

[11] On Miller's reading of *Bleak House* and subsequent critiques by Blake and by P. Morris (Imagining), see the "Materials" section in this volume. For an early response to Miller, see La Capra. Other discussions of *Bleak House* that are influenced by Foucault include Robbins (in part a critique of Miller's reading); Danahay; Fasick; and Reitz's recent study, which argues for a strong connection between Victorian detective fiction and the imperial project.

[12] For insights into the impact of class politics on such efforts see R. Johnson; Gowan. On Victorian professionalism see Perkin and, with reference to *Bleak House*, P. Morris, "*Bleak House*."

[13] Students might be asked to look for other instances in which the novel represents government metaphorically; likewise, they might want to think about the kinds of metaphors used to describe private and public sectors in our own popular culture.

[14] In early essays such as "Civilization" (1836) and again in *On Liberty* (1859), Mill argues that material progress tends to deteriorate character and diminish individual power.

[15] The purpose of *Bleak House*'s antifeminism is specifically to shield feminine domesticity's crucial harborage of personalized pastorship. For Dickens, that quality is vitiated once domestic functions take on the cast of administrative machinery, a trend similarly lamented by Thomas Carlyle in his 1829 essay "Signs of the Times" (467). On organized charity see Behlmer, *Friends*; on women's importance to organized charity see also Summers and Prochaska. For a critique of the recent interest in "faith-based" alternatives to social welfare, see Willis.

[16] Gender is a crucial feature of this process: the dramatic "rise" of professional society described by historians such as Perkin developed partly through the appropriation of modes of pastoral authority associated with women and femininity. Women's "feminine" claims on voluntary social work eventually lost out to men's "masculine" claims on professional employment. But whereas the emergence of the welfare state was thus facilitated

by the appropriation of feminine pastoral credentials, the ongoing neoliberal assault on welfare entails a reversed gender strategy—as when the welfare state is derided in popular British media as an infantilizing nanny state.

[17] The novel produces a vigorous critique of market value that, for all its bleakness, could not be further from today's quasi-religious faith in the market. According to Frank, the market has become the purest expression of the people, "*more* democratic than any of the formal institutions of democracy" (29). To imagine Dickens as affirming such a view, one would need to envision novels that glamorize the antics of Scrooge, Bounderby, Smallweed, the Veneerings, et al. (see Bigelow).

Teaching *Bleak House* in a Comparative Literature Course: Dickens, Hugo, and the Social Question

Michal Peled Ginsburg

One of the ways the social, ideological, and formal features of *Bleak House* can be presented to students in a critical fashion is by teaching the novel together with other nineteenth-century novels dealing with social disparity or social injustice. Such a course can include Elizabeth Gaskell's *Mary Barton*, Victor Hugo's *Les Misérables*, and Emile Zola's *Germinal*; with a somewhat different emphasis, Fyodor Dostoyevsky's *Brothers Karamzov* can be substituted for the novels by Gaskell and Zola. In what follows I limit myself to *Bleak House* and *Les Misérables*.[1] Assuming that readers of this volume are more familiar with Dickens's novel than with Hugo's, my emphasis will be primarily on *Les Misérables*, which I compare to *Bleak House* at appropriate points; for further discussion of the social question in *Bleak House* readers will usefully consult other essays in this volume, especially those by Timothy Carens, Janice Carlisle, and Lauren Goodlad. Since Hugo's novel is too long to be taught in its entirety and abridged versions distort its focus, I suggest reading the novel's first part, "Fantine," and complementing it with the viewing of one of the novel's filmic adaptations. Discussion of *Les Misérables* should precede that of *Bleak House* (despite chronology) since it more directly deals with the issues of poverty, delinquency, and social injustice.

To begin discussion of *Les Misérables*, instructors can ask students to reflect on the novel's title. They quickly discover that "misérable" means not only wretched and unfortunate but also despicable and that the noun "un misérable" means a wretch, a scoundrel, a rascal. Hugo, in other words, equates the poor with the delinquent, and students can be asked to speculate on the reasons for this choice (and thus about Dickens's choice to represent the "good poor," such as Charley). The discussion of the title can then focus on the difference between titles that refer to an individual and those that refer to a category, especially since the novel was originally entitled *Jean Tréjean* (as Jean Valjean was first named). This discussion can help highlight, later on, the particularity of *Bleak House* as a title. The change in title raises the question of the status of Jean Valjean as a hero (an outstanding individual) and as a type (an example for a larger category), a question that can lead to an examination of the novel's structure. A quick look at the table of contents will show students that Jean Valjean gives his name to the last book of the novel. In the first part, it takes 52 pages for Valjean to appear and another 13 pages for him to be named. Similarly, Fantine does not appear until 120 pages into the part of the novel that bears her name. Students can be asked to consider this peculiar way of beginning the novel and the extent to which it contradicts our reading expectations.

The peculiar way the novel begins means that Jean Valjean appears against the background of Monseigneur Myriel. Students' first reaction may be that Myriel is unrealistically good whereas Jean Valjean, who steals a loaf of bread to feed his hungry family, is both real and typical. It is relatively easy to show students that Myriel is in fact both typical and real. As the title of the part of the novel that centers on him suggests, he is the type of the "just man" and, as he himself says, "To be a saint is the exception; to be a just man is the rule" (*Les Misérables* [ed. Gohin] 49; *Les Misérables* [trans. Denny] 29–30).[2] Myriel is also the character most clearly modeled on a real person, Monseigneur Miollis, a former bishop of Digne. If Myriel's behavior is atypical in the sense of different from that of all around him, it is because as the type of the true Christian, he reenacts the radical reversal of established social order that is at the origin of Christianity. Clarifying this point will allow students to formulate the fundamental difference between the French and the British approach to the social question as that between a revolutionary tradition and a tradition of reform (it will also help them understand Myriel's encounter with the "conventionnel" in vol. 1, bk. 1, ch. 10).

Students' sense that Myriel is not realistic may have to do with their understanding of type as representing an average. Dickens and Hugo resemble each other in creating types that are extremes rather than averages; the difference in the way they use these extreme types is related to the fundamental difference between their social agendas. Hugo uses types (Myriel, Javert) to show the limits of certain positions, their inadequacy for solving the social question, thus suggesting the need for a radical change. Dickens's extreme types (Chadband, Mrs. Jellyby) are parodies used to expose the abuse of certain social practices; the parody implies that these practices, if not abused, would be beneficial for the social order, so the parody serves as a call for reform. The example of Vholes is particularly interesting. Vholes is not only the perfect type of the small-time lawyer, "diligent, persevering, steady, acute in business" (622), but also the embodiment of the "one great principle of the English law," which is "to make business for itself" (621). But in parodying Vholes, Dickens suggests that the lawyer's exploitation of his clients to make a living is merely an abuse of a practice (which can be reformed) rather than the inevitable product of the current social structure. By contrast, Hugo never parodies Javert, the man who represents absolute adherence to the letter of the law; he thus suggests the limits of a legalistic understanding of social relations.

The delayed appearance of Jean Valjean indicates that the *misérables* become subjects (and thus possible characters in a novel) only through their becoming subject *to* the law and to charity. The same is true about the way Jo, Jenny, and Charley enter *Bleak House*, and a comparison along these lines can structure the discussion of the two novels.

The life story of Jean before his encounter with the law and with charity shows that the misery of the *misérables* is not only the lack of money, food, and work. It is also the lack of identity, of history, of interiority (thoughts, sentiments, desires)—that is, the lack of everything we deem essential to being, and being recognized as, a human being. Representing *les misérables* otherwise would be to falsify their predicament by reducing the enormity of their deprivation. Students can be asked to discuss how (and whether) one *can* represent them without either falsifying their condition or rendering them totally other.

A comparison of Dickens's treatment of Jo with Hugo's presentation of Jean Valjean can help focus such a discussion and prepare students for evaluating the solutions adopted by Dickens and Hugo. In the inquest passage (176–77) Dickens presents Jo through the parodied lens of the law. The distance we as readers feel from the formal and complacent attitude of the impersonal authority of the law allows us to sympathize with Jo despite his difference (especially since he shows moral sense by knowing "it's wicked to tell a lie" [177]). In the passage speculating on what Jo's thoughts may be (257–58) the narrator insists on Jo's difference from us, his strangeness, while at the same time attributing to Jo some consciousness of his difference (which is, actually, a verbalization of our reading experience). By giving Jo rudimentary morality and consciousness, Dickens thus mitigates Jo's strangeness even while emphasizing it. Hugo, on the other hand, attempts to tell Valjean's story (in the chapter that bears his name, vol. 1, bk. 2, ch. 6) in a way that reveals his complete lack of subjecthood (voice, thoughts, memory). This chapter should be the focus of close reading since it shows most clearly Hugo's understanding of *les misérables* through his particular manipulation of syntax, style, and narrative voice. Discussing the differences between the English translation and the original can be an effective way of making Hugo's emphasis visible to students.[3]

Jean's lack of identity is indicated by his lack of name. Jean, a common name, is also his father's; his mother and sister have the same name, Jeanne, the feminine version of Jean. He does not have a true family name (Valjean, a contraction of "voilà Jean," is merely a nickname repeating the given name). The sister's children are called "the Valjean children" though her married name must have been different. Jean's lack of social identity is indicated also by his lack of a specific place in the family: in his relation to his sister, he occupies the positions of brother, son, and husband.

Jean lacks interiority: though characterized as "thoughtful" and affectionate, he is also "dull" [*endormi*] and "insignificant" (135; 92); he hardly talks; he does not have a sweetheart. His care for his sister and her children is described without attributing to him either agency ("This was done simply, as a duty" [135; 92]) or intention (he paid for the neighbor's milk, "and the children were not punished" [136; 92]). His life story, told primarily in the imperfect, lacks events; it is "the same story" (138; 94) as that of all the *misérables*. Barely individuated, the *misérables* are invisible to the social world that surrounds them and from which they disappear without leaving a trace: "The church-tower of what had once been their village forgot them; the boundary-stone of what had once been their field forgot them" (138; 94). The *misérables* are so reduced in their humanity that they apparently lack even the ability to forget; they are so ignored by other human beings that only the inanimate objects that define social life around them—the church steeple, the boundary stone—forget them (and in so doing appear more human than they do).

The passage describing the theft of the loaf of bread, on the other hand, begins with a clear temporal indication, Sunday evening (later on the year is mentioned), and is told in the past perfect (136; 93). The subject of the actions is a character designated by his proper name, family name, profession, and place of employment. While describing what the baker heard, saw, and did, the passage also sketches the process by which a specific person emerges out of indistinction ("a violent blow," "an arm," "a thief") and is recognized: "It was Jean Valjean." The paragraph reads like a legal deposition, though we know (and if we don't, Dickens would remind us) that a real legal deposition would not be in fact anything like this. Whereas Dickens presents the language of the law as an abuse of human communication (Kenge's correspondence with Esther), Hugo chooses to represent the point of view of the law in a language that any schoolchild would understand (students can note the textbook examples of the interplay of perfect and imperfect tenses as well as the use of the most basic vocabulary). This simplicity is enhanced by an impression of neutrality: the short narrative seems to lack a point of view; it is as if the facts speak for themselves. The point of view of the law, which renders visible Jean Valjean, a criminal, is that of standard language, index of social normativity.

Students easily understand that under the gaze of the law Jean Valjean would emerge as a specific, recognizable individual, a character in a particular story: the law cannot register a crime without identifying an individual and an act, located in time and space. But Hugo goes even further. Though we are told that in prison Valjean has lost all individual identity (137; 94), we know that this identity was attenuated to begin with. On the other hand, in what reads like a Foucauldian analysis *avant la lettre*, Hugo shows how under the gaze of the law (and its attendant disciplines) Valjean becomes a character endowed with affectivity (he weeps), speech (he repeats, "I was a pruner at Faverolles"), and intentions (his hand movements indicate that he committed the crime to feed seven little children [137; 94]). The events of his life are now dated and correlated with historical events; he is remembered by others (the turnkey); he has his own story—that of his failed escapes—which, though repetitive, shows some variations; he undergoes change, he "develops" (140; 96).

If both Hugo and Dickens show that the poor, the *misérables*, become visible to society only when they become subject to the law and to charity, Hugo claims that this encounter also prevents them from ever becoming part of society. This argument (elaborated in vol. 1, bk. 2, ch. 7) is based on the notion that justice, whose function is to regulate social relations, means a balance (between crime and punishment, between debt and payment) and that while this balanced economy functions within society, it does not apply to the *misérables* who, by this very fact, remain always outside it. In *Bleak House*, by contrast, Dickens's insistence on the way the destinies of people from different walks of life are interwoven means that the relation of Esther to Charley, Jenny, and Jo, a relation that brings those three characters into our field of vision as objects of charity, is as much part of this interconnectedness as the relation between Tulkinghorn and George or that between Jo and Jenny. Though the objectification of the poor through charity is made visible (Charley is a "gift" to Esther from Jarndyce) and class distinctions are clearly marked (Charley will never learn proper English), society, as a web of relations, encompasses them all.

Students readily understand how the law in *Les Misérables* fails to mete justice. The punishment, which was supposed to pay for the crime, was so out of proportion to the crime that it created a new debt, this time, of society toward the individual. Jean Valjean's sense that society has incurred a debt toward him pushes him to seek restitution by committing further crimes (the theft of the bishop's silverware), which would cause new punishments, and so on, ad infinitum. But this is not all: if the punishment is a payment exacted for the crime, having paid for his crime (indeed, in excess of his crime) Jean Valjean should now be considered innocent. The yellow passport he has to carry marks him, however, as a criminal: not only an ex-convict but a "very dangerous man" (124; 85). Jean Valjean was neither a criminal nor a dangerous man when he entered prison but has become one there; the punishment neither erases the crime nor reforms a criminal but creates the criminal whom society then continues to punish. This injustice is expressed as a lack of balance: Jean Valjean feels that he is forever caught "entre un défaut et un excès" 'between lack and excess' (142; 97).

The act of charity of the bishop, by its very excess (he not only forgives the theft of the silverware but gives Jean the candlesticks), is meant to counter the excess of the law. It is intended by Myriel, and understood subsequently by Jean Valjean, as an act of redemptive love, of grace, that goes beyond (in)justice and annuls all debts. Students should be challenged to question this understanding by noting some details in the scene between Myriel and Valjean (163; 111) that strike a wrong note: Myriel evokes a promise Jean Valjean has never made; rather than give him the gift of love, he makes him a party to an exchange and demands something in return (a promise); we normally associate the purchase of a man's soul with the devil rather than with God's emissary. Tellingly, the bishop uses the word *achète* ("buy") and not the word *rachète* ("redeem"); though he is generous and compassionate, he does not sacrifice himself for Jean Valjean's sake; he gives not his blood but his candlesticks. This is, of course, as it should be; the bishop is not a saint but a "just man" (and justice is a matter of balanced exchange, not of sacrifice). Though the words the bishop speaks are supposed to perform Jean Valjean's conversion ("you no longer belong to what is evil but to what is good"), this is not quite what happens: leaving the bishop's house for the second time, Jean Valjean commits the crime against "petit Gervais," arguably a worse one than the theft of bread or of the silverware. The symmetry of conversion—the sinner dies to be reborn as a just man—is disturbed by this act of which Hugo says, "[I]n robbing the boy he had committed an act of which he was no longer capable" (171; 117). Belonging neither to the man he was nor to the man he will become, this crime is an excess that prevents the balancing of accounts.

Though repentant and reformed, Jean Valjean can never stop being a *misérable*, that is, become part of society. As M. Madeleine, Valjean clearly models himself on Myriel, but subsequent events show the difference between them. The Champmathieu episode (vol. 1, bk. 7), like the incident with Fauchelevent (vol. 1, bk. 5, ch. 6), shows that a *misérable* has no other choice but to be a *misérable*: if he remains silent and lets Champmathieu die in his stead, he commits a despicable act and is indeed *un misérable*; if he reveals his identity and saves Champmathieu, he becomes again Jean Valjean, a *misérable*. Jean Valjean saves Fauchelevant, crushed under the cart, and saves Champmathieu, as he will later on save Marius and Javert. But every moral act means for him a sacrifice: it entails both risking his life and rebecoming a *misérable*. Esther (somewhat like Myriel) also risks her life by caring for others (giving shelter to Jo, she catches his disease). But though Esther's selflessness is admirable (and made all the more so by contrast to Skimpole's selfishness), she is never called on to make a choice between her moral integrity and her place in society. The heroic excess of Jean Valjean should be read then less as an admirable character trait than as the result and expression of his being outside society, a *misérable*.

Like Dickens, Hugo is often accused of simplifying reality by presenting it in black and white and idealizing it by showing the triumph of good over evil. This issue can be a topic for discussion after both novels have been read. With regard to *Bleak House*, the important point in the context of the social problem is that Esther's perfect goodness, her difference from the parodied characters, and her marriage with Woodcourt at the end of the novel suggest that society can be reformed through discrete, personal acts of goodness and selflessness (rather than through a direct change to institutions such as Chancery). With regard to *Les Misérables*, the instructor should challenge students' initial impression that the bishop and Javert represent the opposites of good and evil by showing them both the limits of the bishop's goodness and Hugo's insistence on Javert's positive qualities. Javert incarnates not evil as opposed to goodness but rather "tout le mauvais du bon" " 'all the evil of what is good' " (389; 268). Similarly, the opposition between Javert and Valjean (the hunter and the hunted) is nuanced: like Valjean, Javert is an outcast ("there are two classes of men whom society keeps inexorably out of bounds: those who attack it and those who protect it" [240; 165]); their similarity is indicated by the anagrammatic relation between their names (Ja-vert, Val-jean). Thus good and evil are far from opposed to each other.

The first part of *Les Misérables* certainly does not end in the triumph of good over evil; the description of Fantine's death, despite its reference to God, does not communicate the sense of closure we find in Jo's death scene. There, a final change has occurred: "The light is come upon the dark benighted way" (734), whereas for Fantine no such change takes place: "She was put [literally, thrown, not "laid to rest," as the English translation has it] in a public grave. Her tomb resembled her bed" (400; 275). By the end of the novel, Jean Valjean is dead too, his grave nameless; his heroic sacrifices have not produced a better world. Unlike Dickens, Hugo does not offer a solution to the social problem. And yet the novel by its very existence implies a hope for a better world, a hope that, as Hugo acknowledges, is incompatible with strict realism: a realist author, he says, an "observant physiologist" (not "psychologist," as the English translation has it) would never have written a novel about *les misérables* and, by thus turning his back on them, "would have effaced from that life the word which God's finger has written on the brow of every man: Hope" (144; 98–99). By writing his novel, Hugo expresses hope since doing otherwise would be denying *les misérables* their humanity.

NOTES

[1] My discussion of *Les Misérables* is greatly indebted to Guy Rosa's *Victor Hugo:* Les Misérables, especially the essays by Rosa ("Histoire sociale") and Richard; to Rosa et al.'s *Lire* Les Misérables, especially the essays by Rosa ("Jean Valjean [1, 2, 6]") and Vernier ("*Les Misérables*: Un texte intraitable"); and to Vernier's "*Les Misérables*: Ce livre est dangereux."

[2] All further references to the novel will be to these editions and will be given parenthetically in the text, French original followed by English translation. Translation was silently modified when necessary.

[3] For example, Hugo writes about Jean Valjean, "Quand il eut l'âge d'homme, il était émondeur à Faverolles" (135). Literally: "When he reached adulthood, he was a pruner at Faverolles." This wording sounds as strange in French as in English: what we expect to read is "he became." As written, the sentence creates the impression that he has always been a pruner; his life lacks events (just as he lacks individuality and interiority). The strangeness of the sentence (especially when opposed to the textbook grammaticality of the account of the theft) suggests the difficulty of representing the life of the *misérables* in normal language. The Penguin translation renders this sentence as "When he was old enough he had gone to work as a tree-pruner at Faverolles" (92). Not only does it create an event, it also adds agency (he does not passively "become" but actively "goes to work"); the rendering of "eut l'âge d'homme" as "when he was old enough" carries a suggestion, absent in the original, that his childhood was not affected by the need to work. The Signet translation (by Fahnestock and MacAfee, based on Wilbour) goes even further by saying, "When he had come of age, he chose the occupation of a pruner at Faverolles" (168). This is a middle-class Jean Valjean, choosing a profession! As happens quite often, older translations are more accurate. An 1893 translation by William Walton says, "When he was of man's age he was a pruner of trees at Faverolles" (168). The repetition of "was" eliminates, however, the difference between "eut" and "était" and thus eliminates the shock we get when we read the perfect where we expected the imperfect.

Fever and AIDS:
Teaching *Bleak House* in South Africa

Carrol Clarkson

In chapter 2 of *Our Mutual Friend*, guests at the Veneerings' banquet engage in stagey dinner-table talk about the Man from Somewhere. It is no simple matter to determine just precisely where he comes from: Jamaica? No. "Tobago, then . . . Man from Nowhere, perhaps! . . . Man from Tumwhere!" Eventually Mortimer Lightwood languidly promises to enlighten the company:

> "Sorry to destroy romance by fixing him with a local habitation, but he comes from the place, the name of which escapes me, but will suggest itself to everybody else here, where they make the wine."
>
> Eugene suggests "Day and Martin's."
>
> "No, not that place," returns the unmoved Mortimer, "that's where they make the Port. My man comes from the country where they make the Cape Wine." (55)

It is in this exotic, unnamed country that I teach *Bleak House*. It is a curious sensation to be placed, by a literary text, in foreign parts, to feel subject to being "softened by distance and unfamiliarity," in the paradoxical instant of reading about Jo as "the ordinary home-made article" (*Bleak House* 724). Dickens writes in his preface to *Bleak House* that he has "purposely dwelt upon the romantic side of familiar things" (7), but clearly, from our perspective, that which constitutes the familiar in the first place is up for discussion. In what ways can a text establish a connection between the familiar and the unfamiliar, between different continents and different centuries? More than a hundred and fifty years after the publication of *Bleak House*, students in an English literature classroom in Africa invariably ask, "How does this text speak to and engage *us, here, today*?" One way I address this question is through a discussion of *Bleak House* in relation to a contemporary South African novel: Phaswane Mpe's *Welcome to Our Hillbrow* (2001). I focus the discussion on questions of urban community and social responsibility, making particular reference to Dickens's representation of fever in Tom-all-Alone's and Mpe's representation of HIV/AIDS in contemporary Hillbrow, an inner-city neighborhood of Johannesburg.

My point of departure, in ascertaining what constitutes the familiar for Dickens, is to show students photographs of nineteenth-century London. Excerpts from Peter Ackroyd's biography provide a gruesome if attention-capturing narrative for the images, as, for example, the graveyard worker's report: "I have been up to my knees in human flesh by jumping on the bodies so as to cram them into the least possible space at the bottom of the graves in which fresh bodies were afterwards placed" (384). The passage lends graphic intensity to Jo's account of Nemo's burial: "They put him wery nigh the top. They was obliged to stamp upon it to git it in. I could unkiver it for you with my broom" (262). Students are interested and appalled to hear that the new London sewers were only built in the 1860s. Ackroyd's account makes for riveting and horrifying reading:

> The Fleet Ditch which ran beside Holborn Hill was no more than an open sewer which emptied out into the Thames; as did two hundred other sewers. . . . And yet the very same Thames water was pumped into the domestic cisterns of London householders or into standing pipes, without any attempt at filtration. It is recorded that the water had a strange taste and was brownish in colour.   (*Dickens* [1990] 383)

Dickens's London seems worlds apart from that beautiful country where they make the Cape wine, except that one of the photographs I will have shown at this point (unbeknownst to the students) is not of nineteenth-century London at all but of Hillbrow, Johannesburg, 2004. More often than not, the students have not noticed, and this failure provides dramatic and uncomfortable pause for thought; the implications of the unrecognized photograph inform much of our discussion for the rest of the term.

Hillbrow, where Mpe's novel is set, is a residential and commercial area adjacent to the city center of Johannesburg. The neighborhood (which covers less than one square kilometer) has undergone momentous social change in the last century. In 1896 the estimated population of Hillbrow was 300 (Smith, dust jacket); by 1993 it was approximately 30,000 (A. Morris 3), and by 2003 the population was estimated to be over 100,000 during the week and possibly over 200,000 during weekends (Mpe, "'Missing Store'" 190). It is hardly surprising that overflowing sewage, reminiscent of London's cesspools, is sometimes seen there today. Alan Morris cites a managing agent of residential apartments, in Hillbrow in 1993, who recalls that in 1982 she managed thirty-two flats, each with one occupant. By 1993, landlords had placed as many as eighteen occupants in each flat (100). One recalled, "[W]e used to have one handyman servicing eight buildings. We've now got full-time plumbers and electricians. . . . [T]he domestic effluent is a major expense" (100). Until 1991, when the Group Areas Act of 1950 was scrapped, Hillbrow was the legal preserve of white residents, but by 1970 people classified as Indian and Coloured had started moving into the area, and by mid-1993 approximately eighty-five percent of Hillbrow's population was black (Morris 3). Today the population of Hillbrow consists largely of immigrants from the rural areas of South Africa and from other countries in Africa (Mpe, "Missing Store" 188).

This is the setting for Phaswane Mpe's novel. Like Jo of *Bleak House*, the characters are "moving on," as the narrative voice of *Welcome to Our Hillbrow* points out:

There are very few Hillbrowans, if you think about it, who were not originally wanderers from Tiragalong and other rural villages, who have come here, as we have, in search of education and work. Many of the *Makwerekwere* [i.e., foreigners from other parts of Africa] you accuse of this and that are no different to us – *sojourners*, here in search of green pastures.

(18, my emphasis)

The chapter entitled "Refilwe on the Move" ends with Refilwe's "journey to AIDS" (113). Refilwe knows that she will be denied welcome even in her home village of Tiragalong: a return home means "exiting this world amidst the ignorant talk of people who turn . . . diseases into crimes" (116). The links back to Dickens are readily made.

The effects of mass migration into the city invite further comparison between nineteenth-century London and today's Johannesburg. Ackroyd depicts in graphic detail the effects of the sheer pressure of human numbers on the infrastructure of the city; recent accounts of Hillbrow are no less shocking:

I have always seen violent incidents [in the stretch between Goldreich and Caroline streets]: a single shot to the head, or even an *assengai* [sic], a short spear, quickly thrust and removed. Crowds gather, mostly in silence, as calls are made to the police officers who are in sight just a few blocks away, stopping cars in the cocaine zone.

The next block is inhabited by homeless squatters, whose cardboard edifices and stolen shopping carts line mounds of burnt ash from fires they use to cook and keep warm. There is an acrid smell and the incessant sounds of whistles and catcalls. (Simone 414)

The characters in Phaswane Mpe's novel walk a carefully detailed route through the streets of Hillbrow, and since the novel is written entirely in the second person, Mpe's representation of the walk has the effect of taking the reader on a guided tour:

If you are coming from the city centre, the best way to get to Cousin's place is by driving or walking through Twist Street. . . . You cross Wolmarans and three rather obscure streets, Kapteijn, Ockerse and Pieterse. . . . You will then cross Van der Merwe and Goldreich streets. . . . Just cross to the other side of Caroline. On your left-hand side is Christ Church. . . . On your right-hand side is a block of flats called Vickers Place. (6)

On 14 March 2004, I went walking with Phaswane Mpe; his brother, Tamela; and his friend, Thabiso Mohlele; we retraced the footsteps of the characters in the novel. I took the photographs that I show to students, juxtaposing them with passages from Dickens. A photograph of a gutted but occupied apartment block in Twist Street resonates in disturbing ways with the description of Tom-all-Alone's in chapter 16 of *Bleak House*:

> It is a black dilapidated street, avoided by all decent people; [¹] where the crazy houses were seized upon, when their decay was far advanced, by some bold vagrants, who, after establishing their own possession, took to letting them out in lodgings. Now, these tumbling tenements contain, by night, a swarm of misery. As, on the ruined human wretch, vermin parasites appear, so, these ruined shelters have bred a crowd of foul existence that crawls in and out of gaps in walls and boards; and coils itself to sleep, in maggot numbers, where the rain drips in; and comes and goes, fetching and carrying fever, and sowing more evil in its every footprint than Lord Coodle and Sir Thomas Doodle, and the Duke of Foodle and all the fine gentlemen in office, down to Zoodle, shall set right in five hundred years—though born expressly to do it.   (256–57)

In another juxtaposition of image and text, I show students a photograph of a deserted alleyway between Hillbrow and the neighboring area of Braamfontein. In many places in Hillbrow the surface of the street is slimy wet. The smells range through urine, liquor, excrement, rotting refuse, vomit, burning oil, hot tar, offal, exhaust fumes, and something else I have never smelled before or since. I am reminded of Edwin Chadwick's "All smell is disease" (qtd. in Ackroyd, *Dickens* [1990] 383).² We read about the "fever-houses" in *Bleak House*:

> Mr Snagsby passes along the middle of a villainous street, undrained, unventilated, deep in black mud and corrupt water—though the roads are dry elsewhere—and reeking with such smells and sights that he, who has lived in London all his life, can scarce believe his senses.   (358)

By this stage the point is clear: at first glance *Bleak House* appears to have little bearing on matters of contemporary concern for students in South Africa, but the world Dickens evokes is closer to home than we may feel comfortable admitting. This revelation has students going back to chapter 4 of *Bleak House*, "Telescopic Philanthropy," and leafing through the novel to find the passage about Jo in chapter 47:

> He is not one of Mrs Jellyby's lambs, being wholly unconnected with Borrioboola-Gha; he is not softened by distance and unfamiliarity; [he is not a comfort or convenience to anyone, as a pretence afar off for leaving evil things at hand alone;³] he is not a genuine foreign-grown savage; he is the ordinary home-made article.   (724)

In this moment of discomfort students realize that ethical questions Dickens raises about social responsibility in the nineteenth century resonate with preoccupations pertinent to our own time and place. This realization puts a teasing philosophical spin on the notion of what constitutes the familiar and home. Students begin to ask questions about the potential of a literary text to reconfigure the boundaries of these concepts: Jo is from a different century and a different continent—in fact, he is a fictional construct—and yet what the narrative voice says about Jo being "homely" (696) suddenly seems true, for us, in that country where they make the Cape wine. I return to this point on an aesthetic and philosophical level later, but for the moment the discussion turns to disease and social responsibility.

Mr. Bucket asks the constable about the fever-houses. He replies that "for months and months, the people 'have been down by dozens,' and have been carried out, dead and dying 'like sheep with the rot'" (358). Students often ask for contextual information on fever in the nineteenth century. Two sources I find at once deft and useful are Ackroyd's biography (380–85) and an article by Socrates Litsios, "Dickens and the Movement for Sanitary Reform." There were four epidemics of cholera in Dickens's lifetime, Ackroyd tells us, and several other diseases fell under the general label of fevers. Cholera first came to England in the summer of 1831 but was officially recognized only in October (Litsios 183); typhus and typhoid fever were initially thought to be the same disease, and there were ignorance and controversy about their causes (Litsios 187–98). It is not always easy to determine which disease is in question when Dickens speaks of fever, especially since the fever dreams of his characters often operate on figurative as much as on literal levels (see esp. chapter 35 of *Bleak House*). Esther Summerson almost certainly has smallpox, but there were many other potentially fatal diseases in nineteenth-century London, such as dysentery, epidemic diarrhea, typhus, typhoid fever, and influenza. Ackroyd cites harrowing statistics of infection and mortality rates in nineteenth-century London (384), but the HIV/AIDS statistics in today's Johannesburg are just as sobering. According to the Johannesburg's official Web site:

> Of children tested on admission to the paediatric wards [at Johannesburg Hospital], 40% are HIV-positive, and 75% of paediatric deaths—mostly children under the age of two—are AIDS related. The overall infection rate for Johannesburg [is] 26%. . . . The total number of AIDS orphans will increase from 76,623 in 2000 to a cumulative total of 139,419 in 2010.

The *Mail and Guardian* in September 2005 put the number of HIV sufferers in Hillbrow between 20% and 40% (Beresford).

Students read Dickens's speech to the Metropolitan Sanitary Association (10 May 1851), where he asserts unambiguously, "Searching Sanitary Reform must precede all other social remedies. . . . [E]ven Education and Religion can do nothing where they are most needed, until the way is paved for their ministrations by Cleanliness and Decency" (*Speeches* 129). In the same speech, we see Dickens's understanding that disease is carried in particles of air (I refer students to chapter 47 of *Dombey and Son*), but the important point here as it relates to *Bleak House* is the question of social responsibility. I ask students to think carefully about the difference between not being responsible, on the one hand, and being irresponsible, on the other. I ask them to consider Dickens's sophisticated narrative deployment of names, titles, and pseudonyms to explore the question of responsibility. And I ask them to think of the extravagant metaphoric titles that instantiate fictive responsibilities in order to abdicate very real ones: "the Women of England, the Daughters of Britain, the Sisters of all the Cardinal Virtues separately, the Females of America, the Ladies of a hundred denominations" (123). Often in Dickens, paronomasia, or the displacement of a character's proper name, becomes an ingenious linguistic indicator of a breach of personal or social accountability. The rhyming and alphabetically arranged Buffies, Cuffies, Boodles, and Coodles constitute a searing attack on the failure of representative government to acknowledge responsibility for Tom-all-Alone's. Nemo, the name adopted by the law writer, is the sign that Captain Hawdon uses to sever all socially responsible ties and that Dickens uses to point to the failure of the legal system to assume responsibility for the likes of Jo. Students like to explore the implications of "Nobody" in their written assignments. If names and language provide points of articulation in human ethical engagements, in what way, precisely, does a nominal displacement, or the refusal to respond from the linguistic site of a proper name, reconfigure one's responsive range, one's field of responsibility? I ask students to read three of Dickens's essays in *Household Words* as part of the theme of responsibility: "Nobody, Somebody and Everybody," "Nobody's Story," and "The Noble Savage" (this last essay is outrageously challenging because there will invariably be Zulu speakers or students of "Hottentot" descent in the classroom).

The question of naming and responsibility is at the very core of controversies surrounding HIV/AIDS. "Nobody ever said AIDS," writes Eddie Vulanie Maluleke. "We died of TB," "Pneumonia, Flu, Cancer." In Mpe's *Welcome to Our Hillbrow*, willful ignorance displaces the name of the disease and hence the responsive field:

> They did not realise that several of the people they had buried in the past two years were victims of AIDS. It was easy to be ignorant of this, because this disease lent itself to lies. Such people were thought to have died of flu, or of stomach-ache. Bone throwers sniffed out the witches responsible, and they were subsequently necklaced.   (121)[4]

In what way, if any, I ask the students, is an ethical demand being made on us in the English literature classroom? through Dickens? through Mpe? Can a literary text realign the sites of naming, responsiveness, and responsibility in ways that open up new channels of discussion through a community of readers?

In a discussion of Ka Ngwenya's poem, "Hillbrow," Mpe emphasizes the image of Hillbrow as a hiding place for the "forsaken." He goes on to comment:

While the poem does not say who the forsaken are, or who has forsaken them, and under what circumstances, it is clear that Hillbrow, in its own way, provides some sanctuary, and that people who do not live or stay in Hillbrow bear some responsibility for their fellow human beings, a responsibility that leads them to discover Hillbrow's sanctuary.

("Missing Store" 192)

Mpe's novel explicitly welcomes the reader to "the world of our Humanity" (113), to "our All" (104), but a readiness to be welcomed to "our Humanity" or "our All" is predicated on a readiness to be welcomed to our Hillbrow. It is only in this multilayered sense that we may be welcomed to, and perhaps find sanctuary in, the world of our fictions. The refrain *"Welcome to Our Hillbrow"* thus becomes a serious plea to you, a community of readers, to respond.[5]

I like to remind students about Emile Benveniste's insights about "I" and "you": namely, that these pronominal forms refer not "to 'reality' or to objective positions in space or time but to the utterance, unique each time, that contains them" (219). The addressee, the anticipated "you" that comes into being in each "reading" of a text across time and space, cannot possibly be contained within the intentional grasp of the "I." "You" are always incipient in, and coincide with, the site and the time of the address, and it is you who recall to yourself an "I" uprooted from the time and the place of writing. But for you and I to be called into being, to effect the relation in language that shares the time of the other, we need to recognize the addressive purchase of the text itself. This, in turn, presupposes a language shared.

At this point I lead students to consider each event of a literary work as an instantiation of and a giving of an "I" to a "you" who hears. Each reading of *Bleak House* or *Welcome to Our Hillbrow*, then, demands on the part of the reader a responsiveness to the work. That gesture, in itself, constitutes an act of sharing in the sense of Jean-Luc Nancy's "partage," which means both sharing and dividing (6, 25). This sharing affirms something in common, but the students come to realize that their responsiveness to the hearing of landscapes other than their own (in Dickens or in Mpe) also constitutes a transgression of supposedly intransigent cultural limits. In responding to *Bleak House* or *Welcome to Our Hillbrow* in a classroom in the Cape in 2005, we are no longer simply in the place we always thought we were.[6]

NOTES

[1] It would have been too dangerous for Phaswane and me to walk alone through Hillbrow: that is why Thabiso and Tamela joined us. On that day there were very few women to be seen, and I did not see one other white person walking in Hillbrow. In some places it was simply too risky, or too painful, to take photos at all.

[2] Edwin Chadwick (1800–90) was a commissioner to the General Board of Health between 1848 and 1854. He instigated the first sanitary commission. Before that he

was secretary to the Poor Law Commissioners (1834–46). (See Dickens, *Speeches* 129; Litsios.)

[3] The portion in square brackets was deleted at the proof stage and does not appear in the 2003 Penguin edition (*Bleak House* [Ford and Monod] 864).

[4] To "necklace" someone is to place a tire around the victim's neck and set it alight.

[5] I speak of the ethical implications of contemporary South African literature in "Locating Identity" and "Visible and Invisible."

[6] Phaswane Mpe died on 12 December 2004. He was thirty-four. I have gained more than I can say from my encounters with him.

Teaching *Bleak House* in Advanced Placement English

Kathleen Breen

AP English. The first-quarter grading period lately over and a group of high school students embarking on a study of *Bleak House*. Implacable November weather. As much confusion in their minds, as if the London fog had but newly enveloped the earth, and it would not be wonderful to meet Mr. Dickens himself manifesting a ghostly presence in the room. "What is this thing called Chancery? Who are Jarndyce and Jarndyce? Is the whole novel like the first four or five pages?"

Such is the beginning scene nearly every time I teach *Bleak House* to high school seniors. The first chapter, after all, as revered as it is by critics, does not immediately engage the average eighteen-year-old reader. The double narration, the topic of an unfamiliar British court system, and the novel's sheer length might all argue against choosing this work. Yet as foggy as the classroom always seems on our first day of reading, we invariably come to the end of the book with universal sadness that it is over. Most of my students enjoy the novel; learn to read, analyze, and write cogently about fiction; and leave with an appreciation of Dickens that surprises and pleases them. And on the open response question of the AP exam, they invariably find relevant connections to *Bleak House* and write strong essays.

Why *Bleak House*? While official AP reading lists recommend a Dickens novel, *Hard Times* and *Great Expectations* are probably more common choices. Admittedly, my strongest reason for choosing *Bleak House* is my affection for the novel and its characters. Most teachers do a better job teaching what they themselves enjoy, and I am no exception. Over a period of sixteen years as an advanced placement and international baccalaureate English teacher at Sacred Heart Academy, Louisville, Kentucky, I taught *Bleak House* eleven times, to an average of sixty students each year (divided into three sections). Sacred Heart is a Catholic girls' school with a college-prep curriculum. My students came to AP English having studied a variety of American and British authors, but with little knowledge of Dickens. Following a unit on short stories in which the focus was on individual elements of fiction, our study of *Bleak House* also met my goals for teaching the novel as a genre. As an example of how fiction is put together, *Bleak House* has it all—plots, subplots, foreshadowing, suspense, coincidence, caricature, motifs, powerful themes, and flat, round, static and dynamic characters. It is well suited to the College Board's objectives for AP English Literature and Composition, particularly as it demonstrates how a novel reflects its social and historical context, yet remains timelessly relevant. While learning skills in close reading and textual analysis, my students also grapple with such issues as the widening gulf between the rich and the poor and the contrast between those who say a great deal while doing very little and those who do a great deal while saying nothing about it. *Bleak House* also fits the AP focus on writing to understand, explain, and evaluate a literary work. For composition students, it offers endless examples of the writer's plying his craft and experimenting with purpose, tone, point of view, poetic devices, and narrative structure.

Schedule

In my early teaching of the novel, I divided it into ten sections assigned between 1 November and 15 December, but these divisions were dictated by the teaching schedule rather than by the structure of the novel itself. After attending the NEH Seminar, *Bleak House*: Charles Dickens and Serial Production at the Dickens Project, University of California, Santa Cruz, in summer 1997, I restructured my course to match the serialization and taught the novel over nine weeks between mid-October and mid-December. This schedule provided a class meeting for each installment, plus one to introduce the novel and three at the end for review, a character tea party, and a test. To supplement the text, students also read Vladimir Nabokov's lectures on *Bleak House*.

The great advantage of teaching the novel in its serial structure is the effect this has on students' engagement in the suspense orchestrated by Dickens. Almost every number concludes in some mysterious event or statement, with dramatic turnings at the end of numbers 5 (Sir Leicester hears the step of the Ghost Walk louder than ever at Chesney Wold), 10 (Spontaneous Combustion!), and 15 (George's arrest for murder). Reading it as it was written heightens students' interest in what will happen next, particularly in the Esther–Lady Dedlock subplot, and creates an experience closer to that of the original audience. After students get caught up in the suspense, I ask them, "How would you like to have to wait another month (or more) for the answer to your questions?"

Prereading Materials

As we begin the novel, I distribute a variety of handouts either adapted or created: maps of England, London, and the neighborhood of Chancery Lane, with specific sites marked; a two-column outline of chapters depicting the shifts in narrator; a character list (one that doesn't give away all the relationships as *Cliffs Notes* does); an outline of the serial structure; a copy of the first paragraph in Dickens's hand; a list of historical topics for research; a list of paragraphs for prose analysis; and complete directions for the reading log.

The Reading Log

As a major assessment of my students' engagement and evaluation of the novel, the reading log carries the weight of two test grades. To begin, students acquire a one-inch binder, stock it with loose-leaf, and divide it into twenty-three parts as follows:

> Preliminary: all the handouts distributed in class
>
> Parts 1–19: a section for each installment, containing "the clouds" (discussed below), plus description of characters as they appear, questions needing answers, class notes, and in-class writings
>
> Part 20: research—ten one-page explanations of historical topics that students select from a list, each synthesizing information from at least two sources
>
> Part 21: prose analyses—ten one-page close readings of assigned paragraphs
>
> Part 22: one creative response, either taken from the list provided or approved separately. If the creative response (such as a painting or a videotaped scene) does not fit into the binder, a description is included here.

Topics for research include public houses, sheriff's officers, Lincoln's Inn, opium, mud in London, urban cemeteries, Chancery, and smallpox. Passages selected for analysis are usually one to two paragraphs long. My directions for their prose analyses suggest students write about two hundred words with abundant textual evidence, measurable statements about the prose, attention to both diction and syntax, and conclusions about the effects of the language.

As a method for teaching students how to do prose analysis, I use a handout that focuses attention on the diction and sentence structure of the novel's opening paragraph. Students discover that verbs are few, but nouns abound. Students also list the twenty adjectives in the paragraph, discovering that eight of them are present participles, conveying the activity "of a great (and dirty) city" (13). Realizing that fragments make up the whole paragraph leads students to conclude that Dickens is composing here for a sense of immediacy, placing the reader in the middle of the scene.

In a close reading of a passage from chapter 42 (661), one student recognizes how Dickens links rural Chesney Wold with legal London, focusing on the theme of society's connections. Citing "where the sheep are all made into parchment," she points to a biblical allusion; the baby sheep, a lamb, symbolizes Christ and suggests that goodness is sacrificed to evil in Chancery. Because of this evil, sheep, goats, and pasture become parchment, wigs, and chaff. In addition, she argues that the many active verbs in the passage, for example, "transfers," "walks," "returns," "changes," "talks," and "melts," when preceded by the simple subject "he," reinforce Tulkinghorn's power to bring about changes in people's lives, particularly that of Lady Dedlock.

When we discuss the second half of the novel, I pay additional attention to the structure and style of particular passages with specific in-class activities. For example, using an overhead transparency, we analyze the diction and rhetorical devices in the description of Jo's being brought in to the Shooting Gallery in chapter 47 (274).

Clouds and Daily Quizzes

The "clouds" (so called because I enclosed the notes for each chapter in hand-drawn clouds) are graphic organizers designed to guide students through the reading of a chapter. Each sheet maps one number (either three or four chapters) with important events linked together and blanks left for students to fill in as they read. For example, the cloud for chapter 39, "Attorney and Client," includes the following notes: summer—long vacation (at least a year since ch. 20); paragraph 2—atmosphere like Krook's—irony that ____ is a "respectable man"—depicted as a predator, blood sucker—cat/mouse; "the one great principle of English law is to make ____ for itself"; Guppy and ____ go to Krook's—Mr. ____ is here—death imagery—Smallweeds in a grave of paper. I distribute each sheet of clouds, one installment at a time, before reading, so students can use it to focus on details and connections. Filling in some blanks points them to certain important events, characters, or themes. The clouds also provide a focus for our subsequent discussion of the installment.

At the beginning of each class, before we discuss anything, students take a ten-question reading quiz, measuring their reading comprehension and retention of facts. This exercise motivates them to keep up with the reading, as the ten quizzes add up to a full test grade. Sample questions for chapter 37 include Who is paying Skimpole's expenses in Lincolnshire?, What cause is absorbing all of Richard's interest?, and To whom did Skimpole introduce Richard for the bribe of a five-pound note? In evaluations completed at the end of the unit, students routinely report that both the clouds and the daily quizzes fueled their reading. Rather than allow students to make up missed quizzes, I recommend doubling the score of the next one they take; this circumvents the possibility of students just garnering the answers from class discussions.

Addressing the Challenge of Reading

Since before studying this novel, my students have usually read shorter works in more contemporary language, I address some of the strategies they might apply to improve comprehension. We talk about the challenge of reading lengthy passages of description, and some students confide that when a passage of prose begins to confuse them, they usually don't reread; instead, they speed up, reading faster and faster to elude the pursuing monster in the maze. Students often reveal a second obstacle to comprehension in their failure to translate description into visual images. They do not automatically see as they read. Part of the problem stems from a long-developed habit of skipping description. Being of a video generation, they are inclined to fast-forward to the dialogue. At first, they admit that they skim for quotation marks because they consider dialogue "interesting" and "meaningful," while blocks of prose, whatever their content, are labeled "difficult" and, worst of all, "boring." Therefore we talk about the fact that Dickens was writing for the interior stage of the reader's imagination in a time period when novels would have been read aloud to family and friends gathered in the parlor of an evening.

Visualizing a description yields meaning, not only on a literal level, but ultimately on the interpretive as well. Students who have skimmed the description of Mr. Tulkinghorn's room in chapter 10, for example, will probably miss the allusion to the frescoed ceiling: "and even its painted ceilings, where Allegory, in Roman helmet and celestial linen, sprawls among balustrades and pillars, flowers, clouds, and big-legged boys, and makes the head ache" (158). When Allegory points to the window in chapter 16, Mr. Tulkinghorn does not look and does not see a mysterious woman glide past in the darkness. In chapter 48, Dickens constructs the last two paragraphs from the perspective of Allegory, who points to the half-empty wine bottle and glass, to the table, to the empty chair, to the two candles, "blown out suddenly" (750), and finally to the figure of Tulkinghorn "lying face downward on the floor shot through the heart" (752).

Here the figure on the ceiling becomes almost another character asking the questions that elicit the reader's interpretation. Who was that woman in the street outside? What if he had seen her? Would he have recognized her? Who came late at night to his chambers? Why? Was it someone he recognized? Why were the candles snuffed quickly? Who murdered him and why? Thinking about these questions and their possible answers is central to making sense of the story.

I also find it important to develop students' understanding of the modes of writing that make up a fictional passage, specifically the differences between description and narration and between narration and reverie. For example, in chapter 8, Esther tells us of her visit to the brickmakers:

> Besides ourselves, there were in this damp, offensive room—a woman with a black eye, nursing a poor little gasping baby by the fire; a man, all stained with clay and mud, and looking very dissipated, lying at full length on the ground, smoking a pipe. . . . They all looked up at us as we came in, and the woman seemed to turn her face towards the fire, as if to hide her bruised eye; nobody gave us any welcome.   (130)

Using a graphic organizer, students work in pairs to discern that some words and phrases are purely descriptive: "damp," "woman with a black eye, nursing a little gasping baby by the fire," "man, all stained with clay and mud, . . . lying at full length on the ground, smoking a pipe." The only purely narrative elements are the actions: "they all looked up at us when we came in," and the lack of action: "nobody gave us any welcome." The words "offensive," "poor," "looking very dissipated," and "as if to hide her bruised eye" fall into the category of reverie, Esther's thoughts (as narrator) about the scene and what it means.

Creative Extensions of the Text

Beyond helping students understand and analyze the text, I want them to have fun with it and make personal connections to Dickens. Some activities are simple; for example, distributing copies of a Dickens's head enlarged to eight by eleven inches and matching speech bubbles, I ask students to find a favorite quotation to inscribe in the bubble. They often decorate the final product, as one student did when she added Mr. Boythorn's bird atop Mr. Dickens's head to accompany a Boythorn quotation. Other activities come from my experience at the NEH seminar and are adapted from the work of fellow participants. After reading chapter 11, students work in groups to compose the coroner's report on the death of Nemo; following chapter 42, they construct alibi statements for the suspects in the murder of Tulkinghorn. For example, a student adopting the persona of Mr. Vholes might tell Mr. Bucket, "Well, sir, being the respectable man that I am, I was at the time in question occupied with the interests of my client, Mr. C. I had my shoulder to the wheel, I assure you; my digestion being impaired, I was not able to venture forth that evening." These two ideas, originated by the Connecticut teacher Werner Liepolt, allow students to be imaginative in exploring both events and characters. Another activity, based on the research of the New York librarian Susan Stone, involves giving students copies of cartoons and articles from *Punch*, 1851–53, and asking them to find connections to the novel. One example depicts an empty Parliament chamber framed by cavorting MPs, perhaps Boodle, Coodle, and Doodle themselves. In this activity, students recognize the topicality of the novel.

A culminating creative assignment is part of the reading log. Choices include text-based collages of the contents of Krook's shop, Mrs. Jellyby's closets, and Tom-All-Alone's; London newspapers with accounts of the inquests at the Sol's Arms and reports on the conditions in Tom-all-Alone's; key entries in characters' diaries; missing scenes, such as the conversation between Jarndyce and Woodcourt about Allan's marrying Esther; letters written by Lady Dedlock, Mr. Jarndyce, and Guppy; storyboards, videotaped scenes, paintings, and sculptures.

In celebration of the novel's completion, we have a Character Tea Party, for which students build costumes out of easily acquired items of clothing. Students enjoy bringing the major characters of the novel together for high tea and comparing the multiple versions of a very filthy Jo and an elegant Lady Dedlock. Several times, Mr. Dickens himself, in the person of Professor Burt Hornback (then at Bellarmine University), attended the party and gave us readings from *Bleak House* and *A Christmas Carol*.

In surveys completed at the end of the unit, students assess the level of their efforts as well as the teaching strategies that helped them the most. For some, the spell of *Bleak House* lasts for years. One student wrote to me of her visit to London as a college sophomore: "While we were there, I made sure we went to Chancery Lane and took a tour of the Inns of Court; all I talked about that morning was *Bleak House*."

In short, as Mr. Micawber would say, *Bleak House* is highly adaptable to the AP curriculum. Its particular richness of language and theme make it a novel that one might teach again and again with increasing enthusiasm and creativity. As part of a year-long course incorporating shorter modern works such as Sylvia Plath's *The Bell Jar* and George Orwell's *Nineteen Eighty-Four*, *Bleak House* provides an experience of the best of nineteenth-century literature.

Teaching *Bleak House* and Nothing but *Bleak House*

Nita Moots Kincaid

Teaching *Bleak House* in the context of the two-year urban community college is not, on the face of it, the most electrifying pedagogical notion advanced recently. Using that one novel to generate virtually all the activities of the class and pretty much the entire course content, however, has proved to be highly popular with students and productive of far-reaching effects I would not have predicted.

It turns out that allowing students to move very slowly through the novel, as they think and write on it chapter by chapter and sometimes paragraph by paragraph, generates a cumulative power that runs through their reading and their thinking. Students who are baffled by Dickens for a week or two seem to grow into his language as they start to soak slowly in his dark vision of the world. By mid-point, they have gained considerable competence, and confidence, in their reading and can begin thinking of broader critical issues—issues involving narrative, history, and the construction of meaning. By the end, they are able to explore with some sophistication connections between Dickens's world and their own, between problems that beset nineteenth-century London and, alas, twenty-first century Los Angeles, as well.

The class of twenty-five from Los Angeles City College is part of a college honors program, a casually run operation that is hit-or-miss in its ability to identify fine students but that sometimes does so, almost against its will. Whatever their native abilities, the students identified by the program generally know little or nothing of Dickens himself, literary theory, or Victorian England. I hope in this course to allow Dickens himself, through this great novel, to provide inroads into all three areas and, more important, to ignite the curiosity of students coming to him (and to fiction of this order) for the first time.

This essay provides details on how the course is structured, an analysis of the pedagogical (and ethical) reasoning guiding this model, and an evaluation, provided largely by the students. It is a course that relaxes the anxiety we all have over how much we teach, focusing instead on how we teach. Though students are expected to do a significant amount of research for the class, research that will lure them into historical documents, there is only the one primary text. *Bleak House* is asked to do the job of supplying constant interest and a range of ideas that will keep a group of diverse students alert and engaged over fifteen weeks. I have found that close and relentless attention to this deeply resonant novel does just that—and more.

The course uses *Bleak House* not only as the main text but also as a model for thinking about history and historical method, about the way social issues are constructed and formed into problems, about textual analysis, and about reading.

The idea is that teaching complex reading skills is easily integrated into forms of literary and cultural analysis and that Dickens's *Bleak House* provides a source book almost inexhaustible in its capacity to enrich and surprise. Learning to read this novel, slowly and in thick detail, students discover ways in which their experience with the novel is also an experience in history, sociology, and philosophy.

Description

Los Angeles City College is an urban community college located in North Central Los Angeles. Our students represent a wide range of cultural and ethnic backgrounds but are seldom affluent. They are sometimes of traditional college age but more often are somewhat (to a lot) older. I teach *Bleak House* in a freshman composition class, a course designed to provide students with college-level critical thinking and writing skills. The class meets one and a half hours twice a week for fifteen weeks. We use the Norton Critical Edition of *Bleak House*, and we read and discuss the text by way of the monthly parts in which it originally was published. I assign many of the critical pieces included in this edition in an effort to help the students connect more quickly and realistically with Dickens's world. During the first week, beyond describing the course in general, discussing my rationale for teaching it, and explaining the various writing activities that will be expected of students, I give them the following writing assignment:

> Write an essay in which you discuss what you know about or imagine life in nineteenth-century England to have been. What was going on in England at the time? What were people thinking? What was England's place in the world, politically and economically? How did the country look? What was London like? How did the people live? Be specific. Write at least two pages, even if you have to invent details.

In the second class session, I introduce and lead a discussion on cultural studies—what it is and how it can help us better understand the way social problems are constructed and raised in *Bleak House*, how the Victorians dealt with them, and how we continue to see the world and many of its problems in ways both similar and dissimilar. These first classes are meant to provide a model for thinking and, just as important, to rattle some presuppositions formed by a progressivist ideology.

Response Papers

To encourage students not only to look at the details of the text but also to arrive prepared for class discussions based on how those details offer an understanding of nineteenth-century England, I ask students to write response papers, due every two weeks, over the course of the semester. Each of these two- to three-page (typed) papers is based on the reading assignments, as well as on the students' research activities, and each addresses specific issues that will help students uncover subtleties of the text, the culture formulated there, and our own ideological blinders. While students receive credit for their response papers, I assure them that these papers are not formal academic essays and encourage them to take risks, to play with ideas in these exercises. At the same time, I hope that writing response papers will ease students into writing more formal essays. The following examples of response-paper assignments have been useful in drawing students who have little experience reading nineteenth-century literature into the novel:

> Read the first paragraph of the novel aloud. What is the effect of Dickens's ungrammatical sentences? What is the effect of his language? Discuss.

> Consider Nemo's name and the repetition of the variations on the word *nothing*, particularly those that come from Jo. Why do you suppose Dickens used these powerful and terrible words? What is their effect on us?

These assignments require the students to read carefully—to be attentive to what Dickens is doing with language—and prompt them to continue to do so as they read further into the novel. After a few weeks, students begin to come to class with passages highlighted that they want to discuss to see what information Dickens might really be offering readers beyond a richly detailed description or plot device.

Essays

I design formal essay assignments to help teach students to write effective expository and argumentative essays in response to issues raised by the reading assignments. So that their work on the essays will feed into their research projects, I design writing prompts that help students get a sense of the rich and strange complexity of nineteenth-century England and begin to make connections between the nineteenth- and twenty-first-century worlds. Here are two examples of such assignments:

> Discuss Dickens's view of "telescopic philanthropy." How does he represent it in *Bleak House*, and how do we understand his opinion of it? Compare telescopic philanthropy in nineteenth-century England with how telescopic philanthropy is evident in twenty-first-century United States. You will need to be specific in arguing your case both in reference to England 150 years ago and the United States today, so you will have to investigate what is going on in our country or city that parallels what was happening in Dickens's world.

Consider the recurrent motif of "moving on" as it applies to Jo. Where do people want him to go, or is that a consideration? What are the implications of that phrase in the novel? Discuss how we use similar gestures of dismissal today.

Research Project

In addition to assigning response papers and formal essays, I ask each student to select a topic on which she or he will conduct research, make an oral presentation, and write a research paper. Beyond offering students instruction on how to assemble a research paper, I solicit the assistance of a Los Angeles City College reference librarian, who conducts a research workshop in the college library. She tailors her session to our class, making the students aware of the wealth of information (both traditional and nontraditional sources, print and electronic) available to them and how to access materials that will be useful in their research. I break the research paper assignment into manageable parts, requiring students over the course of a semester to present an annotated bibliography, an oral report on their research, and a formal outline of their research papers—all before the completion of their final projects. I set up the research schedule in this manner to preclude a student's frantic race at the end of the term to throw together, predictably, a less than satisfactory paper. More important, I want students to begin early in the course to speak with authority in reference to some aspect of Dickens's world, as well as their own, and to understand how their issues are intertwined with those of other students, thereby acquiring a fuller sense of what feeds into the social issues on which they are concentrating. Listed below are some of the instructions I provide my students, along with several of the topics from which they can choose:

Instructions

You are to select one of the following topics for your research project. Your oral presentation will address the questions that are printed below in regular font (those focused on nineteenth-century London). Your final research paper will address the questions printed below both in regular and italic fonts (those that require you to integrate the cultures of nineteenth-century London and twenty-first-century Los Angeles).

Topics

What were the Courts of Chancery, and how did they operate? Were there cases anything like *Jarndyce and Jarndyce*, or was Dickens fabricating all this? Be specific.

What are parallel abuses in our court systems today? Are there ways, for instance, in which long delays eat up costs or force people out of the system? Are there ways in which the wealthy and powerful are favored?

Who is Sir Leicester Dedlock and what is a "Baronet"? Explain the class system and the special privileges and responsibilities given to those with titles. What percentage of the population carried titles?

America of course is a classless society—or so we tell ourselves. Is that true? Do we have anything similar to England's class system operating in our culture today? Do we have lords and ladies without the titles attached?

Dickens describes in great detail Tom-all-Alone's and the section of town in which the brickmakers lived. Where were these sections and why were they so bad—or were they? What kind of sanitary conditions actually prevailed in London slums?

What are conditions in Los Angeles slums today? Do we have slums? Find out details. Would Dickens write a similar indictment of conditions here?

Disease plays a large part in the novel, uniting the very poor and others much better off. What was that particular disease? How much was then known about that disease and how it was spread? Were there similar epidemic diseases? How deadly were such diseases? Provide details. What was the social and professional role of the doctor?

Do we have modern epidemic diseases? Where do they come from, and how do they spread? Whom do they target especially and why?

Who is Jo? What is a crossing sweeper? Jo is asked, "Who takes care of you?" He is also asked, "What do you know?" His answers are "Nobody" and "Nothink." How could that be? Were such children around then? Who were they? How did they live? Why isn't Jo in school?

Who are the Jo's of today? What are they doing to survive?

Assessment

About two dozen students filled out detailed assessments for the class, responding to questions about difficulties encountered, presuppositions about Victorian England, how they viewed the idea of connecting nineteenth-century London with twenty-first-century Los Angeles, the usefulness of the investigatory models used in class, and any change in their views of Dickens.

In terms of difficulties, students spoke most often of Dickens's language, how strange it was and, initially, how baffling: "one of the hardest books I've ever encountered for sure!" One student spoke of the problems he had in adjusting his "ear" for this peculiar "voice" coming off the pages. Several said that methods they had developed for reading modern prose more or less automatically were stymied and that they were forced to think about reading itself, developing various methods to retrain their eyes, ears, and quality of thinking, so that they could find a new set of skills. Several tried making lists and reading passages over and over. Most common was the technique of reading aloud, trying for different emphases, different voices in order to make the adjustment. Mainly, however, students simply made the adjustment by forcing themselves to keep going, keep reading and thinking. That is, adjusting to the prose and world of *Bleak House* was, for all the students, more a matter of patience than of technique. Every student said that it took several weeks to feel at home, but all students also said they were at home after that time.

Knowing this, that these abilities seem to develop, à la Chomsky, at a level beneath consciousness, I felt comfortable both encouraging students to keep going—and meaning it—and using more consistently the close analysis of specific passages from the novel in class, allowing strange language patterns to sink in. This emphasis on close reading and focused awareness seems to have had considerable carryover value. Over half the students said their hard work with *Bleak House* made them more alert and successful readers in all their classes, citing disciplines as diverse as art history and psychology. One student remarked on her ability to understand much more clearly the arguments of Freud, mentioning both improved reading skills and a sharper historical knowledge as contributory.

The students' gradual immersion into the language was accompanied, they said, by an equally gradual complicating of their assumptions about Victorian England. Students reported that their initial assumptions about the period tended to overemphasize greatly the dominance of middle-class culture and the strange and alien quality of Victorian morals, manners, and customs. Several mentioned Merchant-Ivory films and a general connection between clichés about Victorian prudery and opulence with an idea that, apart from servants, most people then lived pretty cushy lives. The image of empire also contributed to a sense that England's great power positioned the bulk of its citizens much more comfortably than in fact it did. Learning about the complex class structure; about the enormous problems connected with industrialization, homelessness, and the urban poor; about sanitation and epidemic diseases; about a political and judicial system more bent on preserving its formal structures than solving problems did not seem to tempt students to leap to the opposite error and see Victorian England as absolutely continuous with our world. Instead, they commonly registered something like shock and dismay at the images of suffering, then and now, and at the fact that such horrors persist even in such different worlds. Several students seemed to feel that improvements in one area were countered by regressive moves elsewhere, almost as if the social structure preserved its own problems like a deterministic machine. I did not introduce Michel Foucault specifically in this course, but this sort of student awareness could suggest that others may want to do so (see, e.g., *History of Sexuality* 3–13, 92–96).

Few of the students had read any works by Dickens before engaging with *Bleak House*. Several had only seen film or theatrical representations of *A Christmas Carol* or *David Copperfield,* so initially they had no particular views of Dickens as a writer. All, however, left with an appreciation for his artistry, and many echoed their peer's comment that Dickens was "an impressively astute observer of human behavior; an ingenious creator of believable and lasting characters; a master plot-conceiver; a concerned and alarmed chronicler of social injustice; and a humanist, as well as a humorist." The students also agreed that Dickens's writing provides readers a "gateway into a world, and views, to which they might not otherwise be exposed." One thing is clear in all this: *Bleak House* presents more than enough material for any course concerned with writing, analyzing social issues, and introducing students to cultural studies.

Bleak House in Law School

Robert Googins

My father, a high school history teacher, weaned me from Horatio Alger's novels to the works of Charles Dickens when I was a young teenager; in doing so, he left a legacy for which I am forever grateful. Still, when I began teaching law in 1964, I never imagined that I would introduce a course entitled Dickens and the Law, which I've been teaching for over a decade. Although the structure of my course is of my own design, the idea came from a seminar taught by Robert Coles at Harvard Law School while he was a professor of psychiatry and medical humanities. In his article "The Keen Eye of Charles Dickens," he states:

> Again and again lawyers figure in the penetrating enactments of ethical con-
> flict which Dickens insisted on making a central element of his most impor-
> tant novels. In *Bleak House,* of course, the issue is not just lawyers, but the
> law itself—its awesome, pervasive, perplexing, unnerving presence.   (33)

Along with Coles's essay, the other essential resource for the course is William Holdsworth's *Charles Dickens as a Legal Historian*, particularly chapter 3, "*Bleak House* and the Procedure of the Court of Chancery.*" With these and other re-sources, students in the course learn about the practice of law in Dickens's era, but they are also led to reflect on crucial questions of legal ethics, questions as important to their work today as they were in Dickens's time. Reading *Bleak House*, they begin to understand the force of Grant Gilmore's remark in *The Ages of American Law*, "In Hell there will be nothing but law and due process will be meticulously observed" (111).

Dickens and the Law is an elective course open to second- and third-year law students; the seminar meets once a week for fourteen weeks. Enrollment is limited to ten students, who must read *Bleak House* before the commence-ment of classes. Before the start of the term, I send each registrant for the course a "bookmark" that has a list of all the novel's characters, which they al-ways find helpful. A familiarity quiz is given at the outset of the first class to test for compliance.

In this first class, I ask the students to constantly examine the extent to which the social and legal issues about which Dickens wrote have importance today. Students are often stunned to learn that the legal profession of today is still struggling with some of the same problems Dickens wrote about.

To assist students in understanding both the novel's historical context and its potential relevance to their contemporary legal training, I pass out the following materials:

a "Legal London" map, circa 1850
a sheet explaining the monetary system in use

a 1994 *Hartford Courant* article on spontaneous combustion (Robinson)

two articles from the *Dickensian*: Peter Denman's "Krook's Death and
 Dickens's Authorities" and J. R. Tye's "Legal Caricature"

Dickens's short story "Chambers" from *The Uncommercial Traveller*

The next four class periods are based on *Bleak House* and deal with the story line, the legal characters and the various attorney-client relationships, the depiction of the Chancery Court, and, finally, the court reforms that came about in the 1850s.

Bleak House: The Lawyers

It would be easy for a casual student of Dickens to assume that he abhorred lawyers, since only a smattering of his lawyers possess a modicum of professional generosity—none of whom grace the pages of *Bleak House*. Furthermore, lawyers do not appear to have been afterthoughts to Dickens, as they constitute the largest professional group in his work; at least fifty-five identified characters are spread throughout his writings. Dickens, however, who chose his friends and acquaintances with a fair degree of care, counted among them a number of lawyers, many being prominent members of the bar (Fyfe 31). Even lawyers who wince at his portrayals of their brethren acknowledge the adroitness with which they are woven into the novel (Behen 379). Indeed, as a young man, Dickens thought of entering the profession himself and sought lodging in New Inn, one of the Inns of Chancery, indicating that he intended to enter the bar as soon as his circumstances permitted (*Letters* 1: 43). Dickens's son, Henry Fielding Dickens, who became a prominent member of the bar himself, acknowledged that his father had many prominent friends who were lawyers and was "very fond of lawyers"—but not necessarily the law (Lockwood 23).

But when, as a teenager, Dickens worked in several law offices as a clerk, he found that the legal profession "seemed to have no other purpose than entangling its victims for the profits of its adepts" (qtd. in E. Johnson 1: 52). Subsequently, as a young man, he became a court reporter, which brought him in contact with the solicitors and proceedings of the Chancery Court. Dickens also had a painful personal experience with the Chancery Court when he brought actions against several persons who had "pirated" his *A Christmas Carol*. Ironically, Dickens acquired a fairly timely judgment against the principal pirates but was unable to collect when the defendants declared bankruptcy. This experience occasioned his remark that "[i]t is better to suffer a great wrong than to have recourse to the much greater wrong of the law" (qtd. in E. Johnson 1: 494). Note the similarity in the grand opening of *Bleak House* when the narrator says, regarding the Chancery Court, "Suffer any wrong that can be done you, rather than come here!" (15).

Mr. Tangle

Mr. Tangle is the first lawyer introduced to the reader and is representative for the bar in general. The name Tangle indicates the way he has spent his entire professional life: mired in the case of Jarndyce and Jarndyce.

Mr. Vholes

Mr. Vholes is engaged by Richard Carstone on Richard's reaching the age of majority. He is thought to be modeled after Charles Molloy, for whom Dickens clerked as a teenager (Fyfe 30). Before that time Richard's interest in the Jarndyce estate was handled by Mr. Kenge, who also acted as solicitor for Ada Clare as well as Mr. Jarndyce. It becomes clear that Vholes secures his client by paying Harold Skimpole a fee to induce Richard to switch solicitors. Even the "child" Skimpole seems to appreciate that this is a bribe (605), an unseemly practice at best and akin to what we might refer to as ambulance chasing today. This activity would clearly violate provision 7.2 b of the current rules of professional conduct precluding, in these circumstances, a lawyer from giving anything of value to another person for recommending the lawyer's services (American Bar Association 41).

Chapter 39, "Attorney and Client," starts with a description of Vholes's quarters in Symonds Inn, which "took kindly to the dry rot and to dirt and all things decaying and dismal" (620). It is in this chapter that Dickens delivers his most scathing, satirical indictment of the profession:

> The one great principle of the English law is, to make business for itself. There is no other principle distinctly, certainly, and consistently maintained throughout all its narrow turnings. Viewed by this light it becomes a coherent scheme, and not the monstrous maze the laity are apt to think it. Let them but once clearly perceive that its grand principle is to make business for itself at their expense, and surely they will cease to grumble.
> (621)

Vholes is the exemplar for this position. He comes to represent that part of the legal establishment that survives at the expense of its clients. The very name Vholes is telling. A vole is a shrewlike rodent, small, but especially vicious. Vholes is also described as "cold blooded" (695), a "vampire" (924). And as others have pointed out, a vole is also a circumstance in a card game where the dealer gets the winning hand (Coles 36). Vholes constantly tries to deal himself the high cards through vague assurances of success when Richard seems on the verge of giving up. Equally improper are Vholes's attempts to get continued financial support from Mr. Jarndyce when Richard's funds seemed to be running out; he discusses his client's affairs without his knowledge or consent (696).

Mr. Kenge

Unlike the personally and professionally reprehensible Vholes, Kenge appears interesting and likeable. We know many people who like to hear themselves talk—and some we don't mind listening to. "Conversation" Kenge falls into this category. He is a partner in a firm that seems to be a prosperous and respected member of the legal community.

Personable as he might be, however, Kenge also represents that segment of the bar that profits from the imperfections of the legal process. Moreover, Kenge appears to genuinely believe in the righteousness of this position. On several occasions he roundly defends the Chancery process to Jarndyce.

> "We are a great country, Mr Jarndyce, we are a very great country. This is a great system, Mr Jarndyce, and would you wish a great country to have a little system? Now, really, really!"
>
> He said this at the stair-head, gently moving his right hand as if it were a silver trowel, with which to spread the cement of his words on the structure of the system, and consolidate it for a thousand ages.   (950)

Earlier in chapter 39, Kenge defends the Vholeses of the profession:

> Alter this law, sir, and what will be the effect of your rash proceeding on a class of practitioners very worthily represented, allow me to say to you, by the opposite attorney in the case, Mr Vholes? Sir, that class of practitioners would be swept from the face of the earth. Now you cannot afford—I would say, the social system cannot afford—to lose an order of men like Mr Vholes. . . . As though, Mr Vholes and his relations being minor cannibal chiefs, and it being proposed to abolish cannibalism, indignant champions were to put the case thus: Make man-eating unlawful, and you starve the Vholeses!   (621–23)

Kenge has been characterized as standing for "the charlatan and pettifogger" (Behen 381), but I think this is a misreading. However, to the extent that he represents those perpetuating the system, he does deserve professional condemnation. While reasonable men may have differed about the extent of reform that the Chancery Court process required, the system was perpetuated by its practitioners for their own benefit. Today's practitioners have an enunciated obligation to ensure that their regulation reflects concern for the public interest and not a parochial self-interest of the bar (American Bar Association 1).

At this juncture, the class members are asked to comment on whether the bar has lived up to this obligation—particularly with respect to reform efforts regarding tort litigation. Finally, the class is asked to comment on whether

Kenge's original representation of both Mr. Jarndyce and his wards raised conflicts of interest issues.

Mr. Tulkinghorn

Mr. Tulkinghorn has been described as one of the "malignant" types of Dickens lawyers (Behen 381)—a description with which I agree. He is the "steward of the legal mysteries, the butler of the legal cellar" of his clients and an "Oyster of the old school, whom nobody can open" (24, 158). Dickens modeled his fictional home after the house of his friend John Forster, which can still be seen today at the southwest corner of Lincoln's Inn Fields (Shatto, *Companion* 101). In the novel he turned it into a set of lawyers' chambers where "lawyers lie like maggots in nuts" (158).

An important legal issue involves the identification of just who Tulkinghorn's clients are. When queried, students quickly and quite reasonably identify both Sir Leicester, baronet, and Lady Dedlock as his clients but generally fail to identify whom Tulkinghorn regards as his client. It seems fairly clear, however, that he believes that his client goes beyond living individuals and includes the baronetcy itself. When confronting Lady Dedlock about her "secret," he states:

> When I speak of Sir Leicester being the sole consideration, he and the family credit are one. Sir Leicester and the baronetcy, Sir Leicester and Chesney Wold, Sir Leicester and his ancestors and his patrimony . . . are, I need not say to you, Lady Dedlock, inseparable.   (657–58)

Despite Tulkinghorn's grandiose view, Sir Leicester was his client, and he treated Lady Dedlock as his client as well in the pending Chancery Court action to which she was a party. There is little doubt that his embarking on an investigation of Lady Dedlock's personal history, without the clients' express knowledge and request, violated his obligations to his clients, to say nothing of his subsequent use of the information to threaten and control Lady Dedlock's actions. Under current rules governing professional conduct, a lawyer confronted with Mr. Tulkinghorn's situation would be precluded from acting as he did under a number of rules governing professional conduct, including rule 1.6 (Confidentiality of Information) and rule 1.7 (Conflicts of Interest: Current Clients) (American Bar Association 7, 9). The reader is left with little doubt that Sir Leicester would have fired Tulkinghorn, or worse, had he not been murdered before Sir Leicester could act.

The Chancery Court: Problems and Reforms

While standards of professional conduct in Dickens's time were not as formalized as they are today, there were certain common understandings regarding the obligations of lawyers. In 1851, an eminent lawyer named Samuel Warren delivered a series of lectures for the Incorporated Law Society of the United Kingdom entitled *The Moral, Social, and Professional Duties of Attornies and Solicitors*.

Warren recognized that lawyers possessed formidable powers that should be employed for good in the service and protection of clients but could be misused for evil in the public's harassment and oppression (5). He indicated that lawyers had an obligation to avoid ruinous causes that would serve their purposes but beggar all others concerned (41). He recognized that the oath taken by lawyers required them to act with strict "integrity" (154) and that in the course of their representation of clients they would learn many of their secrets, which were to be preserved "inviolate" (44). If secrets were learned that would prevent an attorney from maintaining his obligation of loyalty to two clients, he would be obliged to withdraw from the representation of both (339). Thus at the time of the novel's publication, we can properly assume that the legal abuses it depicts would have been understood to be unethical.

In the class periods dealing with Dickens's portrayal of Chancery, we also discuss the reforms devised to correct these abuses. Two objectives in these discussions are to get students to consider the effect that those with vested interests in the status quo have in perpetuating current systems and to get them to think critically about today's laws and court procedures from that prospective. These considerations are especially significant, since the key judiciary committees of many of our state legislatures are dominated by lawyers who often dictate the terms of reforms that affect legal practitioners.

Another objective is to determine the time period in which the story is set, in the light of the criticisms leveled against the author and, particularly, Dickens's statements in the preface to the first edition (5) implying that his portrayal of the court's ills was accurate at the time of its writing in 1852–53.

Most commentators have concluded that the story is set around 1827, when Lord Lyndhurst, thought to be the model for the Lord High Chancellor, succeeded to that high post, replacing Lord Eldon (Holdsworth, *Charles Dickens* 79). This time period represented, perhaps, the low point in the court's history. The First Chancery Commission Report of 1826 had just revealed "the monstrous state of affairs" that existed (84). There is little question that all the ills of the court represented in *Bleak House* were accurate in 1827. There is also little question that the Chancery Commission Report of 1850 showed that many ills remained and prior reforms may have been ignored by those benefiting from the old rules (Holdsworth, *History* 9: 340–42).

William Holdsworth indicates that the court's procedures found their roots in medieval canon law, which by the end of the eighteenth century had become cumbersome. Among the court's problems were

> inadequate court officials and staff
> slow and technical court procedures, which caused uncontested cases to
> take forever

poor staff supervision, which allowed old procedures to survive despite
reforms
a particularly egregious rule that demanded that the court not act unless it
handled all the outstanding issues presented in a given case

(*Charles Dickens* 85–87)

The pleading and evidence-taking processes were especially burdensome. And
Dickens's introductory description of these procedures (14–16, 118) is accurate.
Evidence was taken by written interrogatives and affidavits, often by commissioners or clerks who had no understanding of the case. All expenses were paid,
of course, by the parties.

Frequently the cause would be assigned to a master, a court functionary assigned to handle procedural and administrative matters. Some of the worst
delays and costs occurred at this stage, which was considered "inconceivably
dilatory" (Holdsworth, *Charles Dickens* 98). It is no wonder that some cases
lasted until all the estate assets had been consumed in costs. Unscrupulous lawyers struggled to achieve the so-called Rule of 50. This "rule" indicated that if
practitioners were able to get at least fifty parties involved in a case, it ought to
last forever because of the delays created by having to add new parties to represent deceased suitors (91).

As a result of the 1850 Chancery Commission Report, a number of reforms
were enacted by Parliament in the Chancery Procedure Acts of 1852, essentially contemporary with the writing of *Bleak House*. This legislation

abolished masters
provided for additional staffing and facilities
established procedures for taking oral testimony
curtailed certain dilatory practices of the parties with penalties
accelerated the process of continuing cases despite the death of a party
authorized the court to hire experts

(Holdsworth, *Charles Dickens* 114)

Consequently, some of the ills that Dickens identifies in the novel were addressed in the 1852 legislation, but it is clear that some of the practices per-
sisted, despite changes in the law, and that other reforms were still necessary
(see also Shatto, *Companion* 29). *Bleak House* famously represents the Chancery Court as all powerful, "a living presence whose tentacles reach every other
character in the novel" (Glaser and Roth 288); it took time for meaningful reform to take effect.

The law is a noble profession, but, as Dickens continuously pointed out, not all
its practitioners are noble. Moreover, too often the profession fails to lead reform efforts in areas that cry out for action. Several writers have commented
on the failure of the bar, in Dickens's era, to monitor its practitioners. "The
lawyers, as a body, were perhaps the greatest obstacle to the reform of the law"

(Woodward 18), and "self interest" often perverted efforts of Chancery reform (Manchester 13). The bar associations in existence during Dickens's time, the Society of Gentlemen Practisers in the Courts of Law and Equity, and its successor, the Law Society (Smith and Stevens, ch. 3), paid attention to the unfair practices of individual attorneys but failed to address the broader needs of their clients. *Bleak House* causes students to understand this larger responsibility of the bar. If the current institutions representing lawyers were to come to a similar understanding, reform efforts dealing with such issues as abusive class actions, medical malpractice, product liability, and tort reform in general would be substantially advanced. Dickens remains relevant today.

Curating *Bleak House*

Denise Fulbrook

If one is inclined to try a new approach to teaching *Bleak House*, let me recommend designing a course around it. For those already blanching, coughing, and otherwise squinting at that idea—it is, after all, a very long, very muddy text— let me just say that teaching *Bleak House* in this way made for one of the most satisfying, informative, and inspiring experiences I and my students have ever had sharing a text. Not only did it provide a way around some of the more characteristic difficulties of teaching this text—its length, the demands on historical knowledge it makes, its, well, bleakness—it also allowed for an in-depth study of its rich critical and cultural history. Coming from someone with a sometimes short attention span who was fearful of devoting an entire semester to one novel, let alone a novel where even the illustration plates are known for being dark, this is no small recommendation. In fact, I am still not sure that I could have spent a whole semester teaching this novel if I had used only conventional methods to do so.

The approach I used grew out of a fourteen-week undergraduate course I taught at the University of Kentucky called Text and Context. A new course for majors, its one general requirement was that it allow students to study a single major text from a variety of contextual perspectives. For me, as a nineteenth-century scholar, *Bleak House* was an obvious choice. From miasma and motherhood to literacy and illegitimacy, from law and paternity to madness and morbidity, from sanitation to sensation, the animal to the human, few novels are as richly engaged as *Bleak House* with the questions plaguing, perplexing, haunting, and transforming the nineteenth century. Nor are there many novels that lend themselves so readily to discussion of such a diverse array of literary genres and modes—*Bleak House* is at once gothic and urban, realist and romantic, a social problem novel and a fictional autobiography, a fairy tale and a detective plot, a ghost story and a bildungsroman. Finally, one is pressed to think of a major critical or theoretical approach that has not played a substantive role in the making of the literary legacy of this novel. Hence, initially, the imagined future of this class felt like a dream: no more skipping over important critical traditions, sacrificing a multiplicity of readings for the exemplariness of one sustained analytic path; no more trying to cram the reading assignments for this multiplotted megalosaurus of mid-century fiction into two short weeks. What a wonderful luxury! Needless to say, perhaps, this happy, abstract reasoning took place late in the spring semester, long before I actually had to plan anything, and when I was as confident of the course's being successful as Miss Flite was of getting a judgment in her favor any day from the Chancery case.

In August, the panic descended. Other, less favorable aspects of this imagined class came into focus, and I suddenly became certain that Lady Dedlock would not be the only one buried alive and "bored to death" (56) over the course of the semester. Indeed, while there may be as many ways of contextualizing *Bleak House* as there are heaps of paper generated by Jarndyce and Jarndyce, it also became very clear to me that accessing them without getting caught in a relentless replay of the same depressing text for an entire semester seemed as likely as Richard Carstone's escaping the novel without the life blood being sucked out of him. I feared for the curiosity and vitality of my twenty-eight students. I began to wonder if I wasn't "a little—you know!—M—!" (69), when I first agreed to do the course and then chose *Bleak House*. I knew I had to find an alternative to class after class wherein I introduced students to new contexts or methodologies only to return them—inevitably, inexorably—to close readings of a text that by mid-semester, if not sooner, would undoubtedly seem to them more stagnant than the river at Chesney Wold.

The solution: an experimental course organized around the creation of a library exhibit. From a pedagogical perspective, to say that this approach worked well would be an understatement. To share it is the goal of the remainder of this essay. Because of the scope of this approach and because I hope to provide concrete, practical guidance to anyone who wishes to use it either in relation to *Bleak House* or to any number of other nineteenth-century texts (e.g., *Middlemarch*, the Alice books, *Dracula*), my discussion is also oriented toward sharing the logistical details of this unconventional undertaking. To this end, I begin with a snapshot of the event to help the reader envision what such an exhibit might look like as well as to offer an introductory sense of some of the contexts considered, the research materials used, and the engagement level of the students.

The Exhibit

Held in the Special Collections library, the exhibit included eleven student cases, and on the night of the premiere over 150 people from the academic and local community attended. It was entitled, after many class discussions and votes, "Unlocking *Bleak House*: An Exploration of Charles Dickens." Dedicated to such topics as Dickens and the law, Dickens and fairy tales, disease in Victorian England, and the publication and reception history of the book and moving from spontaneous combustion to birds, characterization to biography, women in the nineteenth century to *Bleak House* in the modern world, the exhibit cases were as diverse as they were informative. They represented a range of subjects and reflected in their conception, design, and content the students' interests and semester-long researches. Some were built by individuals and some by small groups; all were noteworthy for their creativity, high level of scholarship, and the way they worked to engage and teach the spectator about *Bleak House* from a variety of perspectives—some conventional, some not. For example, the case on spontaneous combustion not only attended to the famed debate between Dickens and George H. Lewes about both the scientific credibility of spontaneous human combustion and the responsibility an author of fiction has to the laws of science; it also documented the history of spontaneous human combustion before Dickens to highlight the irregularity of the gender of the victim in *Bleak House* (most were, like Miss Havisham, drunken old women), addressed the discourse of spontaneous combustion post-Dickens, was supported by a poster and explanation of the Hablot K. Browne illustration, and, finally, graphically represented Krook's death through the use of an empty pair of boots, a pile of ashes, a drained and dusty bottle of ale, greasy glass, and an antiqued candle holder. Similarly, the case on characterization combined primary and secondary research with explanatory cards offering interpretations of the novel and creative elements geared toward engaging the exhibitgoer on a more visceral level. It coupled a presentation of pictorial and written evidence (e.g., portraits, letters, newspapers from the Victorian period, articles from *Household Words* and *Notes and Queries*) about the relationship between characters in the novel and real people in Dickens's life (e.g., Caroline Chisholm [Mrs. Jellyby], Walter Savage Landor [Boythorn], Inspector Field [Bucket], and, most famously, Leigh Hunt [Harold Skimpole]), with information drawn from critical debates about Dickens's methods of characterization. Along with producing a pamphlet detailing the defining features of characters in *Bleak House*, the student represented the complex interrelations of those characters through the creation of a four-foot interactive electric grid, which, when switches were flipped, lit different chains of connectedness.

Whether showcasing twentieth-century law review articles about Jarndyce and Jarndyce or nineteenth-century books on natural history and woodcuts of Dickens's birds, articles in Victorian periodicals or notes from the office of Stephen King, student-made maps of "diseased" London or playbills, this approach employed a wide range of creative, literary, and historical materials and engaged the novel on multiple levels. At the premiere, visitors were greeted with an illustrated exhibit guide, a chance to smear their fingers with a feather pen and apothecary ink, a sample of Dickens's signature, and an enormous blow-up of the frontispiece of the first bound volume. (The wrapper for the serial edition graced the publicity materials.) Along with various graphic interpretations of the novel, the exhibit also included several poster-sized versions of the original illustrations, a VCR cart playing the 1985 BBC version of *Bleak House*, a computer linked to a Web site with Victorian sounds, piles of paper falling from the ceiling (as if out of the novel), and a food table with offerings made from recipes from Victorian cookbooks. Information cards contextualized these recipes in relation to *Bleak House*. The students, who, by now, called Dickens "Chaz" and themselves "The Dickensians," served as expert guides, donning name tags that specified which case they created and answering questions about their research. Before the event, I asked faculty members from the English department to quiz the students informally and good naturedly; and, while at first students were nervous about these anticipated questions, by the end of the night their discovery of their ability to share their research with others helped them glow with a newly found sense of themselves as respected members of a community of scholars and educators, a feeling many carried beyond the class.

The Plan

As I revisit the exhibit, I recognize why my students were initially more wary of this approach's being successful than Esther was of believing the praise she received in the novel. This unusual approach is not only ambitious but also at times unpredictable. For this reason, it is crucial to acknowledge the students' doubt in the beginning, to present the attempt as a worthwhile endeavor in itself, and to solicit their cooperation in helping to actualize the goal of collective learning from the first day. One of the most critical things to note about this approach is that it is not only not teacher-centered; it requires the active participation of students, who will ultimately be responsible for the researching and building of the exhibit, and of librarians, who will help provide the students with the tools to accomplish their research and create the exhibit. In fact, the first thing I recommend doing for anyone using this idea is to meet with a reference librarian or two and develop a plan for the semester. Their help and expertise are invaluable.

This approach involved extensive library instruction, and several classes were spent with reference librarians who used search examples that related directly to Dickens or *Bleak House* to introduce students to general literary databases (such as *MLA International Bibliography*, *Literature Online*, and *Periodicals Index Online*), resources that specifically addressed nineteenth-century texts and contexts (*Nineteenth-Century Masterfile*, *Victorian Database*, *Index to the London Times*), and special collections holdings, which proved unexpectedly energizing for the students.[1] As I discovered through the presentation prepared by the curator of rare books at my university, Jim Birchfield, nothing inspires students to become interested in primary research more than the original documents. A discussion of Dickens's narcissism or the significance of handwriting in the novel comes alive for students in vivid and graphic detail when his distinctive, heavily underlined signature is actually in front of them. Reading the Penguin edition of *Bleak House* is not nearly as contextually rich or exciting as being able to flip open the illustrated green-blue wrapper of one of the nineteen monthly parts to find the original illustrations and advertisements.

On library instruction days, I gave the students a specific assignment designed to complement the presentation—for example, needing to find a reputable critical essay on *Bleak House* or having to locate and analyze a nineteenth-century source that they thought would be vital to include in the exhibit. This combination kept the students focused, enabled them to learn through hands-on practice in a guided setting, and got them used to working together to solve research problems such as discovering the best search terms or thinking of ways of conceptualizing contexts. In this sense it was never enough simply to find a critical or archival source; the students needed to learn how to articulate why a particular source or approach was important in understanding the text and placing it in context. Hence, the classes immediately following library instruction were devoted to turning individual research projects into the basis for collective learning. In them, students shared their research in roundtable discussions, introducing as a result a more interesting and diverse variety of ways of contextualizing and reading Dickens's *Bleak House* than would have been possible if I had chosen all the contexts in advance or if all students were always contextualizing the text in the same way at the same time. From these discussions, a pattern of peer education was established, and a collective annotated bibliography and conceptual index project began.

This approach required that reading assignments take a variety of forms. For some classes everyone read the same text and examined the same context, and for others the reading assignments were driven by individual and small-group student research. In terms of structure, the class was divided into two overlapping halves of about seven weeks each. The first half involved three weeks spent on a close reading of *Bleak House*, followed by library instruction, small-group research assignments, and the collective study of particular contexts for reading *Bleak House*. Although any number of contexts could be pursued through shared readings, I focused on fairly conventional ones for the sake of helping students gain a basic understanding of the notion of a context and the influential role some contexts have played in understanding Dickens's work. For example, alongside the novel, we read two biographies that could be used for comparative purposes (Fred Kaplan's *Dickens: A Biography* and Peter Ackroyd's *Dickens: Public Life and Private Passions*); a selection of Dickens's letters; contemporary reviews of Dickens's novel, which repeatedly addressed its plotlessness, grotesqueness, or the "problem" with Esther; and selections from Dickens's first "novel," *Sketches by Boz*, which I consider especially relevant to *Bleak House* in terms of introducing characteristic features of genre, theme, description, character, and style.

Assignments for this half of the class included a topical and conceptual index (designed to help students identify and track an idea in a sustained fashion), an analytic essay that made use of index entries as evidence, miniresearch assignments such as the students introducing into class discussion topics they had looked up in the *Oxford Reader's Companion to Dickens* (Schlicke) and *What Jane Austen Ate and Charles Dickens Knew* (Pool) (e.g., Chancery, society, madness, lunacy, money, domesticity), and, finally, as described above, research into the history of the literary criticism about *Bleak House*.

As a transition to the second half of the course, which was designed to optimize the realization of individual and small-group research, we narrowed possible topics for inclusion in the exhibit. To do this and to devise a way around five hundred different topics being proposed, students were asked to list three areas they wanted represented and three areas they felt absolutely had to be in the exhibit. The final list was culled from these. Despite the variety of individual interests, and perhaps as a result of shared contexts and discussions, we had little difficulty settling on the general areas the class would use to structure its research.

In the second half of the semester, individual and small-group research projects intensified, and I worked with students collectively and individually to develop realizable and educationally valuable projects. Sometimes this meant spending hours with individual students helping them understand the productivity of the trial and error of research; sometimes it meant a collective discussion on subjects such as how to narrow a research topic or how to get materials from another library's special collections or whether a particular topic would be worthwhile to research in relation to *Bleak House*. On some research days, students were allowed class time to work as a group so that they could be guaranteed no time conflicts, and I met with the groups to offer them individualized help with their research struggles. On other days, the class continued to read common texts and explore aspects of Dickens's work or life as a collective; however, during this time and because of the sheer amount of outside research students were doing, I kept assigned reading to a minimum and simply worked diligently to keep the learning experience fresh by employing a variety of unconventional tactics. For example, after discussing Dickens's interest in theatricality and history of public readings and as a means of fostering a discussion of affect in the novel, I invited an actor to class to introduce the students to acting techniques. In subsequent class periods, I required them to read selected passages of *Bleak House* not just aloud but with feeling and with an eye toward distinguishing the voices of different characters. After each reading, we discussed the treatment of affect and character in the text. On other days, we read a part of the novel as it would have been read in serial form, discussing the ways in which novels were printed, circulated, and consumed during the Victorian period and the difference this history makes.

Finally, the last two weeks of the semester were spent preparing, organizing, building, and publicizing the actual exhibit and its premiere, which was a great success. Indeed, for as much work as this approach requires, it is not only well worth it, it is an approach from which scholars and teachers, along with the students, also gain. From this class, I learned a good deal more about Dickens and the various worlds of *Bleak House* than I knew going into the class— before this class I would have never focused, for example, on the large role that birds play in his texts and life—and I learned even more about finding new ways of making the reading of old literary texts and contexts relevant, meaningful, and exciting to today's students and their communities.

NOTE

[1] I would like to thank the librarians, curators, staff, and administration at the University of Kentucky's Young Library and Special Collections who helped make this exhibit a success. I also thank the English Department at the University of Kentucky for its support and the "Dickensians" of English 333, without whose efforts such a beautiful, bleak house could never have been built. Special thanks go to Mary Vass, Carla Cantagallo, and Roxanna Jones at Young and to Bill Marshall, Adrienne Stevens, and the indefatigable Jim Birchfield at Special Collections, whose enthusiasm, expertise, and infinite patience deserve a particular note of appreciation and gratitude.

Teaching *Bleak House* in Serial Installments

Joel J. Brattin

I must confess that I began teaching *Bleak House* in serial installments out of concern not for my students but for myself—out of a sort of pedagogical desperation. I arrived at my present university in 1990 to find a new and, from the perspective of my interest in the Victorian novel, highly daunting teaching schedule. The academic calendar at my university, Worcester Polytechnic Institute (WPI), is based on seven-week terms, with most courses meeting four days a week. How could I possibly manage to teach Victorian masterpieces like *Bleak House*, *Our Mutual Friend*, and *Middlemarch* in that brief period of time—with just twenty-eight fifty-minute class sessions in a term? How could I ask undergraduates, mostly freshman and sophomores majoring in science or engineering, to read long and complex novels in just a month and a half?

My solution was to create a course, Popular Fiction: Reading in Installments, in which we read one full-length Dickens novel and George Eliot's *Middlemarch* in serial installments. Where Dickens's first readers read one serial installment a month, I require my students to read one installment a day. Still, they get a rare opportunity to read *Bleak House* at comparative leisure and to puzzle over questions of plot, structure, and theme in a more deliberate way than students who must rush through the novel in a week or two. The catalog description says that students "will have the opportunity to read two major masterpieces of English fiction the way they should be read: slowly, carefully, and with relish." They have a chance to analyze two long books in one short term, "reading the novels in the way in which they were read by their original readers—serially."[1] What seemed at first an impossible schedule helped inspire me to create a new way of teaching that my students and I have found extremely rewarding.

In the seventeen years since I created the course, students have had the chance to read all of Dickens's long novels—*Pickwick Papers*, *Nicholas Nickleby*, *Martin Chuzzlewit*, *Dombey and Son*, *David Copperfield*, *Bleak House*, and *Our Mutual Friend*.[2] I have gone back to some of my favorites, including *Bleak House*, two or even three times. In this essay, I consider *Bleak House*, emphasizing method: what I do, how I do it, and why.

Because I always conclude the course with *Middlemarch*, originally published in eight books at irregular intervals from 1872 to 1874, and because I give a final examination on the last day of class, I have only sixteen days to teach *Bleak House*. On the first day of class, when I cannot expect students to have read anything, I introduce myself, the course, and Dickens; I also ask my students (generally, between twenty-five and fifty of them) to introduce themselves and to retain the same seats for the first several days of class. (I make a seating chart, so I can match names to faces; though the course is sometimes a large one, I want it to be discussion-based, so I find it essential to learn student names as quickly as possible.)

I impress on my students the necessity of reading carefully the assigned installment of *Bleak House* before class and of looking up any unfamiliar words in the *Oxford English Dictionary*; I also stress the importance of mastering small details (which they cannot get by reading plot summaries).

I reinforce that message about the importance of attending to detail by giving a brief, five-question reading quiz at the beginning of each class session. These quizzes do not necessarily focus on main characters, pivotal plot elements, or important themes; my goal is to inspire careful reading and the mastery of detail, so we can have richer discussions in class. I design the questions so that answering them takes very little class time: correct answers are typically a word or two long, and all five answers easily fit on a half-sheet of recycled paper. I find I can read each question aloud twice, collect the quizzes, and announce the correct answers in the first three or four minutes of class, and the sacrifice of time seems well worth it. The quizzes eliminate the need to take roll and encourage punctuality; I begin promptly at the beginning of the hour, and I offer no opportunity to make up a missed quiz. (The total quiz scores account for twenty percent of a student's course grade.) After class, I alphabetize and grade the quizzes and record the grades; this takes no more than five or ten minutes.

I offer at least one question pertaining to each assigned chapter. I try to create questions that are relatively easy to answer, if one has done the reading, and somewhat difficult to guess, if one has not (even if one has consulted a plot summary). My quiz for the fourth monthly installment, published in June 1852, might include such questions as the following:

> What drug finally took the life of the law-copier, Nemo? [Opium or laudanum]
>
> Who speaks of Captain Swosser falling, "raked fore and aft . . . by the fire from my tops"? [Mrs. Badger]
>
> What secret does Ada tell Esther, at the end of chapter 13? [She and Richard love each other.]

My questions for the eleventh installment of January 1853 might include such questions as:

> What friend accompanies Mr. George, when Mr. Smallweed breaks the pipe of peace? [Mr. Bagnet]
>
> What object of household furnishing does Esther notice is missing from her room, when she recovers from her illness? [A mirror]
>
> Miss Flite tells Esther of whose heroism after a shipwreck? [Allan Woodcourt's]

Another important element in the course is my use of the rich collection of Dickensian materials in the Robert D. Fellman Collection, donated to Worcester Polytechnic Institute in 1995 by a generous Dickensian and since supplemented with additional donations and library purchases. Ever since this remarkable collection—which includes first editions, sets of original parts, a rich and varied collection of illustrations, hundreds of volumes of explanatory and critical works, several letters in Dickens's own hand, and even the unique attendance book for the Guild of Literature and Art—came to the university, I have tried to find ways to share it with students, and I find that teaching the installments provides a golden opportunity. When I teach Popular Fiction: Reading in Installments, the curator of Special Collections gives me access to a locking display case, and in that case I put items appropriate to the installment of *Bleak House* that we will consider the next day. Such items may include original illustrations (often displaying variants in the states of the plates and often emphasizing details of Hablot K. Browne's "dark plates"), portraits of Dickens or of people mentioned in an installment, letters Dickens wrote that bear on an installment (either in printed form from the Pilgrim Edition or in manuscript), relevant pages from other Dickens works such as articles in *Household Words*, reproductions of Dickens's manuscript or his plans for the monthly installments of *Bleak House*, advertisements from the serial parts of the novel, or pages of first-edition text that feature significant textual variants from our paperback. When we consider the final, double installment, which includes Dickens's dedication of the novel to the members of the Guild of Literature and Art, I display the attendance book, open to a page showing the signatures of Dickens, John Forster, Wilkie Collins, John Tenniel, and other Victorian luminaries. I usually provide captions for whatever items I display, drawing attention to salient details; I also provide paper arrows, pointing to bits of text or features in an illustration to which I ask students to pay particularly close attention. I change the display for each class session (that is, I create four different displays every week), taking care that the new display is ready by 8:00 a.m each day, and I require the students to review the contents of the display case before class—reinforcing this requirement by announcing that sometimes the answers to quiz questions will depend on careful consideration of the materials in the case and then making sure to create such quiz questions at frequent intervals. My requirement that students visit the display case every day means that all my students learn where the library is located. Equally important, many of them express satisfaction at being able to examine rare nineteenth-century artifacts.

Quiz questions based on displayed items range broadly. Here are some samples:

> In the illustration "The Lord Chancellor Copies from Memory," what is visible in the far left? [Broken scales]
>
> What famous and controversial American novel was advertised in the third serial installment of *Bleak House*? [*Uncle Tom's Cabin*]
>
> Which character was based, in part, on Inspector Field, portrayed as Inspector Wield in the article in *Household Words* on display in the library? [Bucket]

According to the footnote in the letter on display, did the philosopher
John Stuart Mill like *Bleak House*? [No]
What is the subject of Browne's "dark plate" for the fourteenth install-
ment? [Tom-all-Alone's]

Generally, I arrive in the classroom a few minutes early to chat with students;
I write the number and date of publication of the relevant monthly installment
on the blackboard before class begins. I give the quiz promptly at the beginning
of the hour, and after collecting and discussing it, we have a little more than
forty-five minutes to discuss the installment itself.

We take a chronological approach (that is, we discuss chapter 1 before discussing chapter 2), and we usually have at least ten or fifteen minutes to consider each chapter in the novel. We are able to discuss a great many more topics,
in a great deal more detail, than if I were confined to the three (or five or even
ten) lectures I would likely be able to devote to the novel in a conventional
semester's course. In preparing for class, I draw up questions for discussion
that highlight the elements in each chapter I find of greatest interest and importance; these questions form a kind of skeletal outline for the class session. I
add time markers to this outline and try to observe those markers fairly closely
during class, to prevent my giving disproportionate emphasis to a chapter that
appears early in an installment. This fairly tight structure gives me something to
hold on to, should students prove taciturn or my brain freeze up; on the other
hand, if discussion is going well—and it almost invariably does—I can always
depart from the outline and improvise, working with the good ideas my students
develop about the novel.

Studying the novel serially not only teaches skills in close reading but also
allows a different kind of focus on character development and structure than
conventional ways of approaching novels do.

A serial approach to characters can enhance readers' sympathy. Considering characters like Harold Skimpole, the lawyer Vholes, and his client Richard
Carstone over time, as they develop in the novel, students can appreciate not
just Dickens's thematic or satirical point but his subtlety: midway through the
novel, many students discover a complexity in these characters, and even some
feeling for them, which they may have been unlikely to admit if questions about
the characters came up only after the novel's conclusion.

Similarly, studying *Bleak House* in parts prompts students to consider the
structure of the novel more frequently—and perhaps more carefully. The issue
of the two narrators arises early, and we often consider the relative balance of
two voices in a given installment. We also consider the ways the chapters in a
given installment relate to one another—the first installment, for example, with
its juxtapositions of London and Chesney Wold, affords only the first of many
opportunities to consider Dickens's architecture.

I assign three three-to-five-page essays (each of which counts for twenty percent of a student's grade) over the course of the term—two on *Bleak House* and

one on *Middlemarch*. I give very little lead time for the essays: I assign them at the end of class on Tuesday, and the essays are due on the following Thursday (class does not meet on Wednesday, so students have a bit of extra time to read, think, and write). In these essays, I ask the students to find an interesting and argumentative claim they can make about the installment assigned for Thursday, which they can support with evidence from the text. Of course, I insist on accurate citation and careful documentation, with parenthetical page references. I emphasize that I expect no library research for these essays: I want students to come to terms with the novel itself, not with critical opinion about the novel. For each assignment, I provide a list of ideas, methods, topics, themes, and perspectives that students may find worth considering. For the thirteenth installment, for example, I might include such things as the following:

> Imagery: the function of the stars, moon, and sun
> Character analysis: Mr. Vholes's respectability
> Psychology: Lady Dedlock's state of mind
> Description: shade and shadow in Chesney Wold
> Theme and structure: links between and among chapters
> Tulkinghorn's attitude toward women and marriage
> Satire and the function of Volumnia Dedlock
> Good and bad manners: Lady Dedlock, Hortense, and Tulkinghorn
> The significance of names
> Power and passion

I tell students that thinking critically about this list of topics may help them come up with a thesis but that they are also welcome to pick their own topic as long as it pertains to the assigned serial installment—and many do come up with surprising, interesting, and valuable approaches.

I have had no problems with plagiarized essays in this course. Perhaps students aren't tempted to steal an essay because there aren't many such essays, closely focused on a single installment, available on the Internet.

Because of the focus on individual parts of the novel, there's comparatively little time in class to think about the novel as a whole—but I do devote most of one class session, immediately following the day in which we consider the final double installment, to a free-wheeling examination of the major themes in the novel. (I also introduce George Eliot, and *Middlemarch*, on that day.)

The course as I've designed it provides no opportunity to write about the novel as a whole until the final examination (which counts for the remaining twenty percent of a student's grade); I try to create an essay question that allows students to put together an argument based on evidence from the entire novel. As the students have only half of a fifty-minute class period to write about *Bleak House* (there's a second essay question on *Middlemarch*), I help them prepare for the examination by giving them, in the last class session before the exam, a clear idea about what the question will be, suggesting that they think carefully about the themes in the novel and that they locate textual evidence they may wish to use when considering, say, the theme of duty or the concept of vocation in the novel. The final examination question then focuses on the theme I've suggested it would, inviting the students to consider that theme with reference to, for example, three characters from a list of four or five.

I have found that when I teach *Bleak House* in its serial installments, students have the opportunity to examine the novel closely, and with greater care: to attend to fine details of Dickens's writing that might otherwise be glossed over. At the same time, reading the novel in parts also helps emphasize Dickens's mastery of shape and structure. Students enjoy this approach to fiction, and it has been immensely rewarding for me to teach *Bleak House* and other full-length Dickens novels in this manner.

NOTES

[1] On four Mondays over the course of the term, I require students to read not one but two serial installments; this compromise frees up days to consider *Bleak House* and *Middlemarch* as whole novels and provides a day for the final examination.

[2] I teach *Little Dorrit* in a different course.

Bleak House and Narrative Theory

Hilary M. Schor

No question: *Bleak House* is a daunting text to face in any classroom, for graduate students, undergraduates, and faculty members alike. Apart from its length
(and can we ever say enough about that?), it poses the challenges of an unusually
complicated plot, an antiquated and arcane legal system, a troublingly modest
and inarticulate narrator, and, to add to the "trouble with Esther," a split narrative. The shadowy and haunted aspects of the narrative shade into the opacity of
the plot and the snarled web of relationship—and, as these sentences suggest,
the explanatory powers of even the clearest teacher can become tangled when
confronted with the density and subtlety of Dickens's art. So when I claim that
I love to teach *Bleak House* and that I do so whenever the opportunity presents
itself, I expect to receive looks of surprise and disbelief, and I am sure, dear
reader, that you are not disappointing me now.

Nonetheless, this is my claim. I have taught *Bleak House* in a variety of settings—undergraduate courses on women in British and American literature
after 1800, where I pair it effectively with *Villette*; seminars for PhD students
and law students on legal fictions, where I teach it alongside Jeremy Bentham's
critique of Blackstone, Lawrence Stone's history of marriage, and Alexander
Welsh's account of circumstantial evidence; courses, both graduate and undergraduate, on the nineteenth-century novel and the realist tradition. I do not
teach it in our sophomore survey of English literature, where I turn instead
to *Little Dorrit*—but that, as we say, is another story. In all these classrooms, I
have learned to disarm the inevitable questions and challenges from resistant
students: invariably, the modesty of Esther Summerson looks less like irony and
more like cloying sweetness to twenty-first-century readers (as, indeed, it did to
many of Dickens's contemporary readers), and equally without exception, each
class brings several students who simply boggle at the number of characters.
Imagine their confusion when they then confront the difficulty of meeting these
characters once, twice, and often a third time, until they finally come to realize
that, as Robert Newsom memorably noted, "the dark young surgeon" at Miss
Flite's bed, the "young surgeon" at Esther's dinner party, and Allan Woodcourt
are all one person (*Dickens on the Romantic Side* 55, 56). Even before students
encounter the challenge of this "*Bleak House* effect," the repeated experience
of déjà vu, of repetition with (slight but important) differences, there are basic
textual questions to answer. Students who are wondering, as one finally (in week
3 of our reading) posed the question, "Where in London is Chancery, and why
are so many characters 'in' it?" cannot be expected to notice, or even to care,
that they are meeting people in two narratives; that the "first-person" narrator
speaks in the past tense and the "third-person" narrator in the present or that
the Esther Summerson who writes her "portion of these pages" (27) has already
lived through them and is not only keeping secrets and playing dumb but (on

occasion) lying to the reader. They cannot, that is, enjoy the deepest of narrative games that the novel poses, when they are struggling for comprehension and control of a text that seems always to elude them. It is one thing to disarm questions and resistances, filling in the gaps for confused students; it is quite another to find a pedagogical structure that actually turns *Bleak House*'s evident classroom disadvantages into advantages, its seeming weaknesses into strengths.

But this I believe I have done, in a semester-long graduate seminar I designed on *Bleak House* and narrative theory. I dreamed this class up, fittingly, while riding on a train—and its aim was, quite simply, to get students to embrace the complications of narratology not by using (as most narrative theory seminars do) a wide range of fictional examples but by taking one long, dense, and endlessly frustrating novel. The class, as I conceived it, would use a difficult novel to challenge the theorists—and the theorists, in turn, to test the novelist. It satisfied a number of departmental needs (the chair was torn between requesting a course in literary theory and a course in Victorian literature; this class was very much both), and it also allowed me to create something I had always dreamed of, a single-text course that would provide a window onto a complicated cultural moment. But it also allowed theory-challenged students a path into very difficult theoretical material—and forced the department's theory heads to bring their models to bear on a literary text. It remains for me an open question how well such a course would work with a text less complicated than *Bleak House*, which truly seems to contain every kind of narrative problem you can name, but there is no question but that it works to do something else that I believe in: it makes *Bleak House* seem, if anything, far less anomalous and more a kind of laboratory for solving some of the problems inherent in understanding, and in teaching, all fiction.

The syllabus, however, had to do the following things economically: it had to level the playing field of reading, so no student could claim superior knowledge of the novel; it had to offer students a common entryway into narrative theory and provide some kind of thorough grounding in the field; and it had to allow for a range of student interests, including Victorianists, theorists, and generalists alike. The course I designed, I think, answers these challenges. We accomplish the first by reading the novel quickly, together, over two weeks; we accomplish the second by weaving examples of narrative theory into our rereading of *Bleak House*, taking on two number parts each week; and finally, as the course goes on, we add denser and more culturally based "secondary" readings to our perusal of narratology and Dickens.

In the initial seminar meeting, I distribute the syllabus and "perform" (with the students) a reading of chapters 1 and 3. We then establish not so much a collective reading as a set of collective questions over the next two weeks, reading chapters 1–32 one week and the remainder of the novel the next. In addition, we read two short pieces of criticism to set some boundaries for the course. We read John Butt and Kathleen Tillotson's introduction to *Dickens at Work*, "Dickens as a Serial Novelist," which informs students about the situation of

Dickens's first readers and prepares us for the number-part structure of *Bleak House*. The next week, in quite a different experiment in structure, we read Roland Barthes's early piece of narratology, "Introduction to the Structural Analysis of Narratives," which also helps accustom us to the defamiliarizing practices of structuralism. In the first week of our novel reading, I ask the students to think of three questions they want to see answered in the second half of the novel, and I put all our questions on the blackboard; I also ask them to pull a piece of paper out of a hat, in which I place the names of about twenty minor characters in the novel. Generating the questions gets them started on both the most general and the most trivial puzzles of the novel (What is the role of Africa in the novel? Why the critique of Evangelicalism? What are we to do with the narrator's ironic tone? Who is Nemo, and why is he called Nimrod?); once they have chosen the name of a character, however, they are bound not only to detached critical inquiry but to a single "person" in the book for whom they would be responsible for the remainder of the semester. Choosing a character not only guarantees that every student has something to say each week (the shyest students would speak up for their character) but also adds a willful touch of naiveté to the otherwise unrelieved high theoretical tone of the course—nowhere does Barthes say that we might "adopt" James Bond. It licenses, that is, a wide range of readings and a certain resistance to narratology itself.

So, what is the narratology at the heart of this class, and how does it work? We begin with Barthes (*S/Z*), Peter Brooks (*Reading for the Plot*), Leo Bersani (*A Future for Astyanax*), and Tzvetan Todorov (*The Poetics of Prose*), classic narratological studies focused primarily on form and plot, critics with roots in psychoanalysis who nonetheless are intent on displacing humanist models of the self. From there we move on to more psychoanalytic criticism, reading Robert Newsom's study of the "uncanny" Dickens (*Dickens on the Romantic Side of Familiar Things*) and Sigmund Freud ("The 'Uncanny'"), and feminism, drawing primarily on Teresa de Lauretis (*Alice Doesn't*), Nancy K. Miller ("Emphasis Added"), and Susan Winnett ("Coming Unstrung"), critics who engage explicitly with French narrative theory; last in our quick run through classic narratology, we read Gerard Genette's *Narrative Discourse*, at once the most obsessive and most playful of the theoretical texts we engage with. The course has to offer more than a survey of narrative theory, however; it also has to choose theorists who add something particular to the portion of *Bleak House* we have just reached. The week we read *Narrative Discourse*, for instance, we also read Esther's narration of the onset of her fever, when she claims, "I had no thought that night—none, I am quite sure—of what was soon to happen to me. But . . . I had for a moment an undefinable impression of myself as being something different from what I then was" (489). Genette's discussion of time ("order") and narration ("voice") is perfectly tuned for unraveling the difficulties of Esther's self-presentation, the gap between Esther-character and Esther-narrator; the following week, when we read Esther's account of her fever ("Dare I hint at that worse time when, strung together somewhere in great black space, there was a flaming necklace . . . of which *I* was one of the beads!" [556]) we read chapters by D. A. Miller (*The Novel and the Police*), Deidre Lynch (*The Economy of Character*), and Alex Woloch (*The One vs. the Many*), critics who raise the same questions of (fictional) "subjectivity." We then spend several weeks on problems of realism, drawing on Susan Stewart's *On Longing* to discuss the "world in miniature" in *Bleak House*, on M. M. Bakhtin (*The Dialogic Imagination*) and Henry Mayhew (*London Labour and the London Poor*) to examine the way the novel voices social difference, and on contemporary reviews and journalism to illuminate the novel's topicality (Collins, *Dickens: The Critical Heritage*). I close with D. A. Miller's evocative text *Bringing Out Roland Barthes*, seeing in Miller's rewriting of Barthes's journal-like "Soirées de Paris" a return to the problem at the heart of *Bleak House*: what is the difference between reading as an "I" and reading for another?

This emphasis on doubling worked particularly well in my most recent version of the course, and this is what I want to stress in the rest of this essay, giving an example drawn from the course. In the second week of class, when we read Barthes's "Introduction to the Structural Analysis of Narratives," I drew the students' attention to one particularly fascinating episode in *Bleak House*, which runs across chapters 50 and 51: the scenes beginning in "Esther's Narrative" where Esther observes Ada's growing sadness and decides that it bespeaks Ada's fears for Esther's upcoming (and not particularly eagerly anticipated) marriage to John Jarndyce. Only in the second chapter of the number, "Enlightened," does Esther realize ("A light shone in upon me all at once" [786]) that Ada's grief comes from Ada's own marriage to Richard and her plans to leave Bleak House. Every detail can (must) then be reread: the hand under the pillow in chapter 50 is shown, in chapter 51, to be wearing a wedding ring; the needle-work Ada hides is for her own hope chest, or perhaps even for her unborn child. At this point, Esther's evasiveness and relentless cheerfulness are revealed as inadvertent cruelty toward Ada; her fears for Ada, merely the expression of her own ambivalence over her impending nuptials and the loss of Allan Woodcourt, her true love.

In the first discussion of these chapters, we followed Barthes's analysis of plot "functions" (103–17), in essence tracing the narrative tree that leads to Esther's enlightenment. In particular, we focused on the scene where Ada and Esther go to visit Richard Carstone in his chambers. At every turn in the journey, at every narrative hinge, Esther hesitates and Ada turns out to know the way. Although Ada repeatedly says she "thinks" she knows which way to turn, we soon realize she "knows" which way to turn; only once Esther and the reader have been "enlightened," have completed the sequence ("arrival at Richard's door") can we rename the episode: this sequence is not "Ada and Esther visiting Richard" but "Ada taking Esther to her (own) rooms." To draw further on our early readings in structuralism, borrowing here from *S/Z*, the hermeneutic code (what we might, following Barthes's lead, call the "mystery of Ada's feelings") gives way to the symbolic ("marriage as death") as Esther makes her way to Ada's new home, seeing "more funerals passing along the dismal pavements, than I had ever seen before" (783), and again later, when she returns alone that night, and "put my lips to the hearse-like panel of the door, as a kiss for my dear" (790). This is a fine illustration of what classic narratology offers its users. When we returned to these chapters later in the semester, however, we had many more tools available for reading them. Fresh from our reading of Genette, we could notice with far more precision the elements of Esther's hesitation and deliberate misleading of her readers. Esther again plays games with time and voice, interrupting her account of Ada's "mystery," first with her visits to Caddy Jellyby and the ink-stained infant Esther and second with an interposed "first-person" account from Allan Woodcourt of his visit with Richard. She introduces these pages as what "he told me," but they are experienced by a reader as authored by someone other than Esther. The carefulness with which Esther tricks her readers into thinking that we have left her memoir, only to pull us back in with a clever transition ("I now return to the time when Caddy had recovered, and the shade was still between me and my darling" [782]) also allows Dickens to question readerly assumptions about female narrative, as he does throughout the novel. However cunningly she conceals it, the Esther-narrator here has complete control of her text, adding interpolated narrators at whim, moving between the man she loves and the man she is promised to, much like a princess in the folktales at the heart of de Lauretis's analysis, but with far more mobility and autonomy. The attention that the feminist critics paid to the underlining of certain generic effects (what Nancy K. Miller memorably called "emphasis added") becomes a powerful gesture at this moment in *Bleak House*, when Esther's passionate attachment to Ada cuts against the romantic plots of both heroines, when marriage seems another form of narrative death, and when Esther's true love literally interrupts her own (supposed) marriage plot.

Other benefits accrued to the rereading of this portion of the novel, in the light of our explorations of narrative theory. The first came from the surrounding readings, for we read this number along with the number in which Jo dies (ch. 47, "Jo's Will") and a set of readings on what I called "voicing London," in which we focused on Bakhtin, Mayhew, and contemporary reviews of the novel. Looking at Esther's chapters alongside Walter Bagehot's powerful evocation of Dickens as a "special correspondent for posterity" (394) moved us from the emotional content of Esther's pages to their detailed exploration of London's underside: these are chapters in which Esther, Ada, and Jarndyce move to London so she can care for Caddy's baby, but they feature more of the darkness of the streets than her earlier visits to the city do. In this number, George is arrested for the murder of Tulkinghorn, and Esther and Jarndyce visit him in Milbank prison; this chapter and the final chapter of the number (a third-person chapter), in which Inspector Bucket attends Tulkinghorn's great funeral and begins to draw his web tighter (or so we think) around Lady Dedlock, feature far more of the public, criminal world: newspapers, prisons, lawyers, rewards, and anonymous informants. These chapters are also shadowed by a host of female narrators, not only in the person of Hortense, who (invisibly, at this point) writes the letters that accuse Lady Dedlock, but Mrs. Bucket, who (again, with a significance we cannot yet know) is "dependent on their lodger (fortunately an amiable lady in whom she takes an interest) for companionship and conversation" (804). Only on rereading do we realize that the lodger is in fact Hortense, and the Buckets, as a husband-wife tag team, are drawing the noose not around Honoria but around her maid. But in these chapters, where we primarily share Esther's anxiety as the plot draws closer to the revelation of her mother, we are likelier to share the perspective of another anxious female storyteller, Volumnia, who remarks that Inspector Bucket, "that charmingly horrible person is a perfect Blue Chamber" (812). With this invocation of Bluebeard's castle, alongside the shudder we feel, with Esther, when we are told of the "shape so like Miss Summerson's [that went] by [George] in the dark" (800) as he waited on the dead man's stairway, we are moving closer and closer to the dark night of Lady Dedlock's death. A series of deaths will follow, but clever readers, on their second reading, will notice a plot detail unnoticed even by the ever-vigilant Susan Shatto, sections of whose *The Companion to* Bleak House we read for this week. Not only do Jo and Tulkinghorn die on the same night, a night when George, Lady Dedlock, and Hortense are all making their way through Lincoln's Inn Fields, but Esther herself is afoot, walking in shadows, guarded only by Charley, planting her kiss on the "hearse-like" door. Who is to say, or so our seminar asked, that the shadow that is so much like Esther's is not that of our duplicitous heroine herself?

Esther thinks, at this moment in her narrative, that "one of these days I would confess to the visit" (790), but of course she never does. *Bleak House* does not easily yield up its secrets—that is both what makes it the bane of so many courses and what makes it so endlessly fascinating for our students and for us. The seminar I have sketched here began with structuralism, with the formal constraints of number-part publication and Dickens's fascination with the structure of event; in a class in which students played their way across a range of theoretical registers, tracing the fates of characters, objects, and plot strands through fourteen weeks of reading and rereading, these questions truly came to life. The structure of the assignments encouraged students to merge identificatory reading practices and the most clinical of structuralist habits—such, it seems to me, is the divided inheritance of narratological theory today, and something that Dickens, particularly in his later, endlessly complicated fiction, also invites us to do. These divisions do not line up particularly neatly. In the world of narrative theory, we must learn to enjoy the constructedness, the almost mechanical structures that give us a "credible" fictional text, and yet still follow our curiosity, reading for the love of (imaginary) people. Lost in *Bleak House*, we are mesmerized and drawn on by the sheer complexity of the multiple plots of the novel, at the same time that we are repeatedly pulled up short by the dazzling, local effects of the brilliant prose and the heart-stopping pathos of individual characters. Dickens has a way of confounding all our interpretive strategies; narrative theory has a way of rocking us back on our heels, with the unexpectedness of the power of form, the way repetition and difference play across a lengthy text, forcing us (as Dickens also does) to ask, over and over, "What connexion can there be?" (256). In this seminar, I put my faith in the power of Dickens and literary theory, expecting them to teach us something new about what it means to read (nay, to inhabit) a long novel. Our shared habitation of this text and our growing familiarity with it and with one another have made this seminar a remarkable experience each time I have taught it; I can only recommend its techniques to others and encourage them to create new versions of it for themselves. It will repay such attentions, as the Inimitable would say, with compound interest.

Appendix 1: A *Bleak House* Chronology

Robert Tracy

The length of *Bleak House*, and its emphasis on the elephantine processes of the Court of Chancery, often gives readers an impression that many years elapse between the foggy November day of the first chapters and the winding up of the lawsuit in chapter 65. Asked to estimate the duration of the novel's central events, readers have suggested anything between twenty years, the longest estimate, and seven years, the shortest.

The main action of *Bleak House* takes place over three years, indicated by changes of season and by references to the legal calendar as then established, which determined when and for how long the law courts were in session: Hilary Term (c. 11 Jan.–30 Jan.), Easter Term (mid-Apr.–c. 8 May), Trinity Term (c. 22 May–c. 12 June), the Long Vacation (mid-June c.–1 Nov.), and Michaelmas Term (c. 1 Nov.–c. 25 Nov.). Some courts, however, also sat out of session, as Chancery is doing in chapter 1. The events of the story probably take place in the early 1840s, before railroad were common, but Dickens incorporated into his story the unusual summer election of 1852 and the resulting new Parliament that began sitting on 4 November (ch. 48).

Four successive Novembers or Michaelmas Terms define the duration of the action. The novel begins in November, "Michaelmas Term lately over" (13). When Guppy tells Lady Dedlock that Esther Summerson is her daughter (ch. 29), it is November or early December again. In the third November, Parliament meets, Tulkinghorn is murdered, and Lady Dedlock dies. Jarndyce and Jarndyce is wound up, and Richard Carstone dies, in the fourth November.

I suggest, then, the following time scheme for *Bleak House*. For a detailed argument, see my "Time in *Bleak House*" in *Dickens Quarterly*, from which this shortened chronology is adapted.

Year 1

Chapters 1–4, a day in late November. Esther enters in chapter 3 and describes her first twenty years.
Chapters 5–6, the next day.
Chapters 7–8, the third day.
Chapters 9–11, about a week later, in December.
Chapter 12, early January.
Chapters 13–15, probably later in January.
Chapters 16–17, probably February.
Chapters 18–23, the following summer, during the Long Vacation.
Chapters 24–25, November, Michaelmas Term.
Chapters 26–31, November or early December.

Year 2

Chapters 32–33, probably March.
Chapter 34, a little later.
Chapter 35, late April or early May.
Chapter 36, late May.
Chapters 37–38, early June, before the Long Vacation.
Chapters 39–42, during the Long Vacation.
Chapters 43–44, still summer.
Chapter 45, autumn.
Chapters 46–47, a few days later. See Chapter 51.

Year 3

Chapter 48, early November, Michaelmas Term. Tulkinghorn is murdered.
Chapter 49, the next day.
Chapters 50–51, retrospective account of preceding events in September and October. Esther learns of Ada's marriage on the night of Jo's death, synchronizing chapters 47 and 51. For a further discussion of this synchronization, see the essay by Hilary Schor in this volume.
Chapter 52, one day after chapter 49.
Chapter 53, the next couple of days.
Chapter 54, the next day. Sir Leicester learns Lady Dedlock's story. Bucket arrests Hortense for the murder.
Chapters 55–56, the same day.
Chapters 57–59, that night. The pursuit of Lady Dedlock and discovery of her body.
Chapter 60, probably in January.
Chapter 61, "the months were gliding away," so some months later.
Chapter 62, the next day. Esther and Jarndyce agree to marry "[n]ext month." A new Jarndyce will is found and will come to court "next Term," which is also "next month." This would, however, place this episode in October, which conflicts with the late summer of chapter 64.
Chapter 63, summer. George visits his ironmaster brother.
Chapter 64, late summer, during the Long Vacation.
Chapter 65, November, early in Michaelmas Term. The Chancery case ends. Richard dies.

The main action of the novel ends

Coda

Chapter 66, a few years later. Sir Leicester's old age at Chesney Wold.
Chapter 67, seven years later. Esther is now thirty, and a happy wife and mother.

Appendix 2: Borroboola Gha:
A Poem for the Times

A Stranger preached last Sunday,
And crowds of people came
To hear a two-hour sermon
With a barbarous sounding name;
'Twas all about some heathens,
Thousand of miles afar,
Who live in a land of darkness,
"Borroboola Gha."

So well their wants he pictured,
That when the plates were passed,
Each list'ner felt his pockets,
And goodly sums were cast;
For all must lend a shoulder
To push the rolling car,
That carries light and comfort,
To "Borroboola Gha."

That night their wants and sorrows
Lay heavy on my soul,
And deep in meditation
I took my morning stroll;
Till something caught my mantle
With eager grasp and wild,
And, looking down with wonder,
I saw a little child.

A pale and puny creature
In rags and dirt forlorn;
What could she want, I questioned,
Impatient to be gone.
With trembling voice she answered,
"We live just down the street,
And mammy she's a dying,
And we've nothing left to eat."

Down in a wretched basement,
With mold upon the walls,

Thro' whose half-buried windows
God's sunshine never falls;
Where cold, and want, and hunger,
Crouched near her as she lay
I found a fellow-creature,
Gasping her life away.

A chair, a broken table,
A bed of dirty straw;
A hearth all dark and cheerless
But these I scarcely saw;
For the mournful night before me,
The sad and sick'ning show
Oh! Never had I pictured
A scene so full of woe.

The famished and the naked,
The babes that pine for bread,
The squalid group that huddled
Around the dying bed;
All this distress and sorrow
Should be in lands afar:
Was I suddenly transplanted
To "Borroboola Gha"?

Ah, lo! The poor and wretched
Were close behind the door,
And I had passed them heedless
A thousand times before,
Alas for the cold and hungry
That met me every day,
While all my tears were given
To the suffering far away!

There's work enough for Christians
In distant land, we know:
Our Lord commands his servants
Through all the world to go,
Not only for the heathen,
This was his charge to them
"Go preach the word, beginning
First at Jerusalem."

O! Christian, God has promised
Whoe'er to thee has given
A cup of pure cold water
Shall find reward in Heaven.
Would you secure the blessing
You need not seek it far;
Go find in yonder hovel
A "Borroboola Gha."

—*Frederick Douglass' Paper*, 2 February 1855

NOTES ON CONTRIBUTORS

Gordon Bigelow teaches in the English department at Rhodes College. He is the author of *Fiction, Famine, and the Rise of Economics in Victorian Britain and Ireland* (2003).

Joel J. Brattin, professor of English at Worcester Polytechnic Institute, is a past president of the Dickens Society. He has published extensively on Dickens and helped establish the text for Carlyle's *Past and Present* (2005).

Kathleen Breen teaches advanced placement English and is the library media specialist at Saint Francis DeSales High School, Louisville, Kentucky. She holds master's degrees in English and library and information science.

Timothy Carens, associate professor of English at the College of Charleston, focuses on the intersection of English imperial history and ideology, national identity, and the domestic novel. He is the author of *Outlandish English Subjects in the Victorian Domestic Novel,* (2006) and has begun work on a manuscript titled "Imperial Waste Management."

Janice Carlisle is professor of English at Yale University. Her most recent book is *Common Scents: Comparative Encounters in High-Victorian Fiction* (2004). Her study of the visual politics of the 1860s, *Picturing Reform*, is forthcoming.

Carrol Clarkson teaches at the University of Cape Town. Her publications and research interests are in the philosophy of language and in postapartheid South African literature and art. She has published papers on Dickens and on postapartheid jurisprudence. Her current project is on the work of J. M. Coetzee.

Denise Fulbrook teaches in the Department of English at the University of Kentucky. She is coeditor of the book *Rock over the Edge: Transformations in Popular Music and Culture* (2002). She has published on Jane Austen and *Clueless* as well as, with Eve K. Sedgwick, gender and sexuality.

Michal Peled Ginsburg is professor of French and comparative literature at Northwestern University and specialist in the nineteenth-century novel and narrative theory. She is the author of *Flaubert Writing: A Study in Narrative Strategies* (1986) and *Economies of Change: Form and Transformation in the Nineteenth-Century Novel* (1996). She has recently published articles on the scene of recognition in Dickens (in *Partial Answers*) and on house and home in *Dombey and Son* (*Dickens Studies Annual*). She is a frequent participator in the Dickens Project.

Lauren M. E. Goodlad is associate professor of English and a member of the Unit for Criticism and Interpretive Theory at the University of Illinois, Urbana-Champaign. She is the author of *Victorian Literature and the Victorian State* (2003), coeditor of *Goth: Undead Subculture* (2007), and coeditor, with Julia Wright, of *Victorian Internationalisms*, a special 2007 issue of *Romanticism and Victorianism on the Net*. Her current project is "The Victorian Geopolitical Aesthetic: Literature, Internationalism, and 'the South.'"

Robert Googins is the founding director of the Insurance Law Center at the University of Connecticut School of Law, where he taught a seminar on Charles Dickens and the law. He is the founding president of the Connecticut branch of The Dickens Fellowship.

Daniel Hack is associate professor of English at the University of Michigan, Ann Arbor. He is the author of *The Material Interests of the Victorian Novel* (2005).

John O. Jordan is professor of literature at the University of California, Santa Cruz, and director of the Dickens Project. He has written widely on Dickens and Victorian literature and is the editor of *The Cambridge Companion to Charles Dickens* (2001).

Nita Moots Kincaid is associate professor of English at Los Angeles City College, where she teaches literature and composition courses. A number of these courses involve connecting students with community agencies. In addition to work on Dickens, she has done research and published on service learning and on constructions of the outsider in our culture.

Shu-Fang Lai is associate professor at National Sun Yat-Sen University, Taiwan. She has published on Dickens and science and on Dickens's journalism. She is the author of *Charles Reade, George Meredith, and Harriet Martineau as Serial Writers of* Once a Week, *1859–1865* (2008).

Barbara Leckie is associate professor of English at Carleton University. Her publications include *Culture and Adultery: The Novel, the Newspaper, and the Law, 1857–1914.* (1999). She is working on a book-length study of the intersection of architecture, housing for the poor, and Victorian narratives of social reform in journalism and the novel, 1830–98.

Kevin McLaughlin is professor of English and comparative literature at Brown University. He is the author of *Writing in Parts: Imitation and Exchange in Nineteenth-Century Literature* (1995) and *Paperwork: Fiction and Mass Mediacy in the Paper Age* (2005) and cotranslator of Walter Benjamin's *Arcades Project* (1999).

Robert Newsom is professor emeritus of English at the University of California, Irvine. He has written two books about Dickens, the first on *Bleak House* (1977) and the second a general introduction to Dickens for the Twayne's English Authors Series (2000), as well as numerous essays concerning Dickens and a book about the theory of fiction, *A Likely Story: Probability and Play in Fiction* (1988).

Robert L. Patten is Lynette S. Autrey Professor in Humanities and editor of *SEL: Studies in English Literature, 1500–1900* at Rice University. He has published extensively on Dickens, Victorian publishing, and nineteenth-century book illustration.

Timothy Peltason is professor of English and director of the Newhouse Center for the Humanities at Wellesley College. He is the author of *Reading* In Memoriam (1986) and articles about other Victorian topics. He is writing a sequence of essays about literary judgment.

Jennifer Phegley is associate professor of English at the University of Missouri, Kansas City. She is the author of *Educating the Proper Woman Reader: Victorian Family Literary Magazines and the Cultural Health of the Nation* (2004) and coeditor of *Reading Women: Literary Figures and Cultural Icons from the Victorian Age to the Present* (2005).

Hilary M. Schor is professor of English and law at the University of Southern California. She is the author of books on Elizabeth Gaskell and Charles Dickens, as well as articles on Victorian literature and culture, the realist novel, and film.

Richard L. Stein teaches English at the University of Oregon. He has written extensively on relations between Victorian literature and the visual arts. His recent publications include "Dickens and Illustration" in *The Cambridge Companion to Charles Dickens* and "National Portraits" in *Victorian Prism* (2007).

Lisa Sternlieb is associate professor of English at Penn State University. She is the author of *The Female Narrator in the British Novel: Hidden Agendas* (2002).

Robert Tracy is emeritus professor of English and of Celtic Studies at the University of California, Berkeley. He is a frequent lecturer at the Dickens Universe, a member of the *Dickens Studies Annual* Editorial Board, and president of the Dickens Society (2008–09). He has published widely on Victorian and Irish literature and translated a collection of poems by Osip Mandelstam.

Andrew Williams is a research associate at Cardiff University's School of Journalism, Media and Cultural Studies. He recently finished his PhD on advertising and the serial works of Charles Dickens at the university's Centre for Critical and Cultural Theory. He has taught in the departments of English and cultural criticism at Cardiff.

SURVEY PARTICIPANTS

Without the generous and thoughtful responses of the scholars below, this book would not have been possible. We thank them for the work they did in describing how they teach *Bleak House* and for their diverse pedagogical insights. There are several other people whose assistance in this project was apt and essential, and we thank them here as well. Joseph Gibaldi and the anonymous readers who reviewed this project offered perceptive questions and enabling suggestions at all stages. Robert Newsom read drafts of much of our "Materials" section, and his advice was wonderfully helpful. Joel Brattin also provided kind and timely assistance with the "Materials" section. Finally, JoAnna Rottke of The Dickens Project at the University of California, Santa Cruz, supported the book in numerous ways, and we thank her sincerely for her work.

Michelle Allen, *United States Naval Academy*
Helen Bauer, *Iona College*
Joel Brattin, *Worchester Polytechnic Institute*
Kathleen Breen, *Saint Francis DeSales High School, Louisville, Kentucky*
Sarah Anne Brown, *Lucy Cavendish College, Cambridge University*
Gerald Browne, *Kaua'i Community College, University of Hawai'i*
James Buzard, *Massachusetts Institute of Technology*
Timothy Carens, *College of Charleston*
Janice Carlisle, *Yale University*
Carrol Clarkson, *University of Cape Town*
Lindsey Cordery, *Universidad de la República, Montevideo, Uruguay*
Richard Currie, *College of Staten Island, City University of New York*
Suzanne Daly, *University of Massachusetts, Amherst*
April Heath Denny, *independent scholar*
Laura Fasick, *Minnesota State University, Moorhead*
Lynette Felber, *Indiana University-Purdue University, Fort Wayne*
K. J. Fielding, *University of Edinburgh*
Barbara M. Fisher, *emerita, City College of City University of New York*
Denise Fulbrook, *University of Kentucky*
George Goodin, *emeritus, Southern Illinois University, Carbondale*
Lauren M. E. Goodlad, *University of Illinois, Champaign-Urbana*
Robert Googins, *University of Connecticut School of Law*
Sandra Grayson, *Saint Mary's College of California*
Mark Hennelly, *California State University, Sacramento*
Bert Hornback, *emeritus, University of Michigan*
Anne Jackson, *Boston*
Gerhard Joseph, *Lehman College and Graduate Center, City University of New York*
Christopher Keirstead, *Auburn University*
James Kincaid, *University of Southern California*
Nita Moots Kincaid, *Los Angeles City College*
Shu-Fang Lai, *National Sun Yat-Sen University*
Philip Landon, *University of Rochester*

Richard Landsdown, *James Cook University, Australia*
Barbara Leckie, *Carleton University*
Frederick McDowell, *emeritus, University of Iowa*
John McGowan, *University of North Carolina*
Kevin McLaughlin, *Brown University*
Thomas Moore, *University of Maryland University College*
Goldie Morgantaler, *University of Lethbridge*
Deborah Morse, *College of William and Mary*
Margueritte Murphy, *Bentley College*
Harland Nelson, *Luther College*
Robert Newsom, *emeritus, University of California, Irvine*
Midori Niino, *Kobe City University of Foreign Studies*
Robert L. Patten, *Rice University*
Timothy Peltason, *Wellesley College*
Jennifer Phegley, *University of Missouri, Kansas City*
Mary Sanders Pollock, *Stetson University*
Jamieson Ridenhour, *University of Mary*
Evelyn Romig, *Howard Payne University*
Anita Rose, *Converse College*
Hilary Schor, *University of Southern California*
Sambudha Sen, *University of Delhi*
Richard L. Stein, *University of Oregon*
Lisa Sternlieb, *Penn State University*
Deborah Thomas, *Villanova University*
Leona Toker, *Hebrew University, Jerusalem*
Robert Tracy, *emeritus, University of California, Berkeley*
Chris Vanden Bosch, *University of Notre Dame*
Andrew Williams, *University of Cardiff*
Carolyn Williams, *Rutgers University*
George Worth, *emeritus, University of Kansas*

WORKS CITED

Ackroyd, Peter. *Dickens*. New York: Harper, 1990.

———. *Dickens' London: An Imaginative Vision*. London: Headline, 1987.

———. *Dickens: Public Life and Private Passions*. Irvington: Hydra, 2003.

"Alexandre Dumas." *Anglo-African Magazine* Jan. 1859: 4–5.

Allen, William, and T. R. H. Thomson. *A Narrative of the Expedition Sent by Her Majesty's Government to the River Niger in 1841 under the Command of H. D. Trotter*. 2 vols. 1848. London: Cass, 1968.

Allwood, John. *The Great Exhibitions*. London: Studio Vista, 1977.

Altick, Richard. "Education, Print, and Paper in *Our Mutual Friend*." *Nineteenth-Century Literary Perspectives*. Ed. Claude de L. Ryals. Durham: Duke UP, 1974. 237–54.

American Bar Association. *A.B.A. Codes. Martindale-Hubbell Law Digest*. Pt. 3. LexisNexis, 2005.

Arac, Jonathan. *Commissioned Spirits: The Shaping of Social Motion in Dickens, Carlyle, Melville, and Hawthorne*. New York: Columbia UP, 1989.

Auerbach, Jeffrey A. *The Great Exhibition of 1851: A Nation on Display*. New Haven: Yale UP, 1999.

Axton, William F. "'Keystone' Structure in Dickens' Serial Novels." *University of Toronto Quarterly* 37 (1967): 31–50.

———."Religious and Scientific Imagery in *Bleak House*." *Nineteenth-Century Fiction* 22 (1968): 349–59.

———. "The Trouble with Esther." *Modern Language Quarterly* 26 (1965): 545–57.

Bagehot, Walter. "Charles Dickens." P. Collins, *Dickens* 403–11.

Bakhtin, M. M. *The Dialogic Imagination: Four Essays*. Austin: U of Texas P, 1981.

Barthes, Roland. "Introduction to the Structural Analysis of Narratives." *Image/Music/Text*. New York: Hill, 1977. 79–124.

———. *S/Z*. New York: Hill, 1974.

Beer, Gillian. "Origins and Oblivion in Victorian Narrative." *Sex, Politics, and Science in Nineteenth-Century Novels*. Ed. Ruth Bernard Yeazell. Baltimore: Johns Hopkins UP, 1985. 63–87.

Beeton, Isabella. *Mrs. Beeton's Book of Household Management*. 1861. Abr. ed. Ed. Nicola Humble. Oxford: Oxford UP, 2000.

Behen, Denis. "The Lawyers of Dickens-Land." *Green Bag* 24 (1912): 379–92.

Behlmer, George K. "Character Building and the English Family: Continuities in Social Casework, c. 1870–1930." *Singular Continuities: Tradition, Nostalgia, and Identity in Modern British Culture*. Ed. Behlmer and Fred M. Leventhal. Stanford: Stanford UP, 2000. 58–74.

———. *Friends of the Family: The English Home and Its Guardians, 1850–1940*. Stanford: Stanford UP, 1998.

Belasco Smith, Susan. "Serialization and the Nature of *Uncle Tom's Cabin.*" *Periodical Literature in Nineteenth-Century America*. Ed. Kenneth M. Price and Belasco Smith. Charlottesville: UP of Virginia, 1995. 69–89.

Bellamy, Richard. "T. H. Green and the Morality of Victorian Liberalism." Bellamy, *Victorian Liberalism* 131–51.

———, ed. *Victorian Liberalism: Nineteenth-Century Political Thought and Practice.* London: Routledge, 1990.

Benjamin, Walter. *The Arcades Project*. Trans. Howard Eiland and Kevin McLaughlin. Cambridge: Harvard UP, 1999.

———. *Illuminations: Essays and Reflections*. Trans. Harry Zohn. New York: Schocken, 1978.

———. "The Work of Art in the Age of Mechanical Reproduction." Benjamin, *Illuminations* 217–51

Bentham, Jeremy. *An Introduction to the Principles of Morals and Legislation*. Mill and Bentham 65–112.

Bentley, Nicolas, Michael Slater, and Nina Burgis. *The Dickens Index*. Oxford: Oxford UP, 1988.

Benveniste, Emile. *Problems in General Linguistics*. Coral Gables: U of Miami P, 1971.

Beresford, Belinda. "A Spiral of Mini-epidemics." *Mail and Guardian* 16–22 Sept. 2005: 8.

Bersani, Leo. *A Future for Astyanax: Character and Desire in Literature*. Boston: Little, 1976.

Bhabha, Homi K. Introduction. *Nation and Narration*. Ed. Bhabha. New York: Routledge, 1990. 1–7.

Bigelow, Gordon. *Fiction, Famine, and the Rise of Economics in Victorian Britain and Ireland*. Cambridge: Cambridge UP, 2003.

Blain, Virginia. "Double Vision and the Double Standard." *Literature and History* 2 (1985): 31–46. Rpt. in Tambling 65–86.

Blake, Kathleen. "*Bleak House*, Political Economy, Victorian Studies." *Victorian Literature and Culture* 27 (1997): 1–21.

Bleak House wrapper design. U of California, Santa Cruz, Dickens Project. July 2005 <http://humwww.ucsc.edu/dickens/bibliographies/ bleakhousebiblio/Wrapper .Design.jpg>.

Bleak House. By Charles Dickens. Adapt. Andrew Davies. Dir. Justin Chadwick and Susanah White. Perf. Gillian Anderson and Charles Dance. BBC, 2005.

Bleak House. By Charles Dickens. Adapt. Arthur Hopcroft. Dir. Ross Devenish. Perf. Diana Rigg and Denholm Elliott. 1985. Videocassette. BBC Video, 1988.

Bloom, Harold, ed. *Charles Dickens'* Bleak House. New York: Chelsea, 1987.

"Borroboola Gha: A Poem for the Times." *Frederick Douglass' Paper* 2 Feb. 1855: 4.

Bowen, John, and Robert L. Patten, eds. *Palgrave Advances in Charles Dickens Studies*. Basingstoke: Palgrave Macmillan, 2006.

Boyer, Allen. "The Antiquarian and the Utilitarian: Charles Dickens vs. James Fitzjames Stephen." *Tennessee Law Review* 56 (1989): 595–628.

Brattin, Joel J. "Recent Paperback Editions of Dickens." *Dickens Quarterly* 16.1 (1999): 42–48.

Briggs, Asa. *Victorian People: A Reassessment of Persons and Themes, 1851–67.* 1955. New York: Harper, 1963.

Brimley, George. "A Review of *Bleak House* in the *Spectator.*" Dickens, *Bleak House* [ed. Ford and Monod] 933–37.

Brontë, Charlotte. *Villette.* Ed. Mark Lilly. London: Penguin, 1979.

Brooks, Peter. *Reading for the Plot: Design and Intention in Narrative.* New York: Knopf, 1984.

Brown, Wendy. "Neo-liberalism and the End of Liberal Democracy." *Theory and Event* 7.1 (2003): 43 pars. 13 Feb. 2008 <http://muse.jhu.edu/journals/theory_ &_event>.

Brundage, Anthony. *England's "Prussian Minister": Edwin Chadwick and the Politics of Government Growth, 1832–1854.* University Park: Penn State UP, 1988.

Buckland, William. *Geology and Mineralogy Considered with Reference to Natural Theology.* London: Pickering, 1836.

Butt, John, and Kathleen Tillotson. "The Topicality of *Bleak House.*" *Dickens at Work.* By Butt and Tillotson London: Methuen, 1957. 177–200.

Buzard, James. "'Anywhere's Nowhere': *Bleak House* as Metropolitan Autoethnography." *Disorienting Fiction: The Autoethnographic Work of Nineteenth-Century British Novels.* Princeton: Princeton UP, 2005. 105–56.

Carens, Timothy. "The Civilizing Mission at Home: Empire, Gender, and National Reform in *Bleak House.*" *Dickens Studies Annual* 26 (1998): 121–45.

Carey, John, ed. *The Faber Book of Science.* London: Faber, 1995.

Carlyle, Thomas. *A Carlyle Reader.* 1969. Ed. George B. Tennyson. Acton: Copley, 2000.

———. *Chartism.* 1839. *Selected Writings.* Ed. Alan Shelston. New York: Penguin, 1971. 151–232.

———. *The French Revolution.* Oxford: Oxford UP, 1989.

———. *Past and Present.* 1843. Ed. Richard D. Altick. Boston: Houghton, 1965.

———. *Sartor Resartus: The Life and Opinions of Herr Teufelsdröckh.* New York: Odyssey, 1937.

———. "Signs of the Time." 1829. *Carlyle's Works: Centennial Memorial Edition.* Vol. 15. Boston: Estes; n.d. 462–87. 26 vols.

Chadwick, Edwin. *Report to Her Majesty's Principal Secretary of State for the Home Department, from the Poor Law Commissioners, on an Inquiry into the Sanitary Condition of the Labouring Population of Great Britain; with Appendices.* London: Clowes, 1842.

Charles Dickens: A Tale of Ambition and Genius. Biography. Introd. Jack Perkins. A&E, 1995.

Chesterton, G. K. *Charles Dickens: A Critical Study.* 1906. New York: Dodd, 1929.

Childers, Joseph W. *Novel Possibilities: Fiction and the Formation of Early Victorian Culture.* Philadelphia: U of Pennsylvania P, 1995.

Chomsky, Noam. *Language and Responsibility.* New York: Pantheon, 1979.

City of Johannesburg Web site. "What Effect Is the HIV/AIDS Epidemic Having on the City?" 15 Sept. 2005 <http://www.joburg.org.za/content/view/41/75>.

Clarke, John. "Dissolving the Public Realm? The Logics and Limits of Neo-liberalism." *Journal of Social Policy* 33.1 (2004): 27–48.

Clarkson, Carrol. "Locating Identity in Phaswane Mpe's *Welcome to Our Hillbrow.*" *Third World Quarterly* 26 (2005): 451–59.

———. "Visible and Invisible: What Surfaces in Recent Johannesburg Novels?" *Moving Worlds* 5.1 (2005): 84–97.

Cohen, Jane R. *Charles Dickens and His Original Illustrators.* Columbus: Ohio State UP, 1980.

Coles, Robert. "The Keen Eye of Charles Dickens." *Harvard Law School Bulletin* (Summer/Fall 1984): 31–42.

Collins, Philip. "Charles Dickens." *The New Cambridge Bibliography of English Literature.* Ed. George Watson. Vol. 3. Cambridge: Cambridge UP, 1969. 779–850.

———. "Charles Dickens." *Victorian Fiction: A Second Guide to Research.* Ed. George Ford. New York: MLA, 1978. 34–113.

———. *Dickens and Crime.* New York: St. Martin's, 1962.

———, ed. *Dickens: The Critical Heritage.* New York: Barnes, 1971.

Collins, Wilkie. *The Woman in White.* London: Penguin, 1985.

Connor, Steven, ed. *Charles Dickens.* New York: Longman, 1996.

———. Introduction. Connor, *Charles Dickens* 1–33.

Crafts, Hannah. *The Bondwoman's Narrative.* Ed. Henry Louis Gates, Jr. New York: Warner, 2003.

Crowther, M. A. *The Workhouse System, 1834–1929: The History of an English Social Institution.* Athens: U of Georgia P, 1982.

Cummings, Katherine. "Re-reading *Bleak House*: The Chronicle of a 'Little Body' and Its Perverse Defense." *Telling Tales: The Hysteric's Seduction in Fiction and Theory.* Stanford: Stanford UP, 1991. 191–229. Rpt. in Tambling 183–204.

Curtis, Gerard. *Visual Words: Art and the Material Book in Victorian England.* Burlington: Ashgate, 2002.

Danahay, Martin A. "Housekeeping and Hegemony in *Bleak House.*" *Studies in the Novel* 23 (1991): 416–31.

Darwin, Bernard. *The Dickens Advertiser: A Collection of the Advertisements in the Original Parts of Novels by Charles Dickens.* New York: Macmillan, 1930.

Darwin, Charles. *Origin of Species.* 1859. London: Penguin, 1985.

David, Deirdre. *Rule Britannia: Women, Empire, and Victorian Writing.* Ithaca: Cornell UP, 1995.

Davis, John R. *The Great Exhibition.* Stroud: Sutton, 1999.

de Lauretis, Teresa. *Alice Doesn't: Feminism, Semiotics, Cinema.* Bloomington: Indiana UP, 1984.

Denman, Lord. Uncle Tom's Cabin, Bleak House, *Slavery and Slave Trade.* London: Longman, 1853.

Denman, Peter. "Krook's Death and Dickens's Authorities." *Dickensian* 82 (1986): 130–41.

Desmond, Adrian, and James Moore. *Darwin.* 1991. London: Penguin, 1992.

Dever, Carolyn. *Death and the Mother from Dickens to Freud.* Cambridge: Cambridge UP, 1998.

DeVries, Duane. *General Studies of Charles Dickens and His Writings and Collected Editions of His Works: An Annotated Bibliography.* Vol. 1. New York: AMS, 2004.

Dickens. Screenplay by Peter Ackroyd. Dir. Mary Downs and Chris Granlund. Perf. Anton Lesser. BBC, 2002.

Dickens, Charles. *American Notes for General Circulation.* Oxford Illustrated Dickens. Oxford: Oxford UP, 1987.

———. *"The Amusements of the People" and Other Papers: Reports, Essays, and Reviews, 1834–51.* Ed. Michael Slater. Dent Uniform Edition of Dickens' Journalism. Vol. 2. Columbus: Ohio State UP, 1996.

———. *Bleak House.* Ed. Nicola Bradbury. Penguin Classics. London: Penguin, 2003.

———. *Bleak House.* Ed. George Ford and Sylvère Monod. Norton Critical Edition. New York: Norton, 1977.

———. *Bleak House.* Ed. Stephen Gill. Oxford World's Classics. Oxford: Oxford UP, 1999.

———. *Bleak House. Project Gutenberg.* 13 Apr. 2006 <http://www.gutenberg.org/etext/1023>.

———. *Bleak House.* Online searchable text. U of California, Santa Cruz, Dickens Project. 13 Apr. 2006 <http://humwww.ucsc.edu/dickens/searchworks/searchworksindex.html>.

———. "A Child's Dream of a Star." *Household Words* 6 Apr. 1850: 25–26.

———. *Christmas Books.* Oxford Illustrated Dickens. Oxford: Oxford UP, 1987.

———. *David Copperfield.* Introd. Jeremy Tambling. London: Penguin, 2004.

———. *David Copperfield.* Facsim. ed. Bourton-on-the-Water: Durrant, 2004–05.

———. "Dickens' Working Plans." Dickens, *Bleak House* [ed. Ford and Monod] 777–99.

———. *Dombey and Son.* Harmondsworth: Penguin, 1970.

———, ed. "Earliest Man." *All the Year Round* 26 Jan. 1861: 366.

———. "The Eclipse Seen in India" *All the Year Round* ns 1 13 Feb. 1869: 250–53.

———. "Health by Act of Parliament." *Household Words* 10 Aug. 1850: 460–63.

———. "A Home Question." *Household Words* 11 Nov. 1854: 292–96.

———. *The Letters of Charles Dickens.* Ed. Madeleine House, Graham Storey, Kathleen Tillotson, et al. 12 vols. Pilgrim Edition. Oxford: Clarendon, 1965–2002.

———. The Life and Adventures of Nicholas Nickleby: *Reproduced in Facsimile from the Original Monthly Parts of 1838-9.* Ed. Michael Slater. London: Scolar, 1982.

———, ed. "Meteors." [By Warr.] *Household Words* 16 Feb. 1856: 103–05.

———, ed. "Mr. Bubb's Visit to the Moon." [By Hughes.] *Household Words* 17 May 1851: 187–88.

————, ed. "Mr. Bubs on Planetary Disturbances." [By Charles Thomas Hudson.] *Household Words* 12 Apr. 1851: 58–60.

————. *Mudfog Papers.* 1838. New York: Holt, 1880. Rpt. in *Sketches by Boz.* Oxford Illustrated Dickens. Oxford: Oxford UP, 1987. 605–88.

————, ed. "My Annular Eclipse." [By W. H. Wills.] *Household Words* 24 Apr. 1858: 433–36.

————. "The Noble Savage." *Household Words* 11 June 1853: 337–39.

————. "Nobody, Somebody and Everybody." *Household Words* 30 Aug. 1856: 145–47.

————. "Nobody's Story." *Household Words,* Christmas Extra, 1853: 34–36.

————. "On Duty with Inspector Field." *Household Words* 14 June 1851: 265–70.

————. *Our Mutual Friend.* Harmondsworth: Penguin, 1971.

————. *The Pickwick Papers.* Oxford Illustrated Dickens. Oxford, Oxford UP, 1987.

————. "A Preliminary Word." *Household Words* 30 Mar. 1850: 1–2.

————. "Respecting the Sun." *All the Year Round* 22 Apr. 1865: 297–300.

————. Rev. of *A Narrative of the Expedition Sent by Her Majesty's Government to the River Niger in 1841. Examiner* 19 Aug. 1848: 531–33.

————. Rev. of *The Poetry of Science,* by Robert Hunt. *Examiner* 9 Dec. 1848. Slater 2: 129–34.

————. *Sketches by Boz.* Ed. Dennis Walder. London: Penguin, 1995.

———— "Speech Delivered to the Metropolitan Sanitary Association." London, 10 May 1851. *Speeches* 128–29.

————. *The Speeches of Charles Dickens.* Ed. K. J. Fielding. Oxford: Clarendon, 1960.

————, ed. "A Sweep through the Stars." [By Edmund Saul Dixon.] *Household Words* 22 May 1858: 531–35.

————. *The Uncommercial Traveller.* Oxford Illustrated Dickens. Oxford: Oxford UP, 1987.

Dickens of London. Screenplay by Wolf Mankowitz. Dir. Michael Ferguson and Marc Miller. Perf. Roy Dotrice. Yorkshire Television, 1976. Videocassette. BWE Video, 1998.

The Dickens Page. Ed. Mitsuharu Matsuoka. 13 Apr. 2006 <http://www.lang.nagoya-u.ac.jp/~matsuoka/Dickens.html>.

The Dickens Project. Dir. John O. Jordan. U of California. 13 Apr. 2006 <http://humwww.ucsc.edu/dickens>.

Disraeli, Benjamin. *Sybil; or, The Two Nations.* New York: Penguin, 1985.

Doré, Gustave, and Blanchard Jerrold. *London: A Pilgrimage.* 1872–73. New York: Dover, 1970.

Duggan, Lisa. *The Twilight of Equality? Neoliberalism, Cultural Politics, and the Attack on Democracy.* Boston: Beacon, 2003.

Dyson, A. E. *Dickens's* Bleak House*: A Casebook.* 1969. London: Macmillan, 1983.

"Editor's Easy Chair." *Harper's New Monthly Magazine* Feb. 1853: 419–20.

————. *Harper's New Monthly Magazine* Dec. 1853: 132.

————. *Harper's New Monthly Magazine* June 1854: 119–20.

Edwards, Steve. "The Accumulation of Knowledge; or, William Whewell's Eye."
    Purbrick 26–52.

Engels, Friedrich. *The Condition of the Working Class in England*. 1845. Ed. David
    McLellan. Oxford: Oxford UP, 1999.

Faraday, Michael. "On a Candle." 1850. Carey 88–92.

Fasick, Laura. "Dickens and the Diseased Body in *Bleak House*." *Dickens Studies
    Annual* 24 (1996): 135–51.

ffrench, Yvonne. *The Great Exhibition: 1851*. London: Harvill, n.d.

Fielding, K. J., and Shu-Fang Lai. "Dickens's Science, Evolution and 'the Death of
    the Sun.'" *Dickens, Europe and the New Worlds*. Ed. Anny Sadrin. London:
    Macmillan, 1999. 200–11.

Finer, S. E. *The Life and Times of Edwin Chadwick*. London: Methuen, 1952.

Fisch, Audrey. "Uncle Tom and Harriet Beecher Stowe in England." *Cambridge
    Companion to Harriet Beecher Stowe*. Ed. Cindy Weinstein. Cambridge:
    Cambridge UP, 2004. 96–112.

Ford, George H. *Dickens and His Readers*. New York: Norton, 1965.

Forster, John. *The Life of Charles Dickens*. 1872–74. 2 vols. London: Dent, 1966.

Foucault, Michel. *Discipline and Punish: The Birth of the Prison*. Trans. Alan Sheridan.
    New York: Vintage, 1977.

———. "Governmentality." *The Foucault Effect: Studies in Governmentality*. Ed.
    Graham Burchell, Colin Gordon, and Peter Miller. Chicago: U of Chicago P,
    1991. 87–104.

———. *The History of Sexuality: Volume I*. New York: Pantheon, 1978.

———. "Social Security." *Politics, Philosophy, Culture: Interviews and Other Writings,
    1977–1984*. Ed. Lawrence D. Kritzman. Trans. Alan Sheridan et al. New York:
    Routledge, 1988. 159–77.

———. "Space, Knowledge and Power." Rabinow 239–56.

———. "The Subject and Power." *Michel Foucault: Beyond Structuralism and
    Hermeneutics*. Ed. Herbert L. Dreyfus and Paul Rabinow. Chicago: U of
    Chicago P, 1983. 208–26.

Frank, Thomas. *One Market under God: Extreme Capitalism, Market Populism, and
    the End of Economic Democracy*. New York: Doubleday, 2000.

Freeden, Michael. "The New Liberalism and Its Aftermath." Bellamy, *Victorian
    Liberalism* 175–92.

Freud, Sigmund. "The 'Uncanny.'" 1919. *The Standard Edition of the Complete
    Psychological Works of Sigmund Freud*. Vol. 17. Trans. James Strachey. London:
    Hogarth, 1955. 217–56.

Frye, Northrop. *Anatomy of Criticism: Four Essays*. Princeton: Princeton UP, 1957.

Fyfe, Thomas. *Charles Dickens and the Law*. Edinburgh: Hodge, 1910.

Gagnier, Regenia. *The Insatiability of Human Wants: Economics and Aesthetics in
    Market Society*. Chicago: U of Chicago P, 2000.

Gates, Henry Louis, Jr. "The Fugitive: Could a Manuscript Bought at Auction Be the
    Work of a Runaway Slave?" *New Yorker* 18–25 Feb. 2002: 104–08+.

Gates, Henry Louis, Jr., and Hollis Robbins, eds. *In Search of Hannah Crafts: Critical Essays on* The Bondwoman's Narrative. New York: Basic, 2004.

Gaughan, Richard T. "Their Places Are a Blank: The Two Narrators in *Bleak House*." *Dickens Studies Annual* 21 (1992): 79–96.

Genette, Gerard. *Narrative Discourse: An Essay in Method*. Ithaca: Cornell UP, 1980.

Gerard, Curtis. *Visual Words: Art and the Material Book in Victorian England*. Aldershot: Ashgate, 2002.

Gibbs-Smith, C. H. *The Great Exhibition of 1851: A Commemorative Album*. London: HMSO, 1950.

Gikandi, Simon. *Maps of Englishness: Writing Identity in the Culture of Colonialism*. New York: Columbia UP, 1996.

Gilmore, Grant. *The Ages of American Law*. New Haven: Yale UP, 1977.

Ginsburg, Michal Peled. *Economies of Change: Form and Transformation in the Nineteenth-Century Novel*. Stanford: Stanford UP, 1996.

Glaser, Robert, and Stephen Roth. "In the Matter of Heep, Jaggers, Tulkinghorn & Fogg: An Unjarndyced View of the Dickensian Bar." *Rutgers Law Review* 29 (1976): 278–97.

Goodlad, Lauren M. E. "Is There a Pastor in the House? Sanitary Reform and Governing Agency in Dickens's Midcentury Fiction." *Victorian Literature and the Victorian State: Character and Governance in a Liberal Society*. By Goodlad. Baltimore: Johns Hopkins UP, 2003. 86–117.

Gossett, Thomas F. Uncle Tom's Cabin *and American Culture*. Dallas: Southern Methodist UP, 1985.

Gowan, Peter. "The Origins of the Administrative Elite." *New Left Review* 162 (1987): 4–34.

Graver, Suzanne. "Writing in a 'Womanly' Way and the Double Vision of *Bleak House*." *Dickens Quarterly* 4.1 (1987): 3–15.

Greenblatt, Stephen. Preface. *Allegory and Representation: Selected Papers from the English Institute, 1979–80*. Ed. Greenblatt. Baltimore: Johns Hopkins UP, 1981. vii-xiii.

Gunn, Simon. "The Ministry, the Middle Class and the 'Civilising Mission' in Manchester, 1850–80." *Social History* 21.1 (1996): 22–36.

Hack, Daniel. "Close Reading at a Distance: The African-Americanization of *Bleak House*: The African Americanization of *Bleak House*." *Critical Inquiry* 34.2 (2008): 729–53.

———. *The Material Interests of the Victorian Novel*. Charlottesville: U of Virginia P, 2005.

Hadley, Elaine. "The Past Is a Foreign Country: The Neo-conservative Romance with Victorian Liberalism." *Yale Journal of Criticism* 10.1 (1997): 7–38.

Haight, Gordon. "Dickens and Lewes on Spontaneous Combustion." *Nineteenth-Century Fiction* 10 (1955): 53–63.

Halliwell, Stephen. The Poetics *of Aristotle: Translation and Commentary*. London: Duckworth, 1987.

Hardwick, Michael, and Mollie Hardwick. *Dickens's England*. London: Dent, 1970.

Harris, Jose. "Society and the State in Twentieth-Century Britain." *Social Agencies and Institutions*. Ed. F. M. L. Thompson. Cambridge: Cambridge UP, 1990. 63–118. Vol. 3 of *The Cambridge Social History of Britain, 1750–1950*.

Harvey, John R. *Victorian Novelists and Their Illustrators*. New York: New York UP, 1971.

Herschel, John. *Outline of Astronomy*. London: Longman, 1849.

Holdsworth, William. *Charles Dickens as a Legal Historian*. 1928. Union: Lawbook Exchange, 1995.

———. *A History of English Law*. 9 vols. Boston: Little, 1926.

Hopkins, Chris. "Victorian Modernity? Writing the Great Exhibition." *Varieties of Victorianism: The Uses of a Past*. Ed. Gary Day. Houndsmills: Macmillan, 1998. 40–62.

Hornback, Bert G. "The Narrator of *Bleak House*." *Dickens Quarterly* 16 (1999): 3–12.

Hugo, Victor. *Les Misérables*. Trans. Norman Denny. London: Penguin, 1982.

———. *Les Misérables*. Ed. Yves Gohin. Paris: Gallimard–Folio Classique, 1995.

———. *Les Misérables*. Trans. Lee Fahnestock and Norman MacAfee. Based on Trans. by Charles E. Wilbour. New York: Signet, 1987.

———. *Les Misérables*. Trans. William Walton. Philadelphia: Barrie, 1893.

Hunt, Robert. *The Poetry of Science; or, Studies of the Physical Phenomena of Nature*. London: Reeve, 1848.

Jaffe, Audrey. "*David Copperfield* and *Bleak House*: On Dividing the Responsibility of Knowing." Jaffe, *Vanishing Points* 112–49.

———. *Vanishing Points: Dickens, Narrative, and the Subject of Omniscience*. Berkeley: U of California P, 1991.

Johnson, Edgar. *Charles Dickens: His Tragedy and Triumph*. 2 vols. Boston: Little, 1952.

Johnson, Richard. "Administrators in Education before 1870: Patronage, Social Position and Role." *Studies in the Growth of Nineteenth-Century Government*. Ed. Gillian Sutherland. Totowa: Rowman, 1972. 110–38.

Jordan, John O., ed. *The Cambridge Companion to Charles Dickens*. Cambridge: Cambridge UP, 2001.

Ka Ngwenya, S. "Hillbrow." *Dirty Washing: Collective and Individual Poems*. Ed. Ka Ngwenya et al. Johannesburg: Botsotso, 1999. 37.

Kaplan, Fred. *Dickens: A Biography*. New York: Morrow, 1988.

Kingfisher, Catherine. "Introduction: The Global Feminization of Poverty." Kingfisher, *Western Welfare* 3–12.

———, ed. *Western Welfare in Decline: Globalization and Women's Poverty*. Philadelphia: U of Pennsylvania P, 2002.

Kingsley, Charles. *The Life and Works of Charles Kingsley*. 19 vols. London: Macmillan, 1901–03.

Kirby, William. *On the Power, Wisdom and Goodness of God as Manifested in the Creation of Animals and in Their History, Habits and Instincts*. 2 vols. London: Pickering, 1835.

Kirkpatrick, David D. "On Long-Lost Pages, a Female Slave's Voice." *New York Times* 11 Nov. 2001: 1+.

Klancher, Jon. *The Making of English Reading Audiences, 1790–1832.* Madison: U of Wisconsin P, 1987.

La Capra, Dominick. "Ideology and Critique in Dickens's *Bleak House.*" *Representations* 6 (1984): 166–23. Rpt. in Tambling 128–38.

Leavis, Q. D. "*Bleak House*: A Chancery World." *Dickens the Novelist.* By F. R. Leavis and Q. D. Leavis. London: Chatto, 1970. 118–79.

Leigh, Percival. "The Chemistry of a Candle." *Household Words* 3 Aug. 1850: 439–44.

Lenard, Mary. "'Mr. Popular Sentiment': Dickens and the Gender Politics of Sentimentalism and Social Reform Literature." *Dickens Studies Annual* 27 (1998): 45–68.

[Lewes, G. H.] "Dickens in Relation to Criticism." *Fortnightly Review* 18 (1872): 143–51

Lewis, R. A. *Edwin Chadwick and the Public Health Movement.* London: Longmans, 1952.

Lister, Ruth. "The Responsible Citizen: Creating a New British Welfare Contract." Kingfisher, *Western Welfare* 111–27.

Litsios, Socrates. "Charles Dickens and the Movement for Sanitary Reform." *Perspectives in Biology and Medicine* 6.2 (2003): 183–99.

Lockwood, Frank. *The Law and Lawyers of Pickwick: A Lecture.* London: Roxburghe, n.d. [1894].

Logan, Peter. *Nerves and Narratives: A Cultural History of Hysteria in Nineteenth-Century British Prose.* Berkeley: U of California P, 1997.

Lukács, Georg. "Reification and the Consciousness of the Proletariat." *History and Class Consciousness: Studies in Marxist Dialectics.* By Lukács. Trans. Rodney Livingston. Cambridge: MIT, 1968. 83–222.

Lyell, Charles. *Geological Evidence of the Antiquity of Man.* London: Murray, 1863.

———. *Principles of Geology.* 3 vols. London: Murray, 1830–33.

Lynch, Deidre. *The Economy of Character: Novels, Market Culture, and the Business of Inner Meaning.* Chicago: U of Chicago P, 1998.

Mack, M. P. *Jeremy Bentham: An Odyssey of Ideas.* New York: Columbia UP, 1963.

Maluleke, Eddie Vulanie. "Nobody Ever Said AIDS." *Nobody Ever Said AIDS: Stories and Poems from Southern Africa.* Ed. M. Samuelson, N. Rasebotsa, and K. Thomas. Cape Town: Kwela, 2004. 17–20.

Manchester, A. H. *Sources of English Legal History, 1750-1950.* London: Butterworths, 1984.

Mandler, Peter. "The Making of the New Poor Law *Redivivus.*" *Past and Present* 117 (1987): 131–57.

———. "Tories and Paupers: Christian Political Economy and the Making of the New Poor Law." *Historical Journal* 33.1 (1990): 81–103.

Marx, Karl. "The Fetishism of the Commodity and Its Secret." *Capital: A Critique of Political Economy.* By Marx. Vol. 1. Trans. Ben Fowkes. New York: Vintage, 1977. 163–77.

Maxwell, Richard. *The Mysteries of Paris and London*. Charlottesville: UP of Virginia, 1998.

Mayhew, Henry. *London Labour and the London Poor: The Condition and Earnings of Those That Will Work, Cannot Work, and Will Not Work*. 1864. 4 vols. New York: Dover, 1968.

McLaughlin, Kevin. *Paperwork: Fiction and Mass Mediacy in the Paper Age*. Philadelphia: U of Pennsylvania P, 2005.

———. *Writing in Parts: Imitation and Exchange in Nineteenth-Century Literature*. Stanford: Stanford UP, 1995.

Meisel, Martin. *Realizations: Narrative, Pictorial, and Theatrical Arts in Nineteenth-Century England*. Princeton: Princeton UP, 1983.

Michie. Helena. "'Who Is This in Pain?': Scarring, Disfigurement, and Female Identity in *Bleak House* and *Our Mutual Friend*." *Novel: A Forum on Fiction* 22 (1989): 199–218.

Middleton, Robin. "The Magpie of Lincoln's Inn Fields." *AI [Architecture and Ideas]* 3.1 (2001): 24–33.

Mill, John Stuart. *Autobiography*. Ed. Jack Stillinger. Boston: Houghton, 1969.

———. "Civilization." 1836. *Collected Works of John Stuart Mill*. Ed. John M. Robson. Vol. 18. Toronto: Toronto UP, 1977. 119–47.

———. *On Liberty*. 1859. Ed. Edward Alexander. Toronto: Broadview, 1999.

Mill, John Stuart, and Jeremy Bentham. Utilitarianism *and Other Essays*. Ed. Alan Ryan. Harmondsworth: Penguin, 1987.

Miller, Andrew H. *Novels behind Glass: Commodity Culture and Victorian Narrative*. Cambridge: Cambridge UP, 1995.

———. "*Vanity Fair* through Plate Glass." *PMLA* 105 (1990): 1042–54.

Miller, D. A.. *Bringing Out Roland Barthes*. Berkeley: U of California P, 1992.

———. "Discipline in Different Voices: Bureaucracy, Police, Family, and *Bleak House*." D. A. Miller, *Novel* 58-107. Rpt. in Tambling 87–127.

———. *The Novel and the Police*. Berkeley: U of California P, 1988.

Miller, J. Hillis. Introduction. *Bleak House*. By Charles Dickens. Ed. Norman Page. Harmondsworth: Penguin, 1971. 11–34. Rpt. as "Interpretation in Dickens's *Bleak House*." *Victorian Subjects*. New York: Harvester, 1990. 179–99. Rpt. in Tambling 29–53.

Miller, Nancy K. "Emphasis Added: Plots and Plausibilities in Women's Fiction." *PMLA* 96 (1981): 36–48.

Morris, Alan. *Bleakness and Light: Inner-City Transition in Hillbrow, Johannesburg*. Johannesburg: Witwatersrand UP, 1999.

Morris, Pam. "*Bleak House* and the Struggle for the State Domain." *ELH* 68 (2001): 679–98.

———. *Imagining Inclusive Society in Nineteenth-Century Novels: The Code of Sincerity in the Public Sphere*. Baltimore: Johns Hopkins UP, 2004.

Mpe, Phaswane. "'Our Missing Store of Memories:' City, Literature and Representation." *Shifting Selves: Post-apartheid Essays on Mass Media, Culture and Identity*. Ed. H. Wasserman and S. Jacobs. Cape Town: Kwela, 2003. 181–98.

———. *Welcome to Our Hillbrow*. Pietermaritzburg: U of Natal P, 2001.

Mulvey, Laura. "Pandora: Topographies of the Mask and Curiousity." *Sexuality and Space*. Ed. Beatrice Colomina. New York: Princeton Architectural P, 1992. 53–71.

The Mystery of Charles Dickens. Screenplay by Peter Ackroyd. Dir. Patrick Garland. Perf. Simon Callow. Ovation Channel, 2000. DVD. Kultur Films, 2000.

Nabokov, Vladimir. "*Bleak House* (1852–1853)." *Lectures on Literature*. Ed. Fredson Bowers. New York: Harcourt, 1980. 63–124.

Nancy, Jean-Luc. *The Inoperative Community*. Trans. Peter Connor, Lisa Garbus, Michael Holland, and Simona Shawney. Minneapolis: U of Minnesota P, 1991.

Nead, Lynda. *Victorian Babylon: People, Streets, and Images in Nineteenth-Century London*. New Haven: Yale UP, 2000.

Newman, John Henry. *Apologia Pro Vita Sua*. Ed. David J. DeLaura. New York: Norton, 1968.

Newsom, Robert. "Authorizing Women: *Villette* and *Bleak House*." *Nineteenth-Century Literature* 46 (1991): 54–81.

———, comp. Bleak House: *A Bibliography*. Spring 2001. The Dickens Project. 19 Apr. 2006 <http://humwww.ucsc.edu/dickens/bibliographies/bleakhousebiblio/BH_Biblio_clean.html>.

———. *Charles Dickens Revisited*. New York: Twayne, 2000.

———. *Dickens on the Romantic Side of Familiar Things:* Bleak House *and the Novel Tradition*. 1977. Santa Cruz: Dickens Project, 1988.

Nichol, John Pringle. *Views of the Architecture of the Heavens and Thoughts on Some Important Points Relating to the System of the World*. 1837. Edinburgh: Tait, 1854.

Nicholson, Peter. "The Reception and Early Reputation of Mill's Political Thought." *The Cambridge Companion to Mill*. Ed. John Skorupski. Cambridge: Cambridge UP, 1998. 464–96.

Nisbet, Ada. "Charles Dickens." *Victorian Fiction: A Guide to Research*. Ed. Lionel Stevenson. Cambridge: Harvard UP, 1964. 44–153.

Patten, Robert L. *Charles Dickens and His Publishers*. Oxford: Clarendon, 1978.

———. "Hablot Knight Browne." Schlicke, *Oxford Reader's Companion* 58–63.

———. "Illustrators and Book Illustration." Schlicke, *Oxford Reader's Companion* 288–93.

Pearson, Richard. "Thackeray and *Punch* at the Great Exhibition: Authority and Ambivalence in Verbal and Visual Caricatures." Purbrick 179–205.

Peltason, Timothy. "Esther's Will." *ELH* 59 (1992): 671–91. Rpt. in Tambling 205–27.

Perkin, Harold. *The Rise of Professional Society: England since 1880*. London: Routledge, 1989.

Phegley, Jennifer. "Piracy and the Patriotic Woman Reader: Making British Literature American in *Harper's New Monthly Magazine*, 1850–1855." *Educating the Proper Woman Reader: Victorian Family Literary Magazines and the Cultural Health of the Nation*. Columbus: Ohio State UP, 2005. 31–69.

Pool, Daniel. *What Jane Austen Ate and Charles Dickens Knew: From Fox Hunting to Whist: The Facts of Daily Life in Nineteenth-Century England*. New York: Simon, 1993.

Poovey, Mary. *Making a Social Body: British Cultural Formation, 1830–1864*. Chicago: U of Chicago P, 1995.

Pope, Norris. *Dickens and Charity*. New York: Columbia UP, 1978.

Prochaska, F. K. *Women and Philanthropy in Nineteenth-Century England*. Oxford: Clarendon, 1980.

Purbrick, Louise, ed. *The Great Exhibition of 1851: New Interdisciplinary Essays*. Manchester: Manchester UP, 2001.

Rabinow, Paul, ed. *The Foucault Reader*. Trans. Christian Hubert. New York: Pantheon, 1984.

Reitz, Caroline. *Detecting the Nation: Fictions of Detection and the Imperial Venture*. Columbus: Ohio State UP, 2004.

Richard, J.-P. "Petite lecture de Javert." Rosa, *Victor Hugo* 143–55.

Richards, Thomas. *The Commodity Culture of Victorian England: Advertising and Spectacle, 1851–1914*. Stanford: Stanford UP, 1990.

Robbins, Bruce. "Telescopic Philanthropy: Professionalism and Responsibility in *Bleak House*." *Nation and Narration*. Ed. Homi K. Bhabha. London: Routledge, 1991. 213–30. Rpt. in Tambling 139–62.

Robinson, Kenton. "The Burning Question." *Hartford Courant* 31 Oct. 1994: E1+.

Rosa, Guy. "Histoire sociale et roman de la misère." Rosa, *Victor Hugo* 166–82.

———. "Jean Valjean (1,2,6): Réalisme et irréalisme des *Misérables*." Rosa et al., *Lire* 205–38.

———, ed. *Victor Hugo:* Les Misérables. Paris: Klincksieck, 1995.

Rosa, Guy, et al., eds. *Lire* Les Misérables. Paris: Corti, 1985.

Rose, Michael. "The Disappearing Pauper: Victorian Attitudes to the Relief of the Poor." *In Search of Victorian Values*. Ed. Eric M. Sigsworth. Manchester: Routledge, 1988. 159–77.

Ruskin, John. *The Seven Lamps of Architecture*. New York: Dover, 1989.

———. *The Stones of Venice*. Ed. J. G. Links. [New York]: De Capo, [1960].

———. Unto This Last *and Other Writings*. Ed. Clive Wilmer. Harmondsworth: Penguin, 1985.

Salotto, Eleanor. "Detecting Esther Summerson's Secrets: Dickens' *Bleak House* of Representation." *Victorian Literature and Culture* 25 (1997): 333–49.

Samet, Elizabeth Dale. "'When Constabulary Duty's to Be Done': Dickens and the Metropolitan Police." *Dickens Studies Annual* 27 (1998): 131–43.

Saunders, Rebecca. "The Agony and the Allegory: The Concept of the Foreign, the Language of Apartheid, and the Fiction of J. M. Coetzee. *Cultural Critique* 47 (2001): 215–64.

Schlicke, Paul. "Dickens's Public Readings." *Dickens and Popular Entertainment*. London: Allen, 1984. 226–48.

———, ed. *Oxford Reader's Companion to Dickens*. Oxford: Oxford UP, 1999.

Schor, Hilary. "*Bleak House* and the Dead Mother's Property." *Dickens and the Daughter of the House*. Cambridge: Cambridge UP 1999. 101–23

Schwarzbach, F. S. "Deadly Stains: Lady Dedlock's Death." *Dickens Quarterly* 4 (1987): 160–65.

———. "The Fever of *Bleak House*." *English Language Notes* 20 (1983): 21–27.

Searle, Geoffrey. *The Quest for National Efficiency*. Oxford: Oxford UP, 1971.

Senior, Nassau, Edwin Chadwick, et al. "Poor Law Commissioner's Report of 1834: Copy of the Report Made in 1834 by the Commissioners for Inquiring into the Administration and Practical Operation of the Poor Laws." 1834. London: HMSO, 1905. <http://www.econlib.org/library/YPDBooks/Reports/rptPLC14.html>.

Shatto, Susan. *The Companion to* Bleak House. London: Unwin, 1988.

———. "Lady Dedlock and the Plot of *Bleak House*." *Dickens Quarterly* 5 (1988): 185–91.

Simhony, Avital. "T. H. Green's Complex Common Good: Between Liberalism and Communitarianism." Simhony and Weinstein 69–92.

Simhony, Avital, and David Weinstein, eds. *The New Liberalism: Reconciling Liberty and Community*. Cambridge: Cambridge UP, 2001.

Simone, AbdouMaliq. "People as Infrastructure: Intersecting Fragments in Johannesburg." *Johannesburg—The Elusive Metropolis*. Spec. issue of *Public Culture* 16.3 (2004): 407–29.

Slater, Michael, ed. *Dickens' Journalism*. 3 vols. London: Dent, 1994–99.

Smiles, Samuel. *Character*. 1871. New York: Burt, n.d.

Smiley, Jane. *Charles Dickens*. New York: Penguin, 2002.

———. *Moo*. New York: Ballantine, 1995.

Smith, Abel-Smith, and Robert Stevens. *Lawyers and the Courts*. London: Heinemann, 1967.

Smith, Anna H. *Johannesburg Street Names: A Dictionary of Street, Suburb and Other Place-Names, Compiled to the End of 1968*. Cape Town: Juta, 1971.

"Spontaneous Human Combustion." *Wikipedia: The Free Encyclopedia*. 13 Apr. 2006 <http://en.wikipedia.org/wiki/Spontaneous_human_combustion>.

"State of the Market for December, 1852." *Harper's New Monthly Magazine* Feb. 1853: 419–20.

Steig, Michael. *Dickens and Phiz*. Bloomington: Indiana UP, 1978.

Stein, Richard L. "Dickens and Illustration." Jordan 167–88.

Sternlieb, Lisa. "Esther Summerson: Looking Twice." *The Female Narrator in the British Novel: Hidden Agendas*. New York: Palgrave, 2002. 75–105.

Stewart, Susan. *On Longing: Narratives of the Miniature, the Gigantic, the Souvenir, the Collection*. Baltimore: Johns Hopkins UP, 1984.

Stiglitz, Joseph. *Globalization and Its Discontents*. New York: Norton, 2002.

Stokes, Eric. *The English Utilitarians in India*. Oxford: Clarendon, 1959.

Stone, Harry. "Charles Dickens and Harriet Beecher Stowe." *Nineteenth-Century Fiction* 12.3 (1957): 188–202.

———, ed. *Dickens' Working Notes for His Novels*. Chicago: U of Chicago P, 1987.

Stone, Marjorie. "Dickens, Bentham, and the Fictions of the Law: A Victorian Controversy and Its Consequences." *Victorian Studies* 29 (1985): 125–54.

Stonehouse, John H., ed. *Catalogue of the Library of Charles Dickens from Gadshill.* London: Piccadilly Fountain, 1935.

Summers, Anne. "A Home from Home: Women's Philanthropic Work in the Nineteenth Century." *Fit Work for Women.* Ed. Sandra Burman. London: Croom Helm, 1979. 33–63.

Sutherland, John. *Inside* Bleak House*: A Guide for the Modern Dickensian.* London: Duckworth, 2005.

———. "What Kills Lady Dedlock?" *Who Betrays Elizabeth Bennet? Further Puzzles in Classic Fiction.* Oxford: Oxford UP, 1999. 115–27.

Tambling, Jeremy, ed. Bleak House*: Charles Dickens.* 1987. Houndsmills: Macmillan, 1998.

———. "*Martin Chuzzlewit:* Dickens and Architecture." *English: The Journal of the English Association* 48.192 (1999): 147–68.

Temperley, Howard. *White Dreams, Black Africa: The Antislavery Expedition to the River Niger, 1841–1842.* New Haven: Yale UP, 1991.

Thomas, Ronald. "Making Darkness Visible: Capturing the Criminal and Observing the Law in Victorian Photography and Detective Fiction." *Victorian Literature and the Victorian Visual Imagination.* Ed. Carol T. Christ and John O. Jordan. Berkeley: U of California P, 1995. 134–68.

Thompson, F. M. L. *The Rise of Respectable Society.* London: Fontana, 1988.

Todorov, Tzvetan. *The Poetics of Prose.* Ithaca: Cornell UP, 1977.

Tompkins, Jane. "Sentimental Power: *Uncle Tom's Cabin* and the Politics of Literary History." *Sensational Designs: The Cultural Work of American Fiction, 1790–1860.* New York: Oxford UP, 1985. 122–46.

Tracy, Robert. "Lighthousekeeping: *Bleak House* and the Crystal Palace." *Dickens Studies Annual* 33 (2003): 25–53.

———. "Reading and Misreading *Bleak House.*" *Dickens Quarterly* 20 (2003): 166–71.

———. "Time in *Bleak House.*" *Dickens Quarterly* 21 (2004): 225–34.

Tye, J. R. "Legal Caricature: Cruikshank Analogies to the *Bleak House* Cover." *Dickensian* 69 (1973): 39–41.

University of Glasgow, Special Collections Department, "Book of the Month: Charles Dickens, *Bleak House.*" Nov. 2004. July 2005 <http://special.lib.gla.ac.uk/exhibns/month/nov2004.html>.

Vanden Bossche, Chris R. "Class Discourse and Popular Agency in *Bleak House.*" *Victorian Studies* 47.1 (2004): 7–51.

Vernier, France. "*Les Misérables*: Ce livre est dangereux." *L'Arc* 57 (1974): 33–39.

———. "*Les Misérables*: Un texte intraitable." Rosa et al., *Lire* 5–27.

The Victorian Dictionary. By Lee Jackson. 14 Apr. 2006 <http://www.victorianlondon.org>.

The Victorian Web. Ed. George Landow. 13 Apr. 2006 <http://www.victorianweb.org>.

Viswanathan, Gauri. *Masks of Conquest: Literary Study and British Rule in India.* New York: Columbia UP, 1989.

Warren, Samuel. *The Moral, Social, and Professional Duties of Attornies and Solicitors*. 2nd ed. Edinburgh: Blackwood, 1851.

Welsh, Alexander. *Dickens Redressed: The Art of* Bleak House *and* Hard Times. New Haven: Yale UP, 2000.

West, Gillian. "*Bleak House*: Esther's Illness." *English Studies* 73 (1992): 30–34.

Whewell, William. *Astronomy and General Physics Considered with Reference to Natural Theology*. 1833. London: Pickering, 1834.

[Whipple, Edwin P.] "Novels and Novelists: Charles Dickens." *North American Review* 69 (1849): 383–407.

White, Allon H. "Language and Location in Charles Dickens's *Bleak House*." *Critical Quarterly* 20.4 (1978): 73–89.

Wicke, Jennifer. *Advertising Fictions: Literature, Advertisement, and Social Reading*. New York: Columbia UP, 1988.

Wilkinson, Ann Y. "*Bleak House*: From Faraday to Judgment Day." *ELH* 34 (1967): 225–47.

Willis, Ellen. "Freedom from Religion." *Nation*. 19 Feb. 2001. <http://www.thenation.com/docPrint.mhtml?I=20010219&s=willis>.

Wilt, Judith. "Confusion and Consciousness in Dickens's Esther." *Nineteenth-Century Fiction* 32.3 (1977): 285–309.

Winnett, Susan. "Coming Unstrung: Women, Men, Narrative, and Principles of Pleasure." *PMLA* 103 (1990): 505–18.

Woloch, Alex. *The One vs. the Many: Minor Characters and the Space of the Protagonist in the Novel*. Princeton: Princeton UP, 2003.

Wood, Peter. *Poverty and the Workhouse in Victorian Britain*. Stroud: Sutton, 1991.

Woodward, Llewellyn. *The Age of Reform, 1815–1870*. 2nd ed. Oxford: Oxford UP, 1967.

Yellin, Jean Fagan. "Doing It Herself: *Uncle Tom's Cabin* and Woman's Role in the Slavery Crisis." *New Essays on* Uncle Tom's Cabin. Ed. Eric J. Sundquist. Cambridge: Cambridge UP, 1986. 85–106.

Young, Iris Marion. *Justice and the Politics of Difference*. Princeton: Princeton UP, 1990.

Zwerdling, Alex. "Esther Summerson Rehabilitated." *PMLA* 88 (1973): 429–39.

INDEX OF NAMES

Modern Language Association of America

Approaches to Teaching World Literature

Joseph Gibaldi, series editor

Eliot's Middlemarch. Ed. Kathleen Blake. 1990.

Eliot's Poetry and Plays. Ed. Jewel Spears Brooker. 1988.

Shorter Elizabethan Poetry. Ed. Patrick Cheney and Anne Lake Prescott. 2000.

Ellison's Invisible Man. Ed. Susan Resneck Parr and Pancho Savery. 1989.

English Renaissance Drama. Ed. Karen Bamford and Alexander Leggatt. 2002.

Works of Louise Erdrich. Ed. Gregg Sarris, Connie A. Jacobs, and
James R. Giles. 2004.

Dramas of Euripides. Ed. Robin Mitchell-Boyask. 2002.

Faulkner's The Sound and the Fury. Ed. Stephen Hahn and Arthur F. Kinney. 1996.

Flaubert's Madame Bovary. Ed. Laurence M. Porter and Eugene F. Gray. 1995.

García Márquez's One Hundred Years of Solitude. Ed. María Elena de Valdés and
Mario J. Valdés. 1990.

Gilman's "The Yellow Wall-Paper" and Herland. Ed. Denise D. Knight and
Cynthia J. Davis. 2003.

Goethe's Faust. Ed. Douglas J. McMillan. 1987.

Gothic Fiction: The British and American Traditions. Ed. Diane Long Hoeveler
and Tamar Heller. 2003.

Grass's The Tin Drum. Ed. Monika Shafi. 2008.

Hebrew Bible as Literature in Translation. Ed. Barry N. Olshen and
Yael S. Feldman. 1989.

Homer's Iliad *and* Odyssey. Ed. Kostas Myrsiades. 1987.

Ibsen's A Doll House. Ed. Yvonne Shafer. 1985.

Henry James's Daisy Miller *and* The Turn of the Screw. Ed. Kimberly C. Reed and
Peter G. Beidler. 2005.

Works of Samuel Johnson. Ed. David R. Anderson and Gwin J. Kolb. 1993.

Joyce's Ulysses. Ed. Kathleen McCormick and Erwin R. Steinberg. 1993.

Works of Sor Juana Inés de la Cruz. Ed. Emilie L. Bergmann and Stacey Schlau.
2007.

Kafka's Short Fiction. Ed. Richard T. Gray. 1995.

Keats's Poetry. Ed. Walter H. Evert and Jack W. Rhodes. 1991.

Kingston's The Woman Warrior. Ed. Shirley Geok-lin Lim. 1991.

Lafayette's The Princess of Clèves. Ed. Faith E. Beasley and
Katharine Ann Jensen. 1998.

Works of D. H. Lawrence. Ed. M. Elizabeth Sargent and Garry Watson. 2001.

Lazarillo de Tormes *and the Picaresque Tradition.* Ed. Anne J. Cruz. 2009.

Lessing's The Golden Notebook. Ed. Carey Kaplan and Ellen Cronan Rose. 1989.

Mann's Death in Venice *and Other Short Fiction.* Ed. Jeffrey B. Berlin. 1992.

Marguerite de Navarre's Heptameron. Ed. Colette H. Winn. 2007.

Medieval English Drama. Ed. Richard K. Emmerson. 1990.

Melville's Moby-Dick. Ed. Martin Bickman. 1985.

Metaphysical Poets. Ed. Sidney Gottlieb. 1990.

Miller's Death of a Salesman. Ed. Matthew C. Roudané. 1995.

Milton's Paradise Lost. Ed. Galbraith M. Crump. 1986.

Milton's Shorter Poetry and Prose. Ed. Peter C. Herman. 2007.

Molière's Tartuffe *and Other Plays*. Ed. James F. Gaines and
    Michael S. Koppisch. 1995.

Momaday's The Way to Rainy Mountain. Ed. Kenneth M. Roemer. 1988.

Montaigne's Essays. Ed. Patrick Henry. 1994.

Novels of Toni Morrison. Ed. Nellie Y. McKay and Kathryn Earle. 1997.

Murasaki Shikibu's The Tale of Genji. Ed. Edward Kamens. 1993.

Nabokov's Lolita. Ed. Zoran Kuzmanovich and Galya Diment. 2008.

Poe's Prose and Poetry. Ed. Jeffrey Andrew Weinstock and Tony Magistrale. 2008.

Pope's Poetry. Ed. Wallace Jackson and R. Paul Yoder. 1993.

Proust's Fiction and Criticism. Ed. Elyane Dezon-Jones and
    Inge Crosman Wimmers. 2003.

Puig's Kiss of the Spider Woman. Ed. Daniel Balderston and Francine Masiello.
    2007.

Pynchon's The Crying of Lot 49 *and Other Works*. Ed. Thomas H. Schaub. 2008.

Novels of Samuel Richardson. Ed. Lisa Zunshine and Jocelyn Harris. 2006.

Rousseau's Confessions *and* Reveries of the Solitary Walker. Ed. John C. O'Neal
    and Ourida Mostefai. 2003.

Shakespeare's Hamlet. Ed. Bernice W. Kliman. 2001.

Shakespeare's King Lear. Ed. Robert H. Ray. 1986.

Shakespeare's Othello. Ed. Peter Erickson and Maurice Hunt. 2005.

Shakespeare's Romeo and Juliet. Ed. Maurice Hunt. 2000.

Shakespeare's The Tempest *and Other Late Romances*. Ed. Maurice Hunt. 1992.

Shelley's Frankenstein. Ed. Stephen C. Behrendt. 1990.

Shelley's Poetry. Ed. Spencer Hall. 1990.

Sir Gawain and the Green Knight. Ed. Miriam Youngerman Miller and
    Jane Chance. 1986.

Song of Roland. Ed. William W. Kibler and Leslie Zarker Morgan. 2006.

Spenser's Faerie Queene. Ed. David Lee Miller and Alexander Dunlop. 1994.

Stendhal's The Red and the Black. Ed. Dean de la Motte and Stirling Haig. 1999.

Sterne's Tristram Shandy. Ed. Melvyn New. 1989.

Stowe's Uncle Tom's Cabin. Ed. Elizabeth Ammons and Susan Belasco. 2000.

Swift's Gulliver's Travels. Ed. Edward J. Rielly. 1988.

Thoreau's Walden *and Other Works*. Ed. Richard J. Schneider. 1996.

Tolstoy's Anna Karenina. Ed. Liza Knapp and Amy Mandelker. 2003.

Vergil's Aeneid. Ed. William S. Anderson and Lorina N. Quartarone. 2002.

Voltaire's Candide. Ed. Renée Waldinger. 1987.

Whitman's Leaves of Grass. Ed. Donald D. Kummings. 1990.

Wiesel's Night. Ed. Alan Rosen. 2007.

Works of Oscar Wilde. Ed. Philip E. Smith II. 2008.

Woolf's To the Lighthouse. Ed. Beth Rigel Daugherty and Mary Beth Pringle. 2001.

Wordsworth's Poetry. Ed. Spencer Hall, with Jonathan Ramsey. 1986.

Wright's Native Son. Ed. James A. Miller. 1997.